Studies in the
Quantity Theory of Money

This volume is a publication of the
Workshop in Money and Banking

ECONOMICS RESEARCH STUDIES

of the

ECONOMICS RESEARCH CENTER

of the

UNIVERSITY OF CHICAGO

Studies in the Quantity Theory of Money

Edited by

MILTON FRIEDMAN

With Essays by

MILTON FRIEDMAN

PHILLIP CAGAN

JOHN J. KLEIN

EUGENE M. LERNER

RICHARD T. SELDEN

THE UNIVERSITY OF CHICAGO PRESS

CHICAGO & LONDON

THE UNIVERSITY OF CHICAGO PRESS, CHICAGO 60637
The University of Chicago Press, Ltd., London

© 1956 by The University of Chicago. All rights reserved
Published 1956. Sixth Impression 1973. Printed in the
United States of America

International Standard Book Number: 0–226–26404–1
(Clothbound)

Library of Congress Catalog Number: 56–10999

Table of Contents

v

I

The Quantity Theory of Money—A Restatement

MILTON FRIEDMAN

The Quantity Theory of Money—A Restatement

THE quantity theory of money is a term evocative of a general approach rather than a label for a well-defined theory. The exact content of the approach varies from a truism defining the term "velocity" to an allegedly rigid and unchanging ratio between the quantity of money—defined in one way or another—and the price level—also defined in one way or another. Whatever its precise meaning, it is clear that the general approach fell into disrepute after the crash of 1929 and the subsequent Great Depression and only recently has been slowly re-emerging into professional respectability.

The present volume is partly a symptom of this re-emergence and partly a continuance of an aberrant tradition. Chicago was one of the few academic centers at which the quantity theory continued to be a central and vigorous part of the oral tradition throughout the 1930's and 1940's, where students continued to study monetary theory and to write theses on monetary problems. The quantity theory that retained this role differed sharply from the atrophied and rigid caricature that is so frequently described by the proponents of the new income-expenditure approach—and with some justice, to judge by much of the literature on policy that was spawned by quantity theorists. At Chicago, Henry Simons and Lloyd Mints directly, Frank Knight and Jacob Viner at one remove, taught and developed a more subtle and relevant version, one in which the quantity theory was connected and integrated with general price theory and became a flexible and sensitive tool for interpreting movements in aggregate economic activity and for developing relevant policy prescriptions.

To the best of my knowledge, no systematic statement of this theory as developed at Chicago exists, though much can be read between the lines of Simons' and Mints's writings. And this is as it should be, for the Chicago tradition was not a rigid system, an unchangeable orthodoxy, but a way of looking at things. It was a theoretical approach that insisted that money does matter—that any interpretation of short-term movements in economic activity is likely to be seriously at fault if it neglects monetary changes and repercussions and if it leaves unexplained why people are willing to hold the particular nominal quantity of money in existence.

The purpose of this introduction is not to enshrine—or, should I say, inter—a definitive version of the Chicago tradition. To suppose that one could do so would be inconsistent with that tradition itself. The purpose is rather to set down a particular "model" of a quantity theory in an attempt to convey the flavor of the oral tradition which nurtured the remaining essays in this volume. In consonance with this purpose, I shall not attempt to be exhaustive or to give a full justification for every assertion.

1. The quantity theory is in the first instance a theory of the *demand* for money. It is not a theory of output, or of money income, or of the price level. Any statement about these variables requires combining the quantity theory with some specifications about the conditions of supply of money and perhaps about other variables as well.

2. To the ultimate wealth-owning units in the economy, money is one kind of asset, one way of holding wealth. To the productive enterprise, money is a capital good, a source of productive services that are combined with other productive services to yield the products that the enterprise sells. Thus the theory of the demand for money is a special topic in the theory of capital; as such, it has the rather unusual feature of combining a piece from each side of the capital market, the supply of capital (points 3 through 8 that follow), and the demand for capital (points 9 through 12).

3. The analysis of the demand for money on the part of the ultimate wealth-owning units in the society can be made formally identical with that of the demand for a consumption service. As in the usual theory of consumer choice, the demand for money (or any other particular asset) depends on three major sets of factors: (*a*) the total wealth to be held in various forms—the analogue of the budget restraint; (*b*) the price of and return on this form of wealth and alternative forms; and (*c*) the tastes and preferences of the wealth-owning units. The substantive differences from the analysis of the demand for a consumption service are the necessity of taking account of intertemporal rates of substitution in (*b*) and (*c*) and of casting the budget restraint in terms of wealth.

4. From the broadest and most general point of view, total wealth includes all sources of "income" or consumable services. One such source is the productive capacity of human beings, and accordingly this is one form in which wealth can be held. From this point of view, "the" rate of interest expresses the relation between the stock which is wealth and the flow which is income, so if Y be the total flow of income, and r, "the" interest rate, total wealth is

$$W = \frac{Y}{r}. \tag{1}$$

Income in this broadest sense should not be identified with income as it is ordinarily measured. The latter is generally a "gross" stream with respect to human beings, since no deduction is made for the expense of maintaining human productive capacity intact; in addition, it is affected by transitory elements that make it depart more or less widely from the theoretical concept of the stable level of consumption of services that could be maintained indefinitely.

5. Wealth can be held in numerous forms, and the ultimate wealth-owning unit is to be regarded as dividing his wealth among them (point [a] of 3), so as to maximize "utility" (point [c] of 3), subject to whatever restrictions affect the possibility of converting one form of wealth into another (point [b] of 3). As usual, this implies that he will seek an apportionment of his wealth such that the rate at which he *can* substitute one form of wealth for another is equal to the rate at which he is just willing to do so. But this general proposition has some special features in the present instance because of the necessity of considering flows as well as stocks. We can suppose all wealth (except wealth in the form of the productive capacity of human beings) to be expressed in terms of monetary units at the prices of the point of time in question. The rate at which one form can be substituted for another is then simply $1.00 worth for $1.00 worth, regardless of the forms involved. But this is clearly not a complete description, because the holding of one form of wealth instead of another involves a difference in the composition of the income stream, and it is essentially these differences that are fundamental to the "utility" of a particular structure of wealth. In consequence, to describe fully the alternative combinations of forms of wealth that are available to an individual, we must take account not only of their market prices—which except for human wealth can be done simply by expressing them in units worth $1.00—but also of the form and size of the income streams they yield.

It will suffice to bring out the major issues that these considerations raise to consider five different forms in which wealth can be held: (i) money (M), interpreted as claims or commodity units that are generally accepted in payment of debts at a fixed nominal value; (ii) bonds (B), interpreted as claims to time streams of payments that are fixed in nominal units; (iii) equities (E), interpreted as claims to stated pro-rata shares of the returns of enterprises; (iv) physical non-human goods (G); and (v) human capital (H). Consider now the yield of each.

(i) Money may yield a return in the form of money, for example, interest on demand deposits. It will simplify matters, however, and entail no essential loss of generality, to suppose that money yields its return solely in kind, in the usual form of convenience, security, etc. The magnitude of this return in "real" terms per nominal unit of money clearly depends on the volume of goods that unit corresponds to, or on the general price level, which we may designate by P. Since we have decided to take $1.00 worth as the unit for each form of wealth, this will be equally true for other forms of wealth as well, so P is a variable affecting the "real" yield of each.

(ii) If we take the "standard" bond to be a claim to a perpetual income stream of constant nominal amount, then the return to a holder of the bond can take two forms: one, the annual sum he receives—the "coupon"; the other, any change in the price of the bond over time, a return which may of course be positive or negative. If the price is expected to remain constant, then $1.00 worth of a bond yields r_b per year, where r_b is simply the "coupon" sum divided by the market price of the bond, so $1/r_b$ is the price of a bond promising to pay $1.00 per year. We shall call r_b the market bond interest rate. If the price is expected to change, then the yield cannot be calculated so simply, since it must take account of the return in the form of expected appreciation or depreciation of the bond, and it cannot, like r_b, be calculated directly from market prices (so long, at least, as the "standard" bond is the only one traded in).

The nominal income stream purchased for $1.00 at time zero then consists of

$$r_b\,(0) + r_b\,(0)\; d \frac{\left(\dfrac{1}{r_b\,(t)}\right)}{dt} = r_b\,(0) - \frac{r_b\,(0)}{r_b^2\,(t)} \cdot \frac{d\,r_b\,(t)}{dt}, \qquad (2)$$

where t stands for time. For simplicity, we can approximate this functional by its value at time zero, which is

$$r_b - \frac{1}{r_b}\frac{d\,r_b}{dt}. \qquad (3)$$

This sum, together with P already introduced, defines the real return from holding $1.00 of wealth in the form of bonds.

(iii) Analogously to our treatment of bonds, we may take the "standard" unit of equity to be a claim to a perpetual income stream of constant "real" amount; that is, to be a standard bond with a purchasing-power escalator clause, so that it promises a perpetual income stream equal in nominal units to a constant number times a price index, which we may, for convenience, take to be the same price index P introduced in (i).[1] The nominal return to the holder of the equity can then be regarded as taking three forms: the constant nominal amount he would receive per year in

1. This is an oversimplification, because it neglects "leverage" and therefore supposes that any monetary liabilities of an enterprise are balanced by monetary assets.

the absence of any change in P; the increment or decrement to this nominal amount to adjust for changes in P; and any change in the nominal price of the equity over time, which may of course arise from changes either in interest rates or in price levels. Let r_e be the market interest rate on equities defined analogously to r_b, namely, as the ratio of the "coupon" sum at any time (the first two items above) to the price of the equity, so $1/r_e$ is the price of an equity promising to pay \$1.00 per year if the price level does not change, or to pay

$$\frac{P(t)}{P(0)} \cdot 1$$

if the price level varies according to $P(t)$. If $r_e(t)$ is defined analogously, the price of the bond selling for $1/r_e(0)$ at time 0 will be

$$\frac{P(t)}{P(0)\, r_e(t)}$$

at time t, where the ratio of prices is required to adjust for any change in the price level. The nominal stream purchased for \$1.00 at time zero then consists of

$$r_e(0) \cdot \frac{P(t)}{P(0)} + \frac{r_e(0)}{P(0)} \cdot d\frac{\left[\dfrac{P(t)}{r_e(t)}\right]}{dt} = r_e(0) \cdot \frac{P(t)}{P(0)}$$

$$+ \frac{r_e(0)}{r_e(t)} \cdot \frac{1}{P(0)} \cdot \frac{dP(t)}{dt} - \frac{P(t)}{P(0)} \cdot \frac{r_e(0)}{r_e^2(t)} \cdot \frac{d r_e(t)}{dt}. \tag{4}$$

Once again we can approximate this functional by its value at time zero, which is

$$r_e + \frac{1}{P}\frac{dP}{dt} - \frac{1}{r_e}\frac{d r_e}{dt}. \tag{5}$$

This sum, together with P already introduced, defines the "real" return from holding \$1.00 of wealth in the form of equities.

(iv) Physical goods held by ultimate wealth-owning units are similar to equities except that the annual stream they yield is in kind rather than in money. In terms of nominal units, this return, like that from equities, depends on the behavior of prices. In addition, like equities, physical goods must be regarded as yielding a nominal return in the form of appreciation or depreciation in money value. If we suppose the price level P, introduced earlier, to apply equally to the value of these physical goods, then, at time zero,

$$\frac{1}{P}\frac{dP}{dT} \tag{6}$$

is the size of this nominal return per $1.00 of physical goods.[2] Together with P, it defines the "real" return from holding $1.00 in the form of physical goods.

(v) Since there is only a limited market in human capital, at least in modern non-slave societies, we cannot very well define in market prices the terms of substitution of human capital for other forms of capital and so cannot define at any time the physical unit of capital corresponding to $1.00 of human capital. There are some possibilities of substituting non-human capital for human capital in an individual's wealth holdings, as, for example, when he enters into a contract to render personal services for a specified period in return for a definitely specified number of periodic payments, the number not depending on his being physically capable of rendering the services. But, in the main, shifts between human capital and other forms must take place through direct investment and disinvestment in the human agent, and we may as well treat this as if it were the only way. With respect to this form of capital, therefore, the restriction or obstacles affecting the alternative compositions of wealth available to the individual cannot be expressed in terms of market prices or rates of return. At any one point in time there is some division between human and non-human wealth in his portfolio of assets; he may be able to change this over time, but we shall treat it as given at a point in time. Let w be the ratio of non-human to human wealth or, equivalently, of income from non-human wealth to income from human wealth, which means that it is closely allied to what is usually defined as the ratio of wealth to income. This is, then, the variable that needs to be taken into account so far as human wealth is concerned.

6. The tastes and preferences of wealth-owning units for the service streams arising from different forms of wealth must in general simply be taken for granted as determining the form of the demand function. In order to give the theory empirical content, it will generally have to be supposed that tastes are constant over significant stretches of space and time. However, explicit allowance can be made for some changes in tastes in so far as such changes are linked with objective circumstances. For example, it seems reasonable that, other things the same, individuals want

2. In principle, it might be better to let P refer solely to the value of the services of physical goods, which is essentially what it refers to in the preceding cases, and to allow for the fact that the prices of the capital goods themselves must vary also with the rate of capitalization, so that the prices of services and their sources vary at the same rate only if the relevant interest rate is constant. I have neglected this refinement for simplicity; the neglect can perhaps be justified by the rapid depreciation of many of the physical goods held by final wealth-owning units.

to hold a larger fraction of their wealth in the form of money when they are moving around geographically or are subject to unusual uncertainty than otherwise. This is probably one of the major factors explaining a frequent tendency for money holdings to rise relative to income during wartime. But the extent of geographic movement, and perhaps of other kinds of uncertainty, can be represented by objective indexes, such as indexes of migration, miles of railroad travel, and the like. Let u stand for any such variables that can be expected to affect tastes and preferences (for "utility" determining variables).

7. Combining 4, 5, and 6 along the lines suggested by 3 yields the following demand function for money:

$$M = f\left(P,\ r_b - \frac{1}{r_b}\frac{d\,r_b}{dt},\ r_e + \frac{1}{P}\frac{dP}{dt} - \frac{1}{r_e}\frac{d\,r_e}{dt},\ \frac{1}{P}\frac{dP}{dt};\ w;\ \frac{Y}{r};u\right). \quad (7)$$

A number of observations are in order about this function.

(i) Even if we suppose prices and rates of interest unchanged, the function contains three rates of interest: two for specific types of assets, r_b and r_e, and one intended to apply to all types of assets, r. This general rate, r, is to be interpreted as something of a weighted average of the two special rates plus the rates applicable to human wealth and to physical goods. Since the latter two cannot be observed directly, it is perhaps best to regard them as varying in some systematic way with r_b and r_e. On this assumption, we can drop r as an additional explicit variable, treating its influence as fully taken into account by the inclusion of r_b and r_e.

(ii) If there were no differences of opinion about price movements and interest-rate movements, and bonds and equities were equivalent except that the former are expressed in nominal units, arbitrage would of course make

$$r_b - \frac{1}{r_b}\frac{d\,r_b}{dt} = r_e + \frac{1}{P}\frac{dP}{dt} - \frac{1}{r_e}\frac{d\,r_e}{dt}, \quad (8)$$

or, if we suppose rates of interest either stable or changing at the same percentage rate,

$$r_b = r_e + \frac{1}{P}\frac{dP}{dt}, \quad (9)$$

that is, the "money" interest rate equal to the "real" rate plus the percentage rate of change of prices. In application the rate of change of prices must be interpreted as an "expected" rate of change and differences of opinion cannot be neglected, so we cannot suppose (9) to hold; indeed, one of the most consistent features of inflation seems to be that it does not.[3]

(iii) If the range of assets were to be widened to include promises to pay specified sums for a finite number of time units—"short-term" securities as well as "consols"—the rates of change of r_b and r_e would be reflected in the difference between long and short rates of interest. Since at some stage it will doubtless be desirable to introduce securities of different time duration (see point 23 below), we may simplify the present exposition by restricting it to the case in which r_b and r_e are taken to be stable over time. Since the rate of change in prices is required separately in any event, this means that we can replace the cumbrous variables introduced to designate the nominal return on bonds and equities simply by r_b and r_e.

(iv) Y can be interpreted as including the return to all forms of wealth, including money and physical capital goods owned and held directly by ultimate wealth-owning units, and so Y/r can be interpreted as an estimate of total wealth, only if Y is regarded as including some imputed income from the stock of money and directly owned physical capital goods. For monetary analysis the simplest procedure is perhaps to regard Y as referring to the return to all forms of wealth other than the money held directly by ultimate wealth-owning units, and so Y/r as referring to total remaining wealth.

8. A more fundamental point is that, as in all demand analyses resting on maximization of a utility function defined in terms of "real" magnitudes, this demand equation must be considered independent in any essential way of the nominal units used to measure money variables. If the unit in which prices and money income are expressed is changed, the amount of money demanded should change proportionately. More technically, equation (7) must be regarded as homogeneous of the first degree in P and Y, so that

$$f\left(\lambda P, \ r_b, \ r_e, \ \frac{1}{P}\frac{dP}{dt}; \ w; \ \lambda Y; \ u\right)$$
$$= \lambda f\left(P, \ r_b, \ r_e, \ \frac{1}{P}\frac{dP}{dt}; \ w; \ Y; \ u\right). \tag{10}$$

where the variables within the parentheses have been rewritten in simpler form in accordance with comments 7 (i) and 7 (iii).

3. See Reuben Kessel, "Inflation: Theory of Wealth Distribution and Application in Private Investment Policy" (unpublished doctoral dissertation, University of Chicago).

This characteristic of the function enables us to rewrite it in two alternative and more familiar ways.

(i) Let $\lambda = 1/P$. Equation (7) can then be written

$$\frac{M}{P} = f\left(r_b, \; r_e, \; \frac{1}{P}\frac{dP}{dt}; \; w; \; \frac{Y}{P}; \; u\right). \tag{11}$$

In this form the equation expresses the demand for real balances as a function of "real" variables independent of nominal monetary values.

(ii) Let $\lambda = 1/Y$. Equation (7) can then be written

$$\frac{M}{Y} = f\left(r_b, \; r_e, \; \frac{1}{P}\frac{dP}{dt}, \; w, \; \frac{P}{Y}, \; u\right)$$

$$= \frac{1}{v\left(r_b, \; r_e, \; \dfrac{1}{P}\dfrac{dP}{dt}, \; w, \; \dfrac{Y}{P}, \; u\right)}, \tag{12}$$

or

$$Y = v\left(r_b, \; r_e, \; \frac{1}{P}\frac{dP}{dt}, \; w, \; \frac{Y}{P}, \; u\right) \cdot M. \tag{13}$$

In this form the equation is in the usual quantity theory form, where v is income velocity.

9. These equations are, to this point, solely for money held directly by ultimate wealth-owning units. As noted, money is also held by business enterprises as a productive resource. The counterpart to this business asset in the balance sheet of an ultimate wealth-owning unit is a claim other than money. For example, an individual may buy bonds from a corporation, and the corporation use the proceeds to finance the money holdings which it needs for its operations. Of course, the usual difficulties of separating the accounts of the business and its owner arise with unincorporated enterprises.

10. The amount of money that it pays business enterprises to hold depends, as for any other source of productive services, on the cost of the productive services, the cost of substitute productive services, and the value product yielded by the productive service. Per dollar of money held, the cost depends on how the corresponding capital is raised—whether by raising additional capital in the form of bonds or equities, by substituting cash for real capital goods, etc. These ways of financing money holdings are much the same as the alternative forms in which the ultimate wealth-owning unit can hold its non-human wealth, so that the variables r_b, r_e, P, and $(1/P)(dP/dt)$ introduced into (7) can be taken to represent the cost to the business enterprise of holding money. For some purposes, however, it may be desirable to distinguish between the rate of return re-

ceived by the lender and the rate paid by the borrower; in which case it would be necessary to introduce an additional set of variables.

Substitutes for money as a productive service are numerous and varied, including all ways of economizing on money holdings by using other resources to synchronize more closely payments and receipts, reduce payment periods, extend use of book credit, establish clearing arrangements, and so on in infinite variety. There seem no particularly close substitutes whose prices deserve to be singled out for inclusion in the business demand for money.

The value product yielded by the productive services of money per unit of output depends on production conditions: the production function. It is likely to be especially dependent on features of production conditions affecting the smoothness and regularity of operations as well as on those determining the size and scope of enterprises, degree of vertical integration, etc. Again there seem no variables that deserve to be singled out on the present level of abstraction for special attention; these factors can be taken into account by interpreting u as including variables affecting not only the tastes of wealth-owners but also the relevant technological conditions of production. Given the amount of money demanded per unit of output, the total amount demanded is proportional to total output, which can be represented by Y.

11. One variable that has traditionally been singled out in considering the demand for money on the part of business enterprises is the volume of transactions, or of transactions per dollar of final products; and, of course, emphasis on transactions has been carried over to the ultimate wealth-owning unit as well as to the business enterprise. The idea that renders this approach attractive is that there is a mechanical link between a dollar of payments per unit time and the average stock of money required to effect it—a fixed technical coefficient of production, as it were. It is clear that this mechanical approach is very different in spirit from the one we have been following. On our approach, the average amount of money held per dollar of transactions is itself to be regarded as a resultant of an economic equilibrating process, not as a physical datum. If, for whatever reason, it becomes more expensive to hold money, then it is worth devoting resources to effecting money transactions in less expensive ways or to reducing the volume of transactions per dollar of final output. In consequence, our ultimate demand function for money in its most general form does not contain as a variable the volume of transactions or of transactions per dollar of final output; it contains rather those more basic technical and cost conditions that affect the costs of conserving money, be it by changing the average amount of money held per dollar of transac-

tions per unit time or by changing the number of dollars of transactions per dollar of final output. This does not, of course, exclude the possibility that, for a particular problem, it may be useful to regard the transactions variables as given and not to dig beneath them and so to include the volume of transactions per dollar of final output as an explicit variable in a special variant of the demand function.

Similar remarks are relevant to various features of payment conditions, frequently described as "institutional conditions," affecting the velocity of circulation of money and taken as somehow mechanically determined— such items as whether workers are paid by the day, or week, or month; the use of book credit; and so on. On our approach these, too, are to be regarded as resultants of an economic equilibrating process, not as physical data. Lengthening the pay period, for example, may save book-keeping and other costs to the employer, who is therefore willing to pay somewhat more than in proportion for a longer than a shorter pay period; on the other hand, it imposes on employees the cost of holding larger cash balances or providing substitutes for cash, and they therefore want to be paid more than in proportion for a longer pay period. Where these will balance depends on how costs vary with length of pay period. The cost to the employee depends in considerable part on the factors entering into his demand curve for money for a fixed pay period. If he would in any event be holding relatively large average balances, the additional costs imposed by a lengthened pay period tend to be less than if he would be holding relatively small average balances, and so it will take less of an inducement to get him to accept a longer pay period. For given cost savings to the employer, therefore, the pay period can be expected to be longer in the first case than in the second. Surely, the increase in the average cash balance over the past century in this country that has oc-curred for other reasons has been a factor producing a lengthening of pay periods and not the other way around. Or, again, experience in hyperin-flations shows how rapidly payment practices change under the impact of drastic changes in the cost of holding money.

12. The upshot of these considerations is that the demand for money on the part of business enterprises can be regarded as expressed by a function of the same kind as equation (7), with the same variables on the right-hand side. And, like (7), since the analysis is based on informed maximization of returns by enterprises, only "real" quantities matter, so it must be homogeneous of the first degree in Y and P. In consequence, we can interpret (7) and its variants (11) and (13) as describing the demand for money on the part of a business enterprise as well as on the part of an

ultimate wealth-owning unit, provided only that we broaden our interpretation of u.

13. Strictly speaking, the equations (7), (11), and (13) are for an individual wealth-owning unit or business enterprise. If we aggregate (7) for
all wealth-owning units and business enterprises in the society, the result,
in principle, depends on the distribution of the units by the several variables. This raises no serious problem about P, r_b, and r_e, for these can be
taken as the same for all, or about u, for this is an unspecified portmanteau
variable to be filled in as the occasion demands. We have been interpreting $(1/P)(dP/dt)$ as the expected rate of price rise, so there is no reason
why this variable should be the same for all, and w and Y clearly differ
substantially among units. An approximation is to neglect these difficulties and take (7) and the associated (11) and (13) as applying to the
aggregate demand for money, with $(1/P)(dP/dt)$ interpreted as some kind
of an average expected rate of change of prices, w as the ratio of total
income from non-human wealth to income from human wealth, and Y as
aggregate income. This is the procedure that has generally been followed,
and it seems the right one until serious departures between this linear
approximation and experience make it necessary to introduce measures of
dispersion with respect to one or more of the variables.

14. It is perhaps worth noting explicitly that the model does not use
the distinction between "active balances" and "idle balances" or the
closely allied distinction between "transaction balances" and "speculative
balances" that is so widely used in the literature. The distinction between
money holdings of ultimate wealth-owners and of business enterprises is
related to this distinction but only distantly so. Each of these categories
of money-holders can be said to demand money partly from "transaction"
motives, partly from "speculative" or "asset" motives, but dollars of
money are not distinguished according as they are said to be held for one
or the other purpose. Rather, each dollar is, as it were, regarded as
rendering a variety of services, and the holder of money as altering his
money holdings until the value to him of the addition to the total flow of
services produced by adding a dollar to his money stock is equal to the
reduction in the flow of services produced by subtracting a dollar from
each of the other forms in which he holds assets.

15. Nothing has been said above about "banks" or producers of
money. This is because their main role is in connection with the supply of
money rather than the demand for it. Their introduction does, however,
blur some of the points in the above analysis: the existence of banks enables productive enterprises to acquire money balances without raising
capital from ultimate wealth-owners. Instead of selling claims (bonds or

equities) to them, it can sell its claims to banks, getting "money" in exchange: in the phrase that was once so common in textbooks on money, the bank coins specific liabilities into generally acceptable liabilities. But this possibility does not alter the preceding analysis in any essential way.

16. Suppose the supply of money in nominal units is regarded as fixed or more generally autonomously determined. Equation (13) then defines the conditions under which this nominal stock of money will be the amount demanded. Even under these conditions, equation (13) alone is not sufficient to determine money income. In order to have a complete model for the determination of money income, it would be necessary to specify the determinants of the structure of interest rates, of real income, and of the path of adjustment in the price level. Even if we suppose interest rates determined independently—by productivity, thrift, and the like—and real income as also given by other forces, equation (13) only determines a unique equilibrium level of money income if we mean by this the level at which prices are stable. More generally, it determines a time path of money income for given initial values of money income.

In order to convert equation (13) into a "complete" model of income determination, therefore, it is necessary to suppose either that the demand for money is highly inelastic with respect to the variables in v or that all these variables are to be taken as rigid and fixed.

17. Even under the most favorable conditions, for example, that the demand for money is quite inelastic with respect to the variables in v, equation (13) gives at most a theory of money income: it then says that changes in money income mirror changes in the nominal quantity of money. But it tells nothing about how much of any change in Y is reflected in real output and how much in prices. To infer this requires bringing in outside information, as, for example, that real output is at its feasible maximum, in which case any increase in money would produce the same or a larger percentage increase in prices; and so on.

18. In light of the preceding exposition, the question arises what it means to say that someone is or is not a "quantity theorist." Almost every economist will accept the general lines of the preceding analysis on a purely formal and abstract level, although each would doubtless choose to express it differently in detail. Yet there clearly are deep and fundamental differences about the importance of this analysis for the understanding of short- and long-term movements in general economic activity. This difference of opinion arises with respect to three different issues: (i) the stability and importance of the demand function for money; (ii) the independence of the factors affecting demand and supply; and (iii) the form of the demand function or related functions.

(i) The quantity theorist accepts the empirical hypothesis that the demand for money is highly stable—more stable than functions such as the consumption function that are offered as alternative key relations. This hypothesis needs to be hedged on both sides. On the one side, the quantity theorist need not, and generally does not, mean that the real quantity of money demanded per unit of output, or the velocity of circulation of money, is to be regarded as numerically constant over time; he does not, for example, regard it as a contradiction to the stability of the demand for money that the velocity of circulation of money rises drastically during hyperinflations. For the stability he expects is in the functional relation between the quantity of money demanded and the variables that determine it, and the sharp rise in the velocity of circulation of money during hyperinflations is entirely consistent with a stable functional relation, as Cagan so clearly demonstrates in his essay. On the other side, the quantity theorist must sharply limit, and be prepared to specify explicitly, the variables that it is empirically important to include in the function. For to expand the number of variables regarded as significant is to empty the hypothesis of its empirical content; there is indeed little if any difference between asserting that the demand for money is highly unstable and asserting that it is a perfectly stable function of an indefinitely large number of variables.

The quantity theorist not only regards the demand function for money as stable; he also regards it as playing a vital role in determining variables that he regards as of great importance for the analysis of the economy as a whole, such as the level of money income or of prices. It is this that leads him to put greater emphasis on the demand for money than on, let us say, the demand for pins, even though the latter might be as stable as the former. It is not easy to state this point precisely, and I cannot pretend to have done so. (See item [iii] below for an example of an argument against the quantity theorist along these lines.)

The reaction against the quantity theory in the 1930's came largely, I believe, under this head. The demand for money, it was asserted, is a will-o'-the-wisp, shifting erratically and unpredictably with every rumor and expectation; one cannot, it was asserted, reliably specify a limited number of variables on which it depends. However, although the reaction came under this head, it was largely rationalized under the two succeeding heads.

(ii) The quantity theorist also holds that there are important factors affecting the supply of money that do not affect the demand for money. Under some circumstances these are technical conditions affecting the supply of specie; under others, political or psychological conditions determining the policies of monetary authorities and the banking system. A stable demand function is useful precisely in order to trace out the effects of changes in supply, which means that it is useful only if supply is affected by at least some factors other than those regarded as affecting demand.

The classical version of the objection under this head to the quantity theory is the so-called real-bills doctrine: that changes in the demand for money call forth corresponding changes in supply and that supply cannot change otherwise, or at least cannot do so under specified institutional arrangements. The forms which this argument takes are legion and are still widespread. Another version is the argument that the "quantity theory" cannot "explain" large price rises, because the price rise produced both the increase in demand for nominal money holdings and the increase in supply of money to meet it; that is, implicitly that the same forces affect both the demand for and the supply of money, and in the same way.

(iii) The attack on the quantity theory associated with the Keynesian underemployment analysis is based primarily on an assertion about the form of (7) or (11). The demand for money, it is said, is infinitely elastic at a "small" positive interest rate. At this interest rate, which can be expected to prevail under underemployment conditions, changes in the real supply of money, whether produced by changes in prices or in the nominal stock of money, have no effect on anything. This is the famous "liquidity trap." A rather more complex version involves the shape of other functions as well: the magnitudes in (7) other than "the" interest rate, it is argued, enter into other relations in the economic system and can be regarded as determined there; the interest rate does not enter into these other functions; it can therefore be regarded as determined by this equation. So the only role of the stock of money and the demand for money is to determine the interest rate.

19. The proof of this pudding is in the eating; and the essays in this book contain much relevant food, of which I may perhaps mention three particularly juicy items.

On cannot read Lerner's description of the effects of monetary reform in the Confederacy in 1864 without recognizing that at least on occasion the supply of money can be a largely autonomous factor and the demand for money highly stable even under extraordinarily unstable circumstances. After three years of war, after widespread destruction and military reverses, in the face of impending defeat, a monetary reform that succeeded in reducing the stock of money halted and reversed for some months a rise in prices that had been going on at the rate of 10 per cent a month most of the war! It would be hard to construct a better controlled experiment to demonstrate the critical importance of the supply of money.

On the other hand, Klein's examination of German experience in World

War II is much less favorable to the stability and importance of the demand for money. Though he shows that defects in the figures account for a sizable part of the crude discrepancy between changes in the recorded stock of money and in recorded prices, correction of these defects still leaves a puzzlingly large discrepancy that it does not seem possible to account for in terms of the variables introduced into the above exposition of the theory. Klein examined German experience precisely because it seemed the most deviant on a casual examination. Both it and other war-time experience will clearly repay further examination.

Cagan's examination of hyperinflations is another important piece of evidence on the stability of the demand for money under highly unstable conditions. It is also an interesting example of the difference between a numerically stable velocity and a stable functional relation: the numerical value of the velocity varied enormously during the hyperinflations, but this was a predictable response to the changes in the expected rate of changes of prices.

20. Though the essays in this book contain evidence relevant to the issues discussed in point 18, this is a by-product rather than their main purpose, which is rather to add to our tested knowledge about the characteristics of the demand function for money. In the process of doing so, they also raise some questions about the theoretical formulation and suggest some modifications it might be desirable to introduce. I shall comment on a few of those without attempting to summarize at all fully the essays themselves.

21. Selden's material covers the longest period of time and the most "normal" conditions. This is at once a virtue and a vice—a virtue, because it means that his results may be applicable most directly to ordinary peacetime experience; a vice, because "normality" is likely to spell little variation in the fundamental variables and hence a small base from which to judge their effect. The one variable that covers a rather broad range is real income, thanks to the length of the period. The secular rise in real income has been accompanied by a rise in real cash balances per unit of output—a decline in velocity—from which Selden concludes that the income elasticity of the demand for real balances is greater than unity—cash balances are a "luxury" in the terminology generally adopted. This entirely plausible result seems to be confirmed by evidence for other countries as well.

22. Selden finds that for cyclical periods velocity rises during expansions and falls during contractions, a result that at first glance seems to contradict the secular result just cited. However, there is an alternative explanation entirely consistent with the secular result. It will be recalled

that Y was introduced into equation (7) as an index of wealth. This has important implications for the measure or concept of income that is relevant. What is required by the theoretical analysis is not usual measured income—which in the main corresponds to current receipts corrected for double counting—but a longer term concept, "expected income," or what I have elsewhere called "permanent income."[4] Now suppose that the variables in the v function of (13) are unchanged for a period. The ratio of Y to M would then be unchanged, provided Y is *permanent* income. Velocity as Selden computes it is the ratio of *measured* income to the stock of money and would not be unchanged. When measured income was above permanent income, measured velocity would be relatively high, and conversely. Now measured income is presumably above permanent income at cyclical peaks and below permanent income at cyclical troughs. The observed positive conformity of measured velocity to cyclical changes of income may therefore reflect simply the difference between measured income and the concept relevant to equation (13).

23. Another point that is raised by Selden's work is the appropriate division of wealth into forms of assets. The division suggested above is, of course, only suggestive. Selden finds more useful the distinction between "short-term" and "long-term" bonds; he treats the former as "substitutes for money" and calls the return on the latter "the cost of holding money." He finds both to be significantly related to the quantity of money demanded. It was suggested above that this is also a way to take into account expectations about changes in interest rates.

Similarly, there is no hard-and-fast line between "money" and other assets, and for some purposes it may be desirable to distinguish between different forms of "money" (e.g., between currency and deposits). Some of these forms of money may pay interest or may involve service charges, in which case the positive or negative return will be a relevant variable in determining the division of money holdings among various forms.

24. By concentrating on hyperinflations, Cagan was able to bring into sharp relief a variable whose effect is generally hard to evaluate, namely, the rate of change of prices. The other side of this coin is the necessity of neglecting practically all the remaining variables. His device for estimating expected rates of change of prices from actual rates of change, which works so well for his data, can be carried over to other variables as well and so is likely to be important in fields other than money. I have already used it to estimate "expected income" as a determinant of consumption,[5]

4. See Milton Friedman, *A Theory of the Consumption Function*, forthcoming publication of the Princeton University Press for the National Bureau of Economic Research.
5. See *ibid*.

and Gary Becker has experimented with using this "expected income" series in a demand function for money along the lines suggested above (in point 22).

Cagan's results make it clear that changes in the rate of change of prices, or in the return to an alternative form of holding wealth, have the expected effect on the quantity of money demanded: the higher the rate of change of prices, and thus the more attractive the alternative, the less the quantity of money demanded. This result is important not only directly but also because it is indirectly relevant to the effect of changes in the returns to other alternatives, such as rates of interest on various kinds of bonds. Our evidence on these is in some way less satisfactory because they have varied over so much smaller a range; tentative findings that the effect of changes in them is in the expected direction are greatly strengthened by Cagan's results.

One point which is suggested by the inapplicability of Cagan's relations to the final stages of the hyperinflations he studies is that it may at times be undesirable to replace the whole expected pattern of price movements by the rate of change expected at the moment, as Cagan does and as is done in point 5 above. For example, a given rate of price rise, expected to continue, say, for only a day, and to be followed by price stability, will clearly mean a higher (real) demand for money than the same rate of price rise expected to continue indefinitely; it will be worth incurring greater costs to avoid paying the latter than the former price. This is the same complication as occurs in demand analysis for a consumer good when it is necessary to include not only the present price but also past prices or future expected prices. This point may help explain not only Cagan's findings for the terminal stages but also Selden's findings that the inclusion of the rate of change of prices as part of the cost of holding money worsened rather than improved his estimated relations, though it may be that this result arises from a different source, namely, that it takes substantial actual rates of price change to produce firm enough and uniform enough expectations about price behavior for this variable to play a crucial role.

Similar comments are clearly relevant for expected changes in interest rates.

25. One of the chief reproaches directed at economics as an allegedly empirical science is that it can offer so few numerical "constants," that it has isolated so few fundamental regularities. The field of money is the chief example one can offer in rebuttal: there is perhaps no other empirical relation in economics that has been observed to recur so uniformly under so wide a variety of circumstances as the relation between substantial

changes over short periods in the stock of money and in prices; the one is invariably linked with the other and is in the same direction; this uniformity is, I suspect, of the same order as many of the uniformities that form the basis of the physical sciences. And the uniformity is in more than direction. There is an extraordinary empirical stability and regularity to such magnitudes as income velocity that cannot but impress anyone who works extensively with monetary data. This very stability and regularity contributed to the downfall of the quantity theory, for it was overstated and expressed in unduly simple form; the numerical value of the velocity itself, whether income or transactions, was treated as a natural "constant." Now this it is not; and its failure to be so, first during and after World War I and then, to a lesser extent, after the crash of 1929, helped greatly to foster the reaction against the quantity theory. The studies in this volume are premised on a stability and regularity in monetary relations of a more sophisticated form than a numerically constant velocity. And they make, I believe, an important contribution toward extracting this stability and regularity, toward isolating the numerical "constants" of monetary behavior. It is by this criterion at any rate that I, and I believe also their authors, would wish them to be judged.

I began this Introduction by referring to the tradition in the field of money at Chicago and to the role of faculty members in promoting it. I think it is fitting to end the Introduction by emphasizing the part which students have played in keeping that tradition alive and vigorous. The essays that follow are one manifestation. Unpublished doctoral dissertations on money are another. In addition, I wish especially to express my own personal appreciation to the students who have participated with me in the Workshop in Money and Banking, of which this volume is the first published fruit. I owe a special debt to David I. Fand, Phillip Cagan, Gary Becker, David Meiselman, and Raymond Zelder, who have at various times helped me to conduct it.

We all of us are indebted also to the Rockefeller Foundation for financial assistance to the Workshop in Money and Banking. This assistance helped to finance some of the research reported in this book and has made possible its publication.

II

The Monetary Dynamics of Hyperinflation

PHILLIP CAGAN

The Monetary Dynamics of Hyperinflation*

I. General Monetary Characteristics
of Hyperinflations

Hyperinflations provide a unique opportunity to study monetary phenomena. The astronomical increases in prices and money dwarf the changes in real income and other real factors. Even a substantial fall in real income, which generally has not occurred in hyperinflations, would be small compared with the typical rise in prices. Relations between monetary factors can be studied, therefore, in what almost amounts to isolation from the real sector of the economy.

This study deals with the relation between changes in the quantity of money and the price level during hyperinflations. One characteristic of such periods is that the ratio of an index of prices to an index of the quantity of money (P/M) tends to rise. Row 6 of Table 1 gives one measure of its rise for seven hyperinflations. (These seven are the only ones for which monthly indexes of prices are available.) Another way to illustrate this characteristic is by the decline in the reciprocal of this ratio, which represents an index of the real value of the quantity of money —real cash balances (M/P). Row 15 in Table 1 gives the minimum value reached by this index. Figures 1–7 also illustrate its tendency to decline. In ordinary inflations real cash balances, instead of declining, often tend to rise. The term *"hyperinflation"* must be properly defined. I shall define hyperinflations as beginning in the month the rise in prices exceeds 50 per cent[1] and as ending in the month before the monthly rise in prices drops below that amount and stays below for at least a year. The definition does not rule out a rise in prices at a rate below 50 per cent per month for the intervening months, and many of these months have rates below

* I owe a great debt to Milton Friedman for his helpful suggestions at every stage of the work. I also benefited from discussions with Jacob Marschak on certain theoretical points. The following people read the manuscript in semifinal form and offered useful suggestions: Gary Becker, Earl J. Hamilton, H. Gregg Lewis, Marc Nerlove, and my wife.

1. The definition is purely arbitrary but serves the purposes of this study satisfactorily. Few ordinary inflations produce such a high rate even momentarily. In Figs. 1–7 rates of change are given as rates per month, compounded continuously. A rate of 41 per cent per month, compounded continuously, equals a rate of 50 per cent per month, compounded monthly.

TABLE 1
MONETARY CHARACTERISTICS OF SEVEN HYPERINFLATIONS*

	COUNTRY						
	Austria	Germany	Greece	Hungary	Hungary	Poland	Russia
1. Approximate beginning month of hyperinflation	Oct., 1921	Aug., 1922	Nov., 1943	Mar., 1923	Aug., 1945	Jan., 1923	Dec., 1921
2. Approximate final month of hyperinflation	Aug., 1922	Nov., 1923	Nov., 1944	Feb., 1924	July, 1946	Jan., 1924	Jan., 1924
3. Approximate number of months of hyperinflation	11	16	13	10	12	11	26
4. Ratio of prices at end of final month to prices at first of beginning month	69.9	1.02×10^{10}	4.70×10^8	44.0	3.81×10^{27}	699.0	1.24×10^5
5. Ratio of quantity of hand-to-hand currency at end of final month to quantity at first of beginning month	19.3	7.32×10^9	3.62×10^6	17.0	1.19×10^{25}†	395.0	3.38×10^4
6. Ratio of (4) to (5)	3.62	1.40	130.0	2.59	320.0	1.77	3.67
7. Average rate of rise in prices (percentage per month)‡	47.1	322.0	365.0	46.0	19,800	81.4	57.0
8. Average rate of rise in quantity of hand-to-hand currency (percentage per month)§	30.9	314.0	220.0	32.7	$12,200$†	72.2	49.3
9. Ratio of (7) to (8)	1.52	1.03	1.66	1.41	1.62	1.13	1.16
10. Month of maximum rise in prices	Aug., 1922	Oct., 1923	Nov., 1944	July, 1923	July, 1946	Oct., 1923	Jan., 1924
11. Maximum monthly rise in prices (percentage per month)	134.0	32.4×10^3‖	85.5×10^6#	98.0	41.9×10^{15}	275.0	213.0
12. Change in quantity of hand-to-hand currency in month of maximum change in prices (percentage per month)	72.0	1.30×10^3**	73.9×10^3#	46.0	1.03×10^{16}	106.0	87.0
13. Ratio of (11) to (12)	1.86	24.9	1,160	2.13	40.7	2.59	2.45
14. Month in which real value of hand-to-hand currency was at a minimum	Aug., 1922	Oct., 1923	Nov., 1944	Feb., 1924	July, 1946	Nov., 1923	Jan., 1924
15. Minimum end-of-month ratio of real value of hand-to-hand currency to value at first of beginning month	0.35	0.030††	0.0069‡‡	0.39	0.0031†	0.34	0.27

* All rates and ratios have three significant figures except those in row 15, which have two. For sources see Appendix B (pp. 96–117).

† Includes bank deposits.

‡ The value of x that sets $(1 + [x/100])^t$ equal to the rise in the index of prices (row 4), where t is the number of months of hyperinflation (row 3).

§ The value of x that sets $(1 + [x/100])^t$ equal to the rise in the quantity of hand-to-hand currency (row 5), where t is the number of months of hyperinflation (row 3).

‖ October 2 to October 30, 1923, at a percentage rate per 30 days.

October 31 to November 10, 1944, at a percentage rate per 30 days.

** September 29 to October 31, 1923, at a percentage rate per 30 days.

†† October 23, 1923.

‡‡ November 10, 1944.

that figure. (The three average rates of increase below 50 per cent per month shown in row 7 of Table 1 reflect low rates in some of the middle months.)

Although real cash balances fall over the whole period of hyperinflation, they do not fall in every month but fluctuate drastically, as Figures 1–7 show. Furthermore, their behavior differs greatly among the seven hyperinflations. The ratios in rows 6 and 15 have an extremely wide range. Only when we bypass short but violent oscillations in the balances by striking an average, as in row 9, do the seven hyperinflations reveal a close similarity. The similarity of the ratios in row 9 suggests that these hyperinflations reflect the same economic process. To confirm this, we need a theory that accounts for the erratic behavior of real cash balances from month to month. This study proposes and tests such a theory.

The theory developed in the following pages involves an extension of the Cambridge cash-balances equation. That equation asserts that real cash balances remain proportional to real income (X) *under given conditions*. ($M/P = kX$; k = a constant.) Numerous writers have discussed what these given conditions are. Indeed, almost any discussion of monetary theory carries implications about the variables that determine the level of real cash balances. In the most general case the balances are a function, not necessarily linear, of real income and many other variables.

The following section discusses the most important of these variables. Because one of them—the rate of change in prices—fluctuates during hyperinflations with such extreme amplitude relative to the others, I advance the hypothesis that variations in real cash balances mainly depend on variations in the expected rate of change in prices. Section III elaborates this hypothesis and relates it to observable data on money and prices. It is supported by the statistical analysis presented in Section IV. The hypothesis, with an additional assumption, implies a dynamic process in which current price movements reflect past and current changes in the quantity of money. Sections V and VI explore certain implications of the model that describes this process. Section VII analyzes the revenue collected from the tax on cash balances, which is the counterpart of the rise in prices. A final section summarizes the theory of hyperinflation that emerges from this study.

II. The Demand for Real Cash Balances

Because money balances serve as a reserve of ready purchasing power for contingencies, the *nominal* amount of money that individuals want to hold at any moment depends primarily on the value of money, or the absolute price level. Their desired *real* cash balances depend in turn on

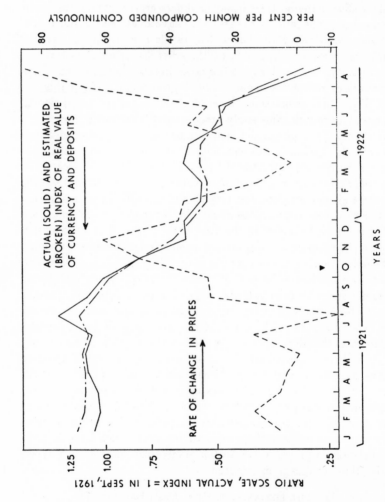

FIG. 1.—Austria—end-of-month rate of change in prices and index of real value of hand-to-hand currency and bank deposits, January, 1921, to August, 1922. (▼ Indicates beginning month of hyperinflation.)

numerous variables. The main variables that affect an individual's desired real cash balances are (1) his wealth in real terms; (2) his current real income; and (3) the expected returns from each form in which wealth can be held, including money.

If an individual's real wealth increases, he will usually desire to hold part of the increase in the form of money, because money is readily accepted in payment for goods and services or debts—it is an asset with a high liquidity.

If his current real income increases, an individual will want to substitute cash balances for part of his illiquid assets, for now he can more readily afford to forego the premium received for holding his assets in an illiquid form, and he may need larger balances to provide conveniently for his expenditures in the periods between income payments.

If the rate of interest on an asset increases, an individual is inclined to substitute this asset for some of his other assets, including his cash balances. His desired real cash balances will decrease. In addition, an increase in the rate of interest reflects a fall in the price of the asset and a decline in the wealth of holders of the asset; this decline in wealth reduces desired real cash balances.

Thus desired real cash balances change in the same direction as real wealth and current real income and in the direction opposite to changes in the return on assets other than money.

A specification of the amount of real cash balances that individuals want to hold for all values of the variables listed above defines a demand function for real cash balances. Other variables usually have only minor effects on desired real cash balances and can be omitted from the demand function. In general, this demand function and the other demand-and-supply functions that characterize the economic system simultaneously determine the equilibrium amount of real cash balances.

A simplified theory of this determination is that the amount of goods and services demanded and supplied and their relative prices are determined independently of the monetary sector of the economy. In one version of this theory—the quantity theory of money—the absolute level of prices is independently determined as the ratio of the quantity of money supplied to a given level of desired real cash balances. Individuals cannot change the nominal amount of money in circulation, but, according to the quantity theory of money, they can influence the real value of their cash balances by attempting to reduce or increase their balances. In this attempt they bid the prices of goods and services up or down, respectively, and thereby alter the real value of cash balances.

During hyperinflation the amount of real cash balances changes

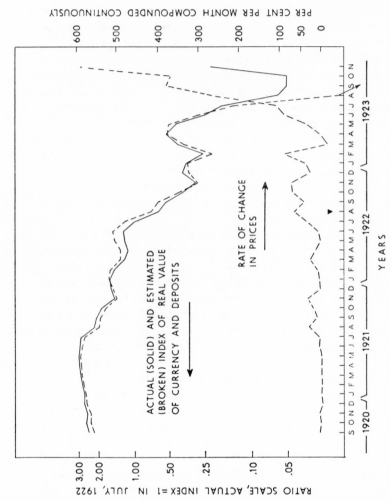

Fig. 2.—Germany—mid-month rate of change in prices and index of real value of hand-to-hand currency and bank deposits, September, 1920, to November, 1923. (▼ Indicates beginning month of hyperinflation.)

drastically (see Table 1). At first sight these changes may appear to reflect changes in individuals' preferences for real cash balances—that is, shifts in the demand function for the balances. But these changes in real cash balances may reflect instead changes in the variables that affect the desired level of the balances. Two of the main variables affecting their desired level, wealth in real terms and real income, seem to be relatively stable during hyperinflation, at least compared with the large fluctuations in an index of real cash balances. Thus to account for these fluctuations as a movement along the demand function for the balances instead of a shift in the function, we must look for large changes in the remaining variables listed above: the expected returns on various forms of holding wealth. Changes in the return on an asset affect real cash balances only if there is a change in the difference between the expected return on the asset and that on money. If this difference rises, individuals will substitute the asset for part of their cash balances. I turn, therefore, to a more detailed consideration of the difference in return on money and on various alternatives to holding money—the cost of holding cash balances.

There is a cost of holding cash balances with respect to each of the alternative forms of holding reserves, and in a wide sense anything that can be exchanged for money is an alternative to holding reserves in the form of cash balances. For practical purposes, these alternatives can be grouped into three main classes: (1) fixed-return assets (bonds); (2) variable-return assets (equities and titles to producers' goods); and (3) non-perishable consumers' goods. The cost of holding cash balances with respect to any of these alternatives is the difference between the money return on a cash balance and the money return on an alternative that is equivalent in value to the cash balance. The money return on a cash balance may be zero, as it typically is for hand-to-hand currency; negative, as it is for demand deposits when there are service charges; or positive, as it is for deposits on which interest is paid. The money return on bonds includes interest and on equities includes dividends, as well as any gains or losses due to a change in the money value of the assets. Variations in the cost of holding cash balances when the alternative is to hold consumers' goods can be determined solely by the change in the real value of a given nominal cash balance—the rate of depreciation in the real value of money. The variation in the real value of goods because of their physical depreciation is fairly constant and can be ignored.

The only cost of holding cash balances that seems to fluctuate widely enough to account for the drastic changes in real cash balances during hyperinflation is the rate of depreciation in the value of money or, equivalently, the rate of change in prices. This observation suggests the hy-

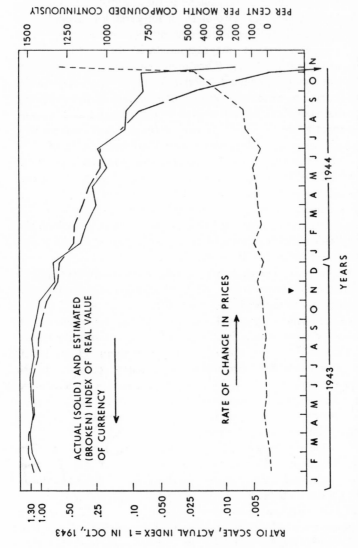

FIG. 3.—Greece—end-of-month rate of change in prices and index of real value of hand-to-hand currency, January, 1943, to October, 1944, and including November 10, 1944. (▼ Indicates beginning month of hyper-inflation.)

pothesis that changes in real cash balances in hyperinflation result from variations in the expected rate of change in prices.

To be valid, this hypothesis requires that the effects of the other variables discussed above be negligible during hyperinflation. For the most part the statistical tests in Section IV uphold the hypothesis that variations in the expected rate of change in prices account for changes in desired real cash balances. For the periods in which the data do not conform to the hypothesis, what evidence there is (see Sec. IV) suggests that taking account of changes in real income would not remedy the limitations of the hypothesis. Another explanation of why the hypothesis fails to hold for these periods is offered instead as a plausible possibility.

In order to test the hypothesis statistically, the two variables, desired real cash balances and the expected rate of change in prices, must be related to observable phenomena. The assumption made about the former is that desired real cash balances are equal to actual real cash balances at all times. This means that any discrepancy that may exist between the two is erased almost immediately by movements in the price level.[2] The assumption made about the expected rate of change in prices is that it depends on the actual rate of change in a way to be explained in the next section.

With the above two assumptions, the hypothesis asserts that time series for the price level and the quantity of money are related by some

2. This assumption can be formulated as follows: Let M^d/P and M/P represent desired and actual real cash balances. Then write

$$\frac{d \log \dfrac{M}{P}}{dt} = \pi\left(\log \frac{M^d}{P} - \log \frac{M}{P}\right), \tag{1}$$

where π is a positive constant. This says that, when desired and actual real cash balances differ, the percentage change in the latter is proportional to the logarithm of their ratio. Prices rise and diminish the actual balances when the latter exceed desired balances. Prices fall and increase the actual balances when the latter fall short of desired balances. If we write the equation as

$$\log \frac{M^d}{P} = \log \frac{M}{P} + \frac{1}{\pi} \frac{d \log \dfrac{M}{P}}{dt},$$

the assumption in the text is equivalent to asserting that π is so large that

$$\frac{1}{\pi} \frac{d \log \dfrac{M}{P}}{dt}$$

is always almost zero.

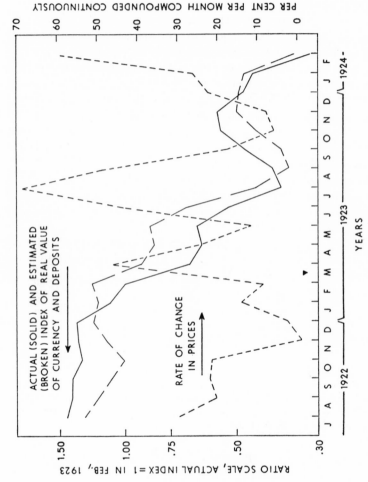

FIG. 4.—Hungary—end-of-month rate of change in prices and index of real value of hand-to-hand currency and bank deposits, July, 1922, to February, 1924. (▼ Indicates beginning month of hyperinflation.)

equation that determines real cash balances. An equation of the following form is able to account for most of the changes in real cash balances in seven hyperinflations:

$$\log_e \frac{M}{P} = -aE - \gamma.$$ (2)

Equation (2) shows the demand for real cash balances for different levels of the expected rate of change in prices. M is an end-of-month index of the quantity of money in circulation, and P is an end-of-month index of the price level. a (which is necessarily positive) and γ are constants. E represents the expected rate of change in prices and is assumed to be a function of the actual rate of change, denoted by C. C stands for $(d \log P)/dt$ and is approximated by the difference between the logarithms of successive values of the index of prices. This difference represents the rate of change in prices per month, compounded continuously, if the logarithms have the base e.[3]

E, being the expected level of C, has the same units of measurement as C, namely, a pure number divided by the number of months. M/P is an index and therefore a pure number. Consequently, the unit of a is "months."

An implication of the above relation is that variations in the expected rate of change in prices have the same effect on real cash balances in percentage terms regardless of the absolute amount of the balances. This follows from the fact that equation (2) is a linear relation between the expected rate of change in prices and the logarithm of real cash balances. This implication seems proper for an equation that is supposed to provide an accurate approximation to the true demand function.

If we write equation (2) in the equivalent form,

$$\frac{M}{P} = e^{-aE - \gamma},$$ (3)

the elasticity of demand for real cash balances with respect to the expected change in prices, implied by the above relation, is

$$\frac{d \frac{M}{P}}{dE} \cdot \frac{E}{M/P} = -aE,$$ (4)

where aE is a pure number. The elasticity is proportional to the expected rate of change in prices. It is positive when E is negative, and negative when E is positive. The elasticity is zero when E is zero.

3. If we view the change in prices from P_{i-t} to P_i in t months as a continuous rate of change at a rate of C per month, $P_i = P_{i-t}e^{Ct}$. When t is one month, $P_i = P_{i-1}e^C$; hence $C = \log_e P_i - \log_e P_{i-1}$.

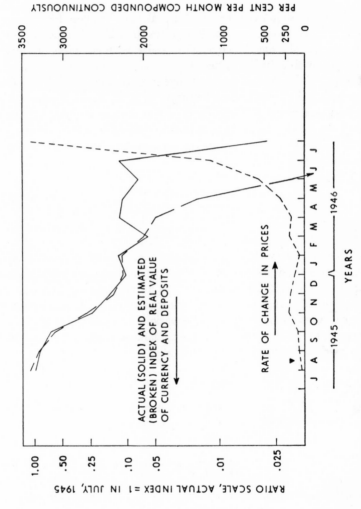

Fig. 5.—Hungary—end-of-month rate of change in prices and index of real value of hand-to-hand currency and bank deposits, July, 1945, to July, 1946. (▼ Indicates beginning month of hyperinflation.)

III. The Expected Rate of Change in Prices

The time series for the seven hyperinflations, displayed in Figures 1–7, indicate that, if desired and actual real cash balances are always equal, the actual rate of change in prices at any moment does not account for the amount of the balances at the same moment. In many months when the rates of change in prices were very low, sometimes even zero or negative, real cash balances were still much lower than they were in previous months when the rates were higher. The expected rate of change in prices seems to depend in some way on what the actual rates of change were in the past. One way is implied by the following assumption, which underlies the statistical analysis described in the next section. *The expected rate of change in prices is revised per period of time in proportion to the difference between the actual rate of change in prices and the rate of change that was expected.*

This assumption is expressed by

$$\left(\frac{dE}{dt}\right)_t = \beta\,(C_t - E_t)\,, \qquad\qquad \beta \geq 0\,, \quad (5)$$

where C_t represents $(d \log P)/dt$ at time t, and E_t is the expected level of C_t. β is a constant,[4] which can be described as a "coefficient of expectation," since its magnitude determines the rapidity with which expected rates of change in prices adjust to actual rates. The smaller is β, the slower is the adjustment.

The solution of (5) indicates what the assumption implies about the expected rate of change in prices. Equation (5) is a linear first-order differential equation in E and t with the solution,[5]

$$E_t = H\,e^{-\beta t} + e^{-\beta t}\int_{-T}^{t} \beta C_x e^{\beta x} dx\,, \qquad (6)$$

where H is the constant of integration and $-T$ is an arbitrary lower limit of the integral. If prices had been almost constant before time $-T$, it is reasonable to assume that E was zero at time $-T$; hence

$$E_{-T} = H\,e^{\beta T} = 0\,, \qquad \text{and} \qquad H = 0\,. \qquad (7)$$

4. Since C and E have the units "per month" and dE/dt, the units "per month per month," the units of β are "per month." Equation (5) is mathematically equivalent to

$$E_t = \beta\left(\log P_t - \int_{-\infty}^{t} E_x dx\right) + \text{a const.}\,,$$

where the integral term represents the expected level of prices at time t.

5. See any textbook on differential equations.

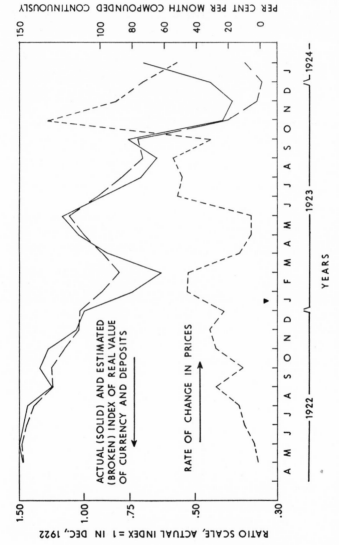

FIG. 6.—Poland—end-of-month rate of change in prices and index of real value of hand-to-hand currency and bank deposits, April, 1922, to January, 1924. (▼ Indicates beginning month of hyperinflation.)

E_t can then be written as

$$E_t = \frac{\int_{-T}^{t} C_x e^{\beta x} d x}{\dfrac{e^{\beta t}}{\beta}}. \tag{8}$$

In this form the expected rate of change in prices is a weighted average of past rates of change with weights given by the exponential function, $e^{\beta x}$. The denominator of the expression represents the sum of the weights, because

$$\int_{-T}^{t} e^{\beta x} d x = \frac{e^{\beta t}}{\beta} (1 - e^{-\beta[T+t]}),$$

and because $-T$ is chosen so that $e^{-\beta(T+t)}$ is sufficiently small to neglect (see [10], p. 41, below).

Since at best there are only monthly observations of prices during most of the hyperinflations, the expected rate of change in prices is approximated by a weighted average of a series of terms, each representing the rate of change in prices for a whole month. That is, if we approximate C_x for $t - 1 < x \leq t$ by C_t,

$$\int_{t-1}^{t} C_x e^{\beta x} d x = C_t \int_{t-1}^{t} e^{\beta x} d x = \frac{C_t e^{\beta t}}{\beta} (1 - e^{-\beta}).$$

Equation (8) is then replaced by a series of terms, each representing a monthly period, as follows:[6]

$$E_t = \frac{(1 - e^{-\beta}) \sum_{x=-T}^{t} C_x e^{\beta x}}{e^{\beta t}}, \qquad t \geq 0. \tag{9}$$

6. A convenient procedure to follow in computing E for a series of months is to calculate the accumulated products of $C_x e^{\beta x}$ for all the months $x \geq -T$, noting the sum of the products for the months $x \geq 0$. Then E_t is simply the quotient of these accumulated products for $x = t$ divided by $e^{\beta t}/(1 - e^{-\beta})$. However, when β is large, say above .7, it is more convenient to compute each E_t separately by the following form of formula (9),

$$E_t = (1 - e^{-\beta}) \sum_{i=0}^{T} C_{t-i} e^{-\beta i}. \tag{9a}$$

In this procedure the weighting pattern, $(1 - e^{-\beta})e^{-\beta i}$, is the same for each E_t and need only be calculated once for each value of β.

We can set the sum of the series of weights at a predetermined level by extending the

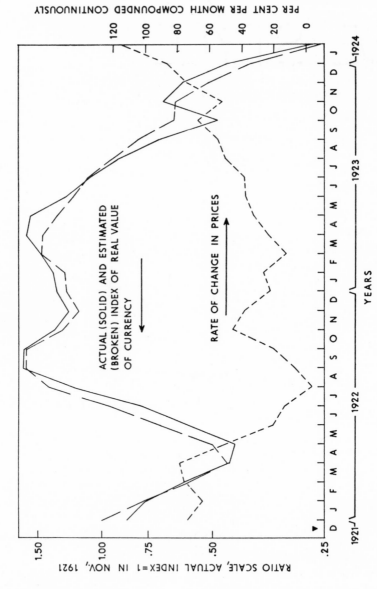

Fig. 7.—Russia—end-of-month rate of change in prices and index of real value of hand-to-hand currency, December, 1921, to January, 1924. (▼ Indicates beginning month of hyperinflation.)

Table 2 illustrates the weighting patterns by the number of months that it takes the weights in equation (9a) to fall by specified percentage amounts for different values of β. The average length of each weighting pattern, shown in the last column, is defined as follows:

$$\frac{-\int_{-\infty}^{0} x\, e^{\beta x} d x}{\dfrac{e^{\beta t}}{\beta}} = +\frac{1}{\beta}.$$

It serves as a measure of the average length of time by which expectations of price changes lag behind the actual changes.

TABLE 2

CHARACTERISTICS OF EXPONENTIAL WEIGHTS
FOR DIFFERENT VALUES OF β

β (PER MONTH)	VALUE OF WEIGHT WHEN $t = 0$ (ROUNDED TO HUNDREDTHS)	APPROXIMATE NUMBER OF MONTHS FOR WEIGHTS TO FALL BY			AVERAGE LENGTH OF WEIGHTING PATTERNS $(1/\beta)$ (MONTHS)
		50 Per Cent	75 Per Cent	90 Per Cent	
.01........	0.01	70	139	230	100.0
.05........	0.05	14	28	46	20.0
.10........	0.10	7	14	23	10.0
.15........	0.14	5	9	15	6.7
.20........	0.18	3	7	12	5.0
.25........	0.22	3	7	9	4.0
.30........	0.26	2	5	8	3.3
.35........	0.30	2	4	7	2.9
.40........	0.33	2	3	6	2.5
.50........	0.39	1	3	5	2.0
.75........	0.53	1	2	3	1.3
1.00........	0.63	1	1	2	1.0
5.00........	0.99	0	0	0	0.5
10.00........	1.00	0	0	0	0.1

IV. STATISTICAL ANALYSIS OF DATA FROM SEVEN HYPERINFLATIONS

Equation (2) and the approximation to the expected rate of change in prices given by equation (9) imply the following equation. The random variable ϵ_t is inserted to account for deviations of the left-hand side from zero.

series. In this study T was set such that

$$(1 - e^{-\beta})\, e^{\beta(-T-t)} < .00005 \tag{10}$$

for $t = 0$ (the first month used in the regressions); using the same T, the inequality is sure to hold for any $t \geq 0$. We are then sure that the series of weights for $t \geq 0$ adds up to $1 \pm .00005$ for $\beta \geq .01$.

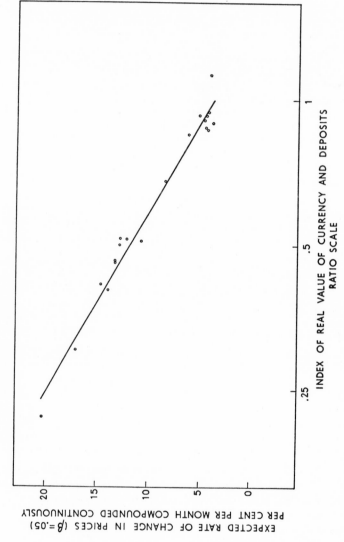

INDEX OF REAL VALUE OF CURRENCY AND DEPOSITS
RATIO SCALE

EXPECTED RATE OF CHANGE IN PRICES (β=.05)
PER CENT PER MONTH COMPOUNDED CONTINUOUSLY

FIG. 8.—Austria—scatter diagram of end-of-month expected rates of change in prices and indexes of real value of hand-to-hand currency and bank deposits, and regression line ($\alpha = 8.55$), January, 1921, to August, 1922.

$$\log_e \left(\frac{M}{P}\right)_t + \alpha \, \frac{(1 - e^{-\beta})}{e^{\beta t}} \sum_{x=-T}^{t} C_x e^{\beta x} + \gamma = \epsilon_t \,. \tag{11}$$

Table 3 contains estimates of the parameters α and β and the correlation coefficients derived by fitting equation (11) to the data from seven hyperinflations.[7] The method of fitting was by least squares. Figures 8–14 show the scatter diagrams of the regressions. Time series of real cash balances estimated from the regression functions have been plotted in

TABLE 3

LEAST-SQUARES ESTIMATES OF α AND β AND CORRELATION COEFFICIENTS FOR SEVEN HYPERINFLATIONS*

COUNTRY	TIME PERIOD (END OF MONTH)	DE-GREES OF FREE-DOM	ESTI-MATED VALUE OF α (MONTHS)	ESTI-MATED VALUE OF β ($\pm .05$) (PER MONTH)	CONFIDENCE INTERVALS†		TOTAL CORR. COEF.
					α (Months)	β (Per Month)	
Austria.........	Jan., 1921–Aug., 1922	17	8.55	.05	4.43–31.0	.01 –.15	.989
Germany.....	Sept., 1920–July, 1923	32	5.46	.20	5.05– 6.13	.15 –.25	.992
Greece‡.......	Jan., 1943–Aug., 1944	17	4.09	.15	2.83–32.5§	.01§–.30	.980
Hungary......	July, 1922–Feb., 1924	17	8.70	.10	6.36–42.2§	.01§–.20	.926
Hungary‡.....	July, 1945–Feb., 1946	5	3.63	.15	2.55– 4.73	.10 –.30	.998
Poland.......	Apr., 1922–Nov., 1923	17	2.30	.30	1.74– 3.94	.10 –.60	.972
Russia‡.......	Dec., 1921–Jan., 1924	23	3.06	.35	2.66– 3.76	.25 –.45	.971

* The estimates were computed by maximizing the total correlation coefficient for given values of β rather than by solving the normal equations. The value of β was estimated within an interval of $\pm .05$. The correct value of the correlation coefficient for each sample is therefore slightly greater than the values given in the table. The method of computing the estimates is discussed in Appendix A, and the data used are given in Appendix B.

† Confidence coefficient for intervals of α and β is .90. The confidence intervals for β are the extreme limits of a .05 interval. That is, the lower limits could be as much as .05 higher, and the upper limits could be as much as .05 lower.

‡ Greece has no adjustment to include deposits because the required data are not available. An adjustment to include deposits is not necessary for Russia. The figures for the quantity of money in Hungary following World War II include deposits for each month. See Appendix B.

§ End of confidence interval lies beyond the figure given. The correct figure was not computed because of the unreliability of the estimates of the expected change in prices for the earlier months when β is very small.

Figures 1–7. For all hyperinflations except the Russian, the regressions include observations before the beginning month shown in Table 1 in order to raise the number of degrees of freedom. But observations were not used from earlier periods in which real cash balances were subject to erratic movements. These movements were mostly increases in the balances in periods of rising prices before the beginning of hyperinflation and are inconsistent with the behavior implied by the demand function formulated above. They are discussed more fully below.

For the periods of hyperinflation covered the results indicate that an exponentially weighted average of past rates of change in prices adequate-

7. The method of deriving the estimates is discussed in Appendix A (pp. 92–96).

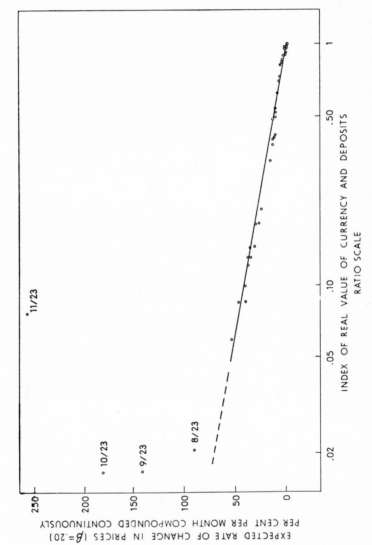

FIG. 9.—Germany—scatter diagram of mid-month expected rates of change in prices and indexes of real value of hand-to-hand currency and bank deposits, and regression line (α = 5.46), September, 1920, to November, 1923. (Points excluded from calculation of regression line are dated.)

ly accounts for movements in real cash balances. Furthermore, the confidence intervals for the estimates of β clearly indicate that expected rates of change in prices are not equal to current actual rates. The value of β that produces this equality is 10.0 (see the second column of Table 2). The highest value of β that does not differ from any of the estimates at the .10 level of significance is only .60.[8]

TABLE 4

Estimates of α and β for Seven Hyperinflations Taken Together and Test of Significance between Estimates for
the Hyperinflations Taken Together and Separately*

Estimated Value of		Total Corr. Coef.	Likelihood-Ratio Test of Significance between Estimates of α and β for the Hyperinflations Taken Together and Separately	
α (Months)	β (±.05) (Per Month)		Likelihood Ratio	.005 Level of Significance for Likelihood Ratio
4.68	.20	.894	72.53	28.3

* See Appendix A for statistical methods.

Table 4 gives estimates of α and β derived by fitting equation (11) to the data for all the hyperinflations taken together. These estimates differ significantly from those computed for each hyperinflation separately.[9]

8. The confidence intervals must be accepted with some caution. Besides relying on asymptotic properties of the likelihood ratio, the method of calculating these intervals assumes the independent normal distribution of the residuals from the least-squares fit. The confidence intervals can at best serve to indicate the approximate amount of random variability in the estimates of the two parameters.

9. Table 4 gives the results of fitting equation (11) to all the data under the assumption that the value of α is the same and the value of β is the same in all the hyperinflations. The value of γ varies among the hyperinflations. That the level of the likelihood ratio is significant for this fit means that the correlation coefficient of the fit is significantly lower than the correlation coefficient based on estimates derived for each hyperinflation separately.

Two other fits of equation (11) were made to all the data. In the first fit, all the hyperinflations have the same value of β, and the values of α and γ vary among the hyperinflations. In the second fit, the value of α is the same in all the hyperinflations, while the values of β and γ vary. The correlation coefficient in these two fits is smaller significantly at the .005 level than the coefficient based on the estimates derived for each hyperinflation separately.

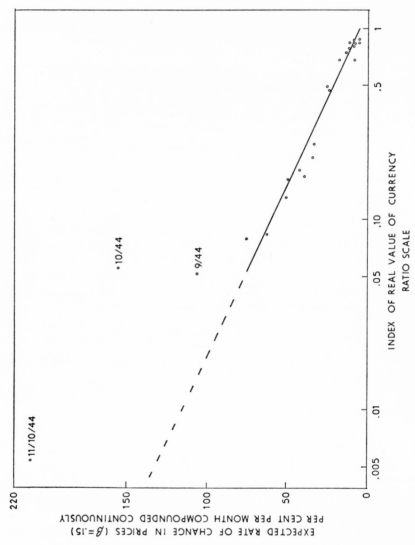

FIG. 10.—Greece—scatter diagram of end-of-month expected rates of change in prices and indexes of real value of hand-to-hand currency, and regression line ($\alpha = 4.09$), January, 1943, to October, 1944, and including November 10, 1944. (Points excluded from calculation of the regression line are dotted.)

Consequently, the differences in the values of the parameters for each hyperinflation cannot be ascribed to random variability in the estimates.

However, we should not overstress these differences. The similarity in the results for the different countries is striking in some important respects. Later sections explore the economic significance of the estimated values of the parameters and point out differences and similarities in the seven hyperinflations. This section deals with the general question of the accuracy of the statistical results. They require certain reservations, not only because of unreliable data but even more because of other difficulties of an economic and statistical nature. These difficulties are taken up below under the following headings: (1) reliability of the data; (2) economic variables ignored in the regression function; (3) observations that do not fit the regressions; and (4) increases in the coefficient of expectation.

1. RELIABILITY OF THE DATA

The data for the statistical analysis are indexes of prices and the quantity of hand-to-hand currency adjusted for all the countries except Greece and Russia to include the quantity of bank deposits. As indicated in Appendix B, which describes the data, they have limited coverage. Hand-to-hand currencies are usually issued by one governmental agency, and official publications report the quantity in circulation with unquestioned accuracy. However, illegal and counterfeit currencies, which are excluded from the money figures because of the unavailability of monthly data, circulated freely in at least one hyperinflation—the German—and were issued to some extent in most of the others. The quantity of bank deposits is based on figures that lack complete coverage. As is shown below, however, an adjustment of the money figures to include deposits has only a small effect on the estimates and cannot be a source of much error. Little can be said about the price indexes except that most of them are averages of prices of economically important commodities. The indexes are far from comprehensive in scope, and their accuracy can be checked only by independent sources. When these exist, they agree on the whole with the index used.

If, as these remarks imply, much of the data could be subject to large errors, why are the correlation coefficients in Table 3 so high? Poor data tend to increase the residual errors of a least-squares fit. The high correlation coefficients suggest that the bulk of the figures are not subject to large random errors. One factor that enhances the reliability of the data is their extreme rates of change. The differences in the rates at which the prices of various commodities rise in hyperinflation are, while no doubt

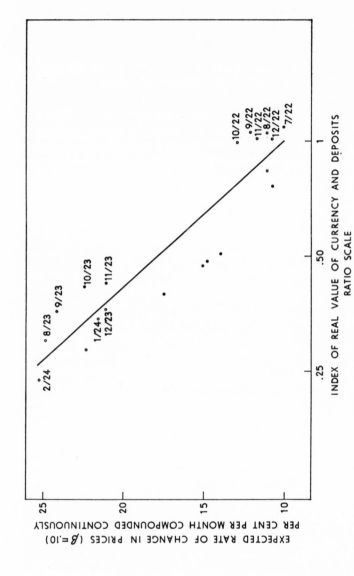

Fig. 11.—Hungary—scatter diagram of end-of-month expected rates of change in prices and indexes of real value of hand-to-hand currency and bank deposits, and regression line ($\alpha = 8.70$), July, 1922, to February, 1924. (Points before January, 1923, and after July, 1923, are dated.)

large in absolute terms, probably small relative to the rates themselves. Therefore, a price index restricted in scope reflects fairly accurately the rate of rise of an index of all prices. The money figures also, while incomplete, are adequate for approximating large changes.

Although apparently free from large random errors, the data could be consistently biased in one direction. The exclusion of illegal and counterfeit currencies tends to lower the estimates of α.[10] Also limiting a price index to wholesale or retail commodities exclusively, as is necessary for want of comprehensive data, tends to make the index too high or too low, respectively. Note, however, that, if the price index used is a constant multiple of a "correct" index, α and β are estimated without bias. To produce bias in the estimates of β, an index must misrepresent the rates of change in prices. Even then, estimates of β will not be biased if there is a linear relation between the rates used and the "correct" rates. It is not unlikely that such a relation holds approximately. In hyperinflation all prices rise so rapidly that almost any group of them registers more or less accurately the time pattern of the movements in all. Consequently, bias resulting from a consistent error in the price index would appear mainly in estimates of α. But they exhibit no signs of this bias. There is no relation between the size of the estimates of α in Table 3 and the kind of index used. The estimates of α for the Austrian and first Hungarian hyperinflations are the two largest, and they are based on indexes of the cost of living and wholesale prices, respectively. The Polish and Russian estimates, which are the two smallest, depend on indexes of wholesale and retail prices, respectively. The bias is apparently not large enough to determine the rank of the estimates. Therefore, we should be able to rely at least on their general magnitude.

The data for the estimates in Table 3 include indexes of hand-to-hand currency and monthly interpolations of an annual index of the quantity of bank deposits held by individuals and enterprises. As one of the notes to Table 3 points out, the data for Greece and Russia do not include deposits; for Hungary after World War II monthly figures on deposits are available, and no interpolations are necessary. For the other four hyperinflations Table 5 gives estimates of α and β computed from data that exclude deposits. A comparison of Tables 3 and 5 indicates that including an estimate of deposits improves the correlation coefficient twice (Germany and Hungary after World War I) and diminishes it twice (Austria

10. Figures for the quantity of money that understate the correct amount by an increasing percentage over time also make the index of real cash balances progressively too low by an increasing percentage and bias the estimate of α downward.

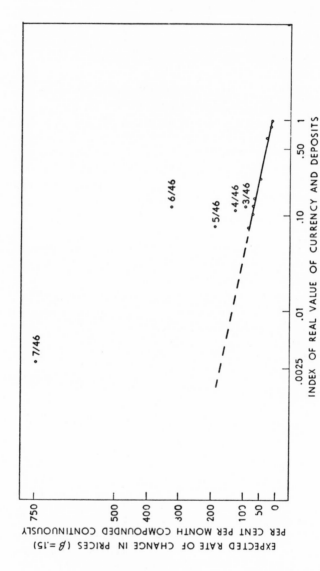

Fig. 12.—Hungary—scatter diagram of end-of-month expected rates of change in prices and indexes of real value of hand-to-hand currency and bank deposits, and regression line ($\alpha = 3.63$), July, 1945, to July, 1946. (Points excluded from calculation of the regression line are dated.)

and Poland).[11] The net effects on the estimates of including deposits are unimportant. It is likely, therefore, that the use of deposit figures in the other hyperinflations would not make an appreciable difference. Moreover, the ratio of deposits to currency is not likely to change rapidly, so that the use of monthly deposit figures, if they were available, would probably not alter these results.

TABLE 5

ESTIMATED VALUES OF α AND β EXCLUDING
BANK DEPOSITS FROM THE DATA*

Country	Estimated Value of α (Months)	Estimated Value of β ($\pm.05$) (Per Month)	Total Correlation Coefficient
Austria.....................	8.78	.05	.996
Germany...................	5.04	.25	.987
Hungary (after World War I)..	6.16	.10	.886
Poland.....................	2.84	.25	.978

* The monthly periods and the degrees of freedom are the same as in Table 3. The remarks in n. * of Table 3 apply to these estimates.

2. ECONOMIC VARIABLES IGNORED IN THE REGRESSION FUNCTION

The figures for the quantity of money exclude all money in circulation during the hyperinflations that did not have a fixed rate of exchange with the depreciating currency. One important type of excluded money is foreign bank notes. In addition, in Russia a stable-valued currency first issued by the government at the end of 1922, the chervonets, circulated along with the depreciating rubles. The Hungarian government issued a new currency in 1946, the tax pengö, which was supposed to keep a constant purchasing power. Its issue was partly successful in that it never depreciated in value at the tremendous rates reached by the regular pengö.

These issues are not counted as part of the quantity of money, because this study concerns the cash balances of rapidly depreciating currencies only. However, the sudden introduction of these other issues opened up new alternatives to holding the depreciating currency in cash balances. The fact that a stable-valued money does not pay interest means little

11. Including deposits should improve the results, because the trend of deposits and that of hand-to-hand currency may differ from each other by a great deal. It is to be expected that using monthly interpolations of an annual index of deposits might increase the residual errors about the regression lines. Therefore, the fact that the variance of the residual errors was increased by the adjustment in two cases does not indicate that the estimates of the parameters were not improved.

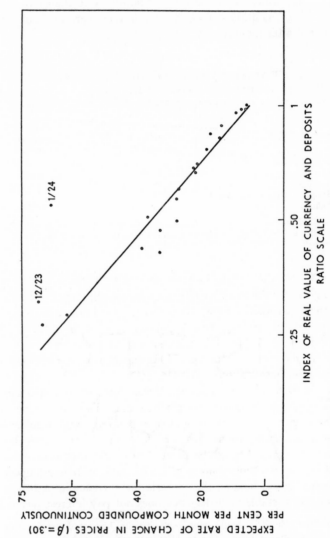

Fig. 13.—Poland—scatter diagram of end-of-month expected rates of change in prices and indexes of real value of hand-to-hand currency and bank deposits, and regression line ($\alpha = 2.30$), April, 1922, to January, 1924. (Points excluded from calculation of regression line are dated.)

in time of hyperinflation. The main concern is to prevent balances of future purchasing power from completely vanishing. Therefore, the effect of issuing a stable-valued currency along with a depreciating one is to hasten the liquidation of balances composed of the latter. It is difficult, however, to find evidence of this effect. As for foreign bank notes, the quantity in circulation during the hyperinflations is not known. It can only be assumed that they could always be held and that their quantity in circulation increased gradually as the rapidly diminishing value of the domestic currency encouraged their use. If so, their gradual increase in circulation does not disrupt the continuity of the data but does make *a* higher than it would be if they could not be obtained. The quantities of chervontsi issued in Russia during 1922–23 are known. The magnitude of their effect on the real value of rubles is difficult to judge. In any event, real cash balances of rubles were not comparatively low in Russia during the last part of the hyperinflation, as the introduction of the chervonets may suggest. There are apparently no figures on the circulation of the tax pengö issued in Hungary in 1946, and so there is no way to determine the magnitude of its effect on the value of the regular pengö.

Other errors in the estimates arising from sources of an economic nature are probably minor. The main variable that was neglected in formulating the demand function for real cash balances is real income. Conceivably, changes in real income could have large effects on the balances. Such changes, however, are probably not a source of much error in the estimates. For some countries there are annual indexes of production and agricultural output to indicate the change in real income. These indexes have small movements compared with the fluctuations in real cash balances, at least until prices rise drastically in the last stages of hyperinflation. A semiannual index of output for Germany declines in the final stage of hyperinflation by as much as one-third in less than half a year.[12] Even so, an adjustment of the data to take account of real-income changes in Germany that assumes income elasticity of demand for the balances to be unity has little effect on the parameter estimates. This effect largely offsets that of the adjustment to include deposits. For the other countries, indexes of output suggest either no great change in real income during the months of hyperinflation or conflicting tendencies from which no conclusions can be drawn.

12. In so far as this drop in real income resulted from measures intentionally adopted to restrict the use of money, there need be no further effect on desired real cash balances.

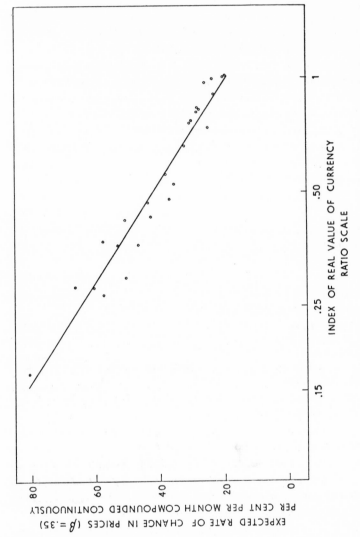

FIG. 14.—Russia—scatter diagram of end-of-month expected rates of change in prices and indexes of real value of hand-to-hand currency, and regression line (α = 3.06), December, 1921, to January, 1924.

3. OBSERVATIONS THAT DO NOT FIT THE REGRESSIONS

The periods covered by the statistical analysis exclude some of the observations near the end of the hyperinflations. The excluded observations are from the German, Greek, and second Hungarian hyperinflations, and they are dated in Figures 8–14. (Some of the points on the scatter diagram for the first Hungarian hyperinflation are also dated, but they were not excluded from the statistical analysis.) All the excluded observations lie considerably to the right of the regression lines, and their inclusion in the statistical analysis would improperly alter the estimates of α and β derived from the earlier observations of the hyperinflations.

One or both of two hypotheses could explain these observations with a much higher level of real cash balances than equation (2) implies. The first one is that in hyperinflation rumors of currency reform encourage the belief that prices will not continue to rise rapidly for more than a certain number of months. This leads individuals to hold higher real cash balances than they would ordinarily desire in view of the rate at which prices are expected to rise in the current month. As long as currency reform remains improbable for the near future, individuals adjust their real cash balances according to the rate at which they expect prices to change for some time. When they believe that the current rate at which they expect prices to rise will not last indefinitely, they are less willing to incur certain costs involved in keeping their balances low. For example, individuals would be unwilling to invest in risky equity stocks or secondhand durable goods whose principal attraction consists in the lack of better alternatives, unless there appeared to be no end to currency depreciation. Firms would not lease warehouses to maintain high inventory stocks as a substitute for cash assets, if the lease were expected to far outrun the rise in prices. Thus, when hyperinflation is expected to end in the near future, real cash balances will gradually rise, even though the expected rate of change in prices for the period preceding the end of hyperinflation remains constant or increases.

The second hypothesis is that the function that determines the demand for real cash balances does not conform to equation (2). This hypothesis suggests that the regression function shown on the scatter diagrams would fit the observations better if it curved upward on the left. To be consistent with the data, this hypothesis requires that all observations that lie to the right of the linear regressions shall fall in order along some curved regression function or, equivalently, that the value of α shall decline as the expected change in prices increases.[13]

13. It is conceivable, of course, that these high levels of real cash balances could be explained by more radical revisions of the model than are considered in the text. For

It would be difficult to test these two hypotheses, and I shall not attempt to do so. But it is not difficult, and is certainly worthwhile, to see to what extent they are consistent with the data plotted on the scatter diagrams. The evidence from these diagrams can be summarized briefly.

The Austrian data (see Fig. 8) do not support either of the two hypotheses. All the observations lie close to a linear regression line. The Russian data (see Fig. 14) only slightly support the two hypotheses. The four observations that lie substantially to the right of the upper half of the linear regression line refer to the last four months of hyperinflation. If these four observations were lowered to take into account the effects of expectations of currency reform, then all the observations might lie near a regression function that curved upward slightly. The Hungarian data after World War I (see Fig. 11) do not seem to support the two hypotheses. However, the four observations that lie to the right of the upper half of the regression line may show a high level of real cash balances because of expectations of currency reform. Figure 4 showed that the observations for August, September, and October, 1923, refer to a period in which the rate of change in prices fell sharply. It is possible that during these three months and the following month, November, there was an expectation that hyperinflation would soon end. A similar expectation may have affected the observations to the right of the lower half of the regression line. August through October, 1922, was a period of falling rates of change in prices. The difficulty of explaining the Hungarian data after World War I in this way is that some of the data from the other hyperinflations are inconsistent with the same explanation. In the Polish hyperinflation, for example (see Fig. 6), the rate of change in prices declined from February to March, 1923, but the data for this period indicate that the estimated level of real cash balances was *not* above the actual level for the entire period.

Observations near the end of the other hyperinflations lie at varying distances to the right of the regression lines, and regression functions that

------

example, new currency could be issued at such a high rate that people could not prevent the real value of their balances from rising even though expenditures rise at an increasing rate. However, a lag in the adjustment of actual real cash balances to their desired level, like that expressed by equation (1) in n. 2, fails to remedy the limitations of the model in the final months of hyperinflation. The lag suggests that the balances should decline when their actual level exceeds the desired level. In fact, they frequently rose still more in the ending months when the model indicates they already exceeded their desired level by large amounts. The failure of this lag to account for the facts reinforces the supposition that the first hypothesis in the text, while it cannot be directly supported, is the main explanation of these limitations.

curved upward would not fit them closely. However, expectations of currency reform may account for these observations. If they were adjusted for the effects of these expectations, it is possible that curvilinear regression functions would then fit the observations better than linear ones. The German hyperinflation provides a good example of this possibility (see Fig. 9). Prices had almost stopped rising in Germany by the middle of November, 1923. (This explains why real cash balances in the middle of that month were relatively so high.) The horizontal distance between the regression line and observations for the three preceding months is progressively greater for the months nearer to the end of hyperinflation. The configuration of these observations is thus consistent with an increasing effect on real cash balances of expectations of currency reform. If taking this effect on the balances into account shifted the points for August, September, and October, 1923, slightly to the left, there is some curvilinear regression function that would fit the data for these three months fairly well.

Similar remarks apply to the later observations for the Greek and Hungarian hyperinflations after World War II and the Polish hyperinflation after World War I (see Figs. 10, 12, and 13). The horizontal distance between the regression line and observations for the later months in these three hyperinflations is progressively greater for the months nearer to the end of the hyperinflations, which, according to the first hypothesis, suggests an increase in the effects of expectations of currency reform. Nevertheless, the observations from these hyperinflations, as well as those from the German one, are not inconsistent with the second hypothesis. Regression functions that curved upward slightly would fit the observations better than linear ones. The scatter diagrams indicate that the functions should begin to curve upward for an expected percentage rate of change in prices per month (compounded continuously) greater than 90–100, except for the Polish hyperinflation where the function should curve upward for a rate greater than 60–70.

The preceding discussion does not provide a direct test of the two hypotheses advanced above, but it does suggest possible revisions to make equation (2) more consistent with the data. Whether these revisions stand up in the light of all the relevant evidence has yet to be confirmed. The first is that expectations of currency reform acted to raise real cash balances near the end of hyperinflation. It is difficult to infer the extent to which this revision is required, because the second revision is also consistent with the data. What the second revision comes to is the possibility that the value of a falls at the higher levels reached by the expected change in prices.

4. INCREASES IN THE COEFFICIENT OF EXPECTATION

Figures 1–7 reveal that the residual errors by which estimated real cash balances differ from the actual levels have marked serial correlation. It is statistically significant at less than the .05 level in all hyperinflations except the second Hungarian.[14] And that one is probably not significant only because so few months were included in the regression. The regressions essentially involve fitting difference equations, in which uncorrelated random disturbances typically produce serial correlation, and its appearance in the results is not surprising. However, some, if not nearly all, of it can be attributed to shifts over time in the true value of the coefficient of expectation. Even if these shifts were purely random, the expected price change, being a sum of terms that contain past values of the coefficient (see eq. [6]), would include a component that involved the sum of successive values of a random variable. As is well known, such a sum will show positive serial correlation.

But random movements in the coefficient account for only part, probably a small part, of the serial correlation, because the evidence indicates that the coefficient does not shift in a purely random fashion but tends to increase over time. The index of real cash balances estimated from the regression functions tends to register in the early months a larger response to fluctuations in contemporaneous price changes than the actual index does, and in the later months a smaller response (see Figs. 1–7). This tendency implies that the estimated coefficients are too high for the early months and too low later on.[15] The tendency stands out clearly in five of the hyperinflations when they are divided into two parts: the Austrian, divided at June, 1921; the Greek, divided at November, 1943; the first Hungarian, divided at August, 1923; the Polish, divided at December, 1922; and the Russian, divided at April, 1923. Of the other two, the second Hungarian was too short for this tendency to show up, and the German (discussed in a moment) seems to show, if anything, the opposite tendency.

This tendency in five of the hyperinflations is confirmed by computed estimates of the coefficient, which have a higher value when the regression

14. For a description of the test for serial correlation used see J. von Neumann, "Distribution of the Ratio of the Mean Square Successive Difference to the Variance," *Annals of Mathematical Statistics*, XII (December, 1941), 367–95. For the significance tables see B. I. Hart and J. von Neumann, "Tabulation of the Probabilities for the Ratio of the Mean Square Successive Difference to the Variance," *Annals of Mathematical Statistics*, XIII (June, 1942), 207–14.

15. This cannot be due to a rising value of a, for then we should observe that points on the scatter diagrams, plotted for a given coefficient, curved downward to the left. Actually the points curve upward, if they curve at all.

fit includes only the later months than when the fit includes all the months. Table 6 gives estimates that were derived by fitting the regression to an arbitrary number of the later months. The three hyperinflations represented in the table were the only ones with an estimate for the later months that exceeded the estimate for all months by .05 or more. For these three, the last column in the table shows that the estimate for the later months as a percentage of the estimate for all months was 150 to over 200 per cent, that is, the former *exceeded* the latter by 50 to over 100 per cent. For Austria and Greece, computations not shown suggest that the estimate for the later months also exceeded the estimate for all months by as much as 50 per cent. However, for these two countries the

TABLE 6

ESTIMATES OF α AND β FOR THE LATER MONTHS
OF THREE HYPERINFLATIONS*

COUNTRY	PERIOD	DEGREES OF FREEDOM	ESTIMATE OF		ESTIMATE OF β FOR LATER MONTHS AS PERCENTAGE OF ESTIMATE FOR ALL MONTHS†
			α (Months)	β (Per Month)	
Hungary...	Feb., 1923–Feb., 1924	10	4.72	.15(± .05)	150
Poland.....	Aug., 1922–Dec., 1923	14	1.72	.45(± .05)	150
Russia.....	Apr., 1923–Jan., 1924	7	2.37	.80(± .10)	230

* Method of estimation and sources are the same as for Table 3.

† Preceding column in this table as a percentage of the corresponding estimates of the coefficient for all months shown in Table 3.

percentage difference between the two estimates could not be judged precisely without more exact estimates than have been computed. (The period covered by the regression for Hungary after World War II was too short to detect any change in the coefficient.) These estimates are of average values of the coefficient in the periods covered. If the coefficient was increasing within the periods, the results indicate that its percentage increase from the beginning to the end of these hyperinflations was at least greater than 50 per cent. Based on so few observations, these estimates are certainly subject to considerable error,[16] but they do suggest that increases in the coefficient over time may have been substantial.

16. It is likely that the percentages in the last column of Table 6 are somewhat too high. Errors of measurement in the index of prices, which is used in the index of real cash balances and of current change in prices, will produce a spurious correlation between these two and thus tend to bias estimates of the coefficient upward. This bias will be

For Germany, on the other hand, an estimate for the later months was about the same as the estimate for all months. The failure of the German data to indicate that the coefficient increased is puzzling in view of the other evidence. It is possible that the estimate for all months is too high for the early months even though the regression appears to fit equally well throughout. This result could occur if the extreme fluctuations in real cash balances for the later months dominated the regression, as appears probable only for Germany, and the relatively stable level of the balances from September, 1920, to July, 1921, contributed little. It is not clear, therefore, that the coefficient did not increase, though the amount could not have been very much.

That the coefficient should generally increase over time is certainly reasonable. It would be strange indeed if the public did not become conditioned by recent inflation to conclude that a fresh spurt in prices was not temporary but foretold more intense inflation to come. The assumption about expectations made in Section III pictured them as determined by a trial-and-error process, whereby expected price changes were adjusted to actual changes at a rate proportional to their difference. That assumption seems to provide an adequate approximation to the facts and sufficed for the model. But there is no reason to stop there. It is also reasonable to assume that with experience the public should make these adjustments more rapidly. We have found this assumption to be generally consistent with the data, though the effect of increases in the coefficient on the level of real cash balances is small compared with the major fluctuations that the balances undergo. Nevertheless, this assumption is important, for it ought to account for the level of the coefficients at the beginning of hyperinflation. The coefficient should be higher when past price rises have been more prolonged or larger.

Table 7 compares the level of the coefficient with the price changes preceding hyperinflation. The figures reveal some relation, though it is far from precise, between the level of the coefficient and the extent of past inflation. To what degree errors in the estimates of the coefficient account for the lack of precision in this relation is difficult to say. The very wide confidence intervals for the estimates (see Table 3) suggest that too

---

greater the shorter is the time period covered by the regression, because the variance of errors in the series, which is unrelated to the length of period covered, is then a larger fraction of the total variance, which is larger for longer periods. The amount of bias is difficult to judge. Indirect evidence that it might be fairly sizable is presented in the next section. But, since over-all fluctuations in the series in the periods covered are so large, it is unlikely to account entirely for all the increase in the coefficient over time shown by the estimates.

much reliance should not be placed on them. Yet it is possible to make sense of these figures "after the fact" and to reach some tentative conclusions. The low Austrian coefficient corresponds to relatively mild inflation in the preceding period, and the high Russian one to vigorous war and postwar inflation. For these two the relation seems clear cut. For the others it is less so. If we disregard Germany for the moment, we can attribute the high Polish coefficient to the large rise in prices over the entire

TABLE 7

COMPARISON OF EXPECTATION COEFFICIENT WITH PRICE
CHANGES PRECEDING HYPERINFLATION*

HYPERINFLATION	COEFFI-CIENT OF EXPECTA-TION	PRICE CHANGE PRECEDING BEGINNING MONTH OF REGRESSIONS		
		Since Prewar (1913–14 or 1937–39) (Per Cent)	One Year (Per Cent)	Two Years (Per Cent per Year)
Austrian.........	.05	6,500	94	82
Hungarian I.....	.10	17,300	314	N.a.
Hungarian II.....	.15	10,400	3,460†	520‡
Greek..........	.15	9,750	424	940§
German.........	.20	1,400	206	156
Polish..........	.30	75,000‖	241#	N.a.
Russian........	.35	28,800,000	1,610	990

N.a. = Not available.
* For sources see Appendix B.
† 13 months at an annual rate.
‡ 25 months at an annual rate.
§ 22 months at an annual rate.
‖ Wholesale price index. A cost-of-living index gives 58,500 per cent.
Cost-of-living index. A wholesale-price index linked to an index of retail food prices gives 137 per cent.

period since 1913–14, and the lower coefficient for Greece and Hungary to a smaller rise over that period, in spite of their larger figures for the year immediately preceding hyperinflation. Apparently the rapid inflation preceding the second Hungarian hyperinflation was also too short to affect the coefficient much. Thus Hungary's experience with hyperinflation the first time does not seem to have influenced behavior appreciably the second time it occurred. This result suggests that memories of currency depreciation fade away in a quarter-century, at least the first time, and that speed of adjustment depends on how prolonged recent experience with inflation has been.

The medium-sized German coefficient at first sight seems out of line

with the others in view of the mild inflation there during and immmediate-
ly after the war. The comparatively high level of this coefficient conceivably results from the advanced development, both financial and industrial, of the German economy at that time. Depreciation in the value of
money may be more apparent, and its effects sooner felt, in an economy
with proportionately less agriculture. Industrial firms and workers rely
on the value of money in selling their products and services; in less urban-
ized economies, money is used much less. While these facts were also
likely to make the coefficient for Austria higher relative to the others, its
value was low primarily because hyperinflation there was milder and
much shorter, ending just about the time the others, after World War I,
were getting started.

By and large, it appears that the coefficient usually increased in response to continual inflation. This increase probably accounts for most
of the serial correlation in the regression residuals. Whether the coefficient increased steadily or suddenly jumped to a higher level during
the hyperinflations cannot be determined, since the data cover too short
a period of time for gradual changes to show up. However, there is some
evidence on this question in the behavior of real cash balances in the
months preceding those included in the regressions. This evidence points
to rather sudden increases in the coefficient from very low or even
negative levels. A negative coefficient in the initial stages of inflation
would indicate that the public expects prices to decline eventually. In
Germany the balances rose throughout World War I, even though prices
were continually going up. Shortly after the war the balances fell sharply
by far more than the model can account for. Moreover, there is no indication that real income fell sharply at the same time. In Austria and Poland
as well, the balances rose in the months preceding hyperinflation, despite
continual inflation. There was also a rapid fall in real cash balances in
these two countries shortly after the war. This fall seems to reflect a belated adjustment to inflation after a long period in which prices were
expected to return to their prewar level.[17] (The figures on money do not
go back far enough in time for Hungary during both world wars and for
Greece during World War II to observe whether the same phenomenon
occurred in these countries.)

17. In Russia, however, real cash balances fell continuously throughout World
War I, even though the rate of change in prices fluctuated fairly closely about the same
average level from the middle of 1917 to the end of 1921. The decline in real income and
political uncertainties during the same period probably account for this steady fall in
the balances.

The erratic changes in the balances preceding hyperinflation imply that the coefficient of expectation makes a sudden upward shift, presumably when the public first loses confidence in the prospect for stable or lower prices.[18] After that, if inflation persists and speeds up, the coefficient (as we have seen) appears to become higher, possibly again by sudden shifts rather than gradual increases. While the exact timing and pattern of these shifts remain unexplained, they bear at least some relation to both the rate and the duration of past inflation. Duration is important, for there is no one rate acting as a threshold that, if pierced, causes the coefficient to jump up. Thus even very mild inflation, if continued long enough, ought eventually to produce a fairly high coefficient. The further question about how high it might go cannot be given a definite answer. After it reaches a certain level this question might seem to lose significance. Russia's coefficient reached close to .8, which gives an average lag in expected behind actual price changes of only one and a quarter months. At that point expectations are extremely responsive to current price movements, and there is not much room for shortening the lag. Yet the exact value of the coefficient at high levels becomes very important in determining whether the price rise is stable or not, that is, whether the rise becomes self-generating. This question forms the subject matter of the next section. The evidence presented there suggests that the coefficients did not, and perhaps never would, reach levels that produce self-generating price rises.

An increasing coefficient of expectation produces an upward bias in estimates of a, because the constant value of the coefficient used in computing the expected rate of change in prices falls short of the true value by increasing amounts for successively later months of hyperinflation. The expected rate of change is then understated by a greater amount for successively later months, since the actual rate of change tends to increase. This understatement biases estimates of a upward.[19] Such bias would partly account for the fact that the estimates of a in Table 6 are lower than those in Table 3. The former would be the more accurate estimates if they were derived with the better estimates of the coefficient. However, the upward bias in estimates of the coefficient (described in n. 16), which bias is larger when the estimates are based on shorter

18. See A. J. Brown, *The Great Inflation, 1939–51* (London: Oxford University Press, 1955), pp. 190–92.

19. It should be pointed out that for this reason an increase in the coefficient is not responsible for pulling observations for the later months of hyperinflation above the regression lines. This could only result from a fall in the coefficient. These high observations can indeed be interpreted as a fall in the coefficient.

periods, also makes the estimates of a in Table 6 somewhat lower than those in Table 3. The true value, therefore, lies somewhere in between the estimates in these two tables, but which estimate is more accurate cannot be determined.

V. The Stability of Equilibrium in Hyperinflation

The coefficient of expectation determines the speed with which individuals revise their expectations of the rate of change in prices. The amount by which they change their real cash balances in accordance with their revised expectations depends on the elasticity of their demand for the balances, which is proportional to the value of a. But the total reaction of a given series of changes in the quantity of money on the price level, and therefore the condition for the stable moving equilibrium of prices, depends on the product of the two parameters.[20] This is proved by deriving the condition for stability from the model.

In a self-generating inflation, a small rise in prices causes such a "flight from money" that prices go up more than in proportion to the initial rise. This cannot occur if, for any change in the price level, its rate of change moves in the opposite direction. Then any increase in prices is dampened by a fall in their rate of rise. This condition for stable moving equilibrium is expressed by

$$\frac{\partial \left(\dfrac{d \log P}{dt} \right)}{\partial P} < 0 .$$

The condition can be derived for hyperinflations from equations (2) and (5). If the indexes of P and M are set at unity in the same month in which E is zero, γ in equation (2) vanishes, and the two equations can be written as follows:

$$\log \frac{M}{P} = - aE , \tag{2a}$$

$$\frac{dE}{dt} = \beta \left(\frac{d \log P}{dt} - E \right) . \tag{5a}$$

---

20. This dependence means that, for given data, the lower is the value of β, the higher is the value of a. As β becomes smaller, the individual weights for the average of past rates of change in prices become more equal, and the weighted average produces a smaller variation in the values of the expected changes. Consequently, a lower β implies a higher a, because the smaller variations in the expected rates of change in prices have to explain the same given variations in real cash balances.

The logarithms have the base e. To reduce the two equations to a single relation between observable variables, equation $(2a)$ is first differentiated with respect to time, which gives

$$-\frac{1}{a}\left(\frac{d\log M}{dt} - \frac{d\log P}{dt}\right) = \frac{dE}{dt}. \qquad (2a')$$

Substituting $(2a)$ and $(2a')$ into $(5a)$ produces the following relation between P and M only:

$$\beta(\log P - \log M) = \frac{d\log M}{dt} - (1 - a\beta)\frac{d\log P}{dt}. \qquad (12)$$

From this it follows that

$$\frac{\partial\left(\frac{d\log P}{dt}\right)}{\partial P} = \frac{-\beta}{1 - a\beta}\left(\frac{1}{P}\right), \qquad (13)$$

since M is independent of P, and, therefore, partial derivatives of M and of its rate of change with respect to P are zero. Since P is never negative, it is apparent from (13) that prices are in stable equilibrium if $a\beta$ is less than unity and that they are not so if $a\beta$ is greater than unity.[21]

What the stability or instability of equilibrium implies about the course of hyperinflation can be inferred from the function that determines prices through time. The function can be derived by solving equation (12) for $\log P$. This equation is a linear first-order differential equation in $\log P$ and t, where M is assumed to be a function of t, independent of P. The solution of $\log P$ in terms of t, assuming for the moment that $a\beta$ is not unity, can be written as

$$(\log P)_t = (\log M)_t + H\,e^{-\beta t/(1-a\beta)}$$

$$+\frac{a\beta}{1-a\beta}\frac{\left(\int_{-T}^{t}\frac{d\log M}{dx}\,e^{\beta x/(1-a\beta)}\,dx\right)}{e^{\beta t/(1-a\beta)}}, \qquad (14)$$

where $-T$ is an arbitrary number to be specified and H is the constant of integration. H is determined by specifying the values of the variables at a particular time. Without any loss of generality we can assume that, prior to the time when $t = 0$, M and P were unity and that, at $t = 0$, M began to increase at the rate $(d\log M/dt)_0 = r_M$ and that prices began

21. The limiting case, when $a\beta$ is unity and the partial derivative in (13) is zero, turns out to be equivalent to stable equilibrium (see eq. [16]). I am indebted to Professor Jacob Marschak for drawing my attention to this way of formulating the criterion of the stability of equilibrium.

to increase at the rate $(d \log P/dt)_0 = r_P$.[22] With these initial conditions, equation (14) takes on the following form:

$$(\log P)_t = (\log M)_t + \frac{\alpha\beta}{1-\alpha\beta} \frac{\left(\int_0^t \frac{d \log M}{d x} e^{\beta x/(1-\alpha\beta)} d x\right)}{e^{\beta t/(1-\alpha\beta)}}$$
$$+ \left(\frac{r_M}{\beta} - \frac{1-\alpha\beta}{\beta} r_P\right) e^{-\beta t/(1-\alpha\beta)}. \tag{15}$$

The course of inflation depends crucially on the value of $\alpha\beta$, the "reaction index."

When the reaction index is less than unity, the terms following the integral in equation (15) approach zero as t increases, so that prices eventually depend on two factors: the quantity of money and the integral, which is an exponentially weighted average of the past rates of change in the quantity of money. The logarithm of real cash balances thus becomes proportional to the negative of this integral.

When the reaction index equals unity, the last term in the original equation (12) drops out, and the level of prices can be derived immediately. We have

$$\log P = \log M + \frac{1}{\beta} \frac{d \log M}{dt},$$

or, since $\alpha\beta = 1$,

$$\log \frac{M}{P} = -\alpha \frac{d \log M}{dt}. \tag{16}$$

Real cash balances in this case are related to the current rate of change in the quantity of money. Adjustments in the balances are not influenced by the past costs of holding money.[23]

22. It is necessary to specify that $r_P > r_M$. In the identity

$$\frac{d \log \frac{M}{P}}{dt} \equiv \frac{d \log M}{dt} - \frac{d \log P}{dt},$$

the assumed initial rates can be substituted in the right-hand side, so that

$$\left(\frac{d \log \frac{M}{P}}{dt}\right)_0 \equiv r_M - r_P.$$

Since real cash balances fall when prices and the quantity of money are rising, it is necessary that each side of the preceding identity be negative.

23. The expected change in prices may still lag behind the actual change in prices unless β (or $1/\alpha$) is sufficiently large. In fact,

$$\left(\frac{d \log P}{dt} - E\right) = \frac{1}{\beta} \frac{d^2 \log M}{dt^2},$$

When the reaction index is greater than unity, the terms following the integral in (15) are positive. The integral term is negative. The exponential weights in the integral are now turned around, so that the largest weight is given to the past rates of change in money. The integral term eventually stays relatively constant,[24] and the price level depends mainly on the logarithm of money and the two terms following the integral. These two terms following the integral rise at an exponential rate. Therefore, log P/M eventually rises at roughly an exponential rate.

The solution of equations (15) and (16) with the quantity of money rising at a constant percentage rate will illustrate the three cases of a reaction index less than, equal to, or greater than unity. Before $t = 0$, suppose that log P and log M are zero and, when $t \geq 0$, that log $M = r_M t$. The equations for prices, the change in prices, and real cash balances are then as follows for $t \geq 0$:

$$(\log P)_t = r_M t + a r_M - \frac{1 - a\beta}{\beta} (r_P - r_M) e^{-\beta t/(1-a\beta)} , \quad (17a)$$

$$\left(\frac{d \log P}{dt}\right)_t = r_M + (r_P - r_M) e^{-\beta t/(1-a\beta)} , \quad (17b)$$

$$\left(\log \frac{M}{P}\right)_t = - a r_M + \frac{1 - a\beta}{\beta} (r_P - r_M) e^{-\beta t/(1-a\beta)} . \quad (17c)$$

---

or, since $a\beta = 1$, the difference also equals $a(d^2 \log M/dt^2)$. This means that, when the quantity of money increases at an increasing rate, the expected rate of change in prices lags behind the actual rate. Actual real cash balances are then never as low as they would be if individuals could foresee the actual rates. This result is a consequence of the form of equation (5a) in the model, which shows how expectations are revised per period of time. Higher orders of revision of expectations are not taken into account. In fact, however, when prices actually rise at increasing rates for some time, individuals appear to revise their expectations with increasing rapidity. Equation (5a) nonetheless is adequate to account for most of the data.

24. This statement is true as long as log M rises at less than an exponential rate. If log M were to start rising at an exponential rate greater than $-\beta/(1 - a\beta)$, the integral term takes on an increasing negative value. The price level would have to become infinite immediately. (This can be done by setting $r_P = \infty$). Otherwise, sooner or later log P would begin to fall even though log M were rising. This is inconsistent with our premises. There is no rising level of prices in this equation that does not immediately rise to infinity and yet is consistent with a log M that rises at an exponential rate greater than $-\beta/(1 - a\beta)$.

The situation in the intermediate cases, in which log M rises exponentially at a rate less than or equal to $-\beta/(1 - a\beta)$ can be found by referring to equation (15). The fact that, when log M rises at a great enough rate, log P must go to infinity, if it is to increase at all, arises more from the limitations of the model than from the realities of hyperinflation. The model is a first approximation to those realities only.

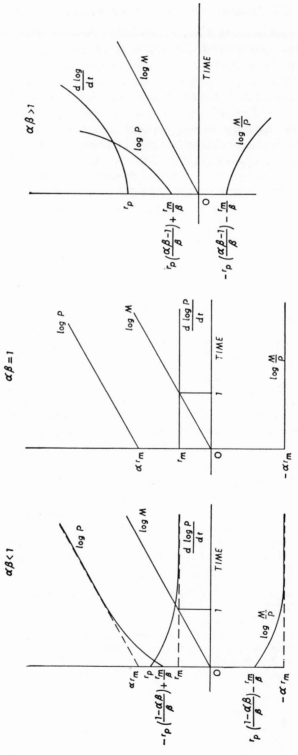

Fig. 15.—Three cases of model for constant rate of increase in quantity of money

These equations are plotted in Figure 15. When the index equals unity, the last term in (17a) and (17c) becomes zero. For this case, direct substitution of the assumed changes in the quantity of money in (16) yields the same result.

Table 8 gives estimates and confidence intervals of the reaction indexes. Only the German and Russian hyperinflations, of those examined, seem to have an index that is greater than unity. Except for the Austrian, Greek, and second Hungarian hyperinflations, however, the confidence intervals are too wide to conclude that the true value of the index is less than unity.

TABLE 8

REACTION INDEXES*

Country	Estimate of $\alpha\beta$	Confidence Intervals for $\alpha\beta$†
Austria..........................	.43	.31 − .66
Germany.........................	1.09	.92 −1.26
Greece..........................	.61	.32‡− .85
Hungary (after World War I)........	.87	.42‡−1.27
Hungary (after World War II).......	.54	.47 − .76
Poland..........................	.69	.39 −1.04
Russia..........................	1.07	.94 −1.20

* For method of estimation see Appendix A.
† The confidence level for the intervals is .90. See Appendix A.
‡ End of confidence interval lies beyond the value shown. See n. § to Table 3.

Increases in the coefficient of expectation over time (for which supporting evidence was discussed under subsection 4 in the last section) do not necessarily produce larger reaction indexes for the later months than the indexes for all months listed in Table 8. As was pointed out, when a constant coefficient is used, these increases bias estimates of α upward and so those in Table 8. Taking these increases into account places only the Russian index above unity. Based on the estimates in Table 6 for the later months, the index for Russia becomes 1.90; but for Poland it becomes only .77, and for Hungary I it falls to .71. Computations not shown for the others indicate that the index does not come up to unity; estimates for the last half of the German hyperinflation reduce its value to .96. This evidence implies that only the Russian index clearly exceeds unity. For the later months the German index seems to stand slightly below; and the others, considerably below.

But this estimate of the Russian index may spuriously exceed unity, because there is another bias making estimates of the indexes too high that has to be considered, even though we cannot exactly calculate its

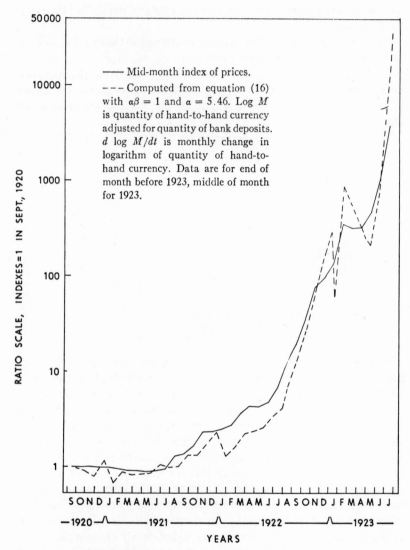

FIG. 16.—Index of prices generated by model and actual index of prices for Germany, September, 1920, to July, 1923.

effect. It is the upward bias in the estimated level of the coefficient of expectation (see n. 16). While this bias makes estimates of a too low, it does not in fact make them proportionately lower; correction for it would mean that the reaction indexes should be lowered somewhat. Its effect on estimates for the whole period of hyperinflation is probably small, but on those for a short period the effect could be substantial. Whether this bias is sufficient to account entirely for the fact that the Russian index exceeds unity is uncertain. There are other minor sources of bias, some operating in the other direction, that might be important when small amounts are crucial.[25] Thus while the true values of the others would all appear to lie below unity, the existence of many sources of possible error places even this conclusion in doubt. The estimate of the German index, being so close to unity, is especially doubtful.

Indirect evidence that the Russian index, as well as the German and others, are actually not greater than unity is provided by the estimated level of prices that can be computed from equation (15). Using the estimated value of the parameters for Germany and Russia from Table 8 in equation (15) to estimate the actual level of prices gives very poor results. Moreover, any other values of the index greater than unity are also unsatisfactory. On the other hand, values equal to, or slightly lower than, unity for Germany and Russia give more reasonable results, as indicated for the German hyperinflation by Figure 16, which compares the actual level of German prices with that generated by equation (16).

25. The two most important sources, which produce downward biases in the parameters, are described below. It is hard to believe that either of them could be very important, even though there is little basis on which to compute the exact amounts involved.

a) The exclusion of illegal currency issues from the series on money undoubtedly makes these data progressively too low by greater percentage amounts, because the incentives to issue without authorization were greatest in the peaks of hyperinflation coming at the end (see the discussion under subsection 1 in Sec. IV). By understating the series for real cash balances, this exclusion makes the estimates of a too low.

b) Least-squares estimates of the coefficient in a first-order difference equation are biased downward. This results from the failure of these estimates to take account of the serial correlation in the regression residuals, which is produced by difference equations even when the original random variable is not autocorrelated (see T. C. Koopmans [ed.], *Statistical Inference in Dynamic Economic Models* [New York: John Wiley & Sons, 1950], pp. 365–83). The regression function (11) is a difference equation of the Tth order. To what extent the estimates in Tables 3 and 8 are subject to the bias found for first-order equations is not known. Such bias, which has nothing to do with any of those mentioned heretofore, implies that estimates of the two parameters are too low. Conceivably it accounts for some of the actual serial correlation in the regression residuals, which was discussed under subsection 4 in Section IV and attributed to increases in the coefficient.

The reason why parameter values estimated from the model in one form are not always appropriate to it in another form is that one introduces biases not present in the other. While the two forms are mathematically identical, the regression functions derived from them involve different time series. For any point in time, the regression used relates the current money supply and prices to past changes in prices. The regression for the other form of the model relates current money and prices to past changes in money. While the former method of estimating the parameters does not sharply distinguish between values of the reaction index above or below unity, the latter does. Thus, even though the true index may lie below unity, the estimated value by the method used will sometimes turn out greater than unity because of random errors and bias.

This interpretation of the results seems inescapable, because a reaction index that exceeds unity is not consistent with the general characteristics of the hyperinflations. When the index exceeds unity, equation (15) implies that changes in the quantity of money, once the quantity initially rises, have very little to do with the course of inflation. The fall in real cash balances is so large that prices continue to rise under the impetus of falling balances *ad infinitum*.[26] This situation did not characterize the whole of the German and Russian hyperinflations, or the others either. Price changes did not always tend to increase at exponential rates. Yet if the reaction index were above unity, the *logarithm* of actual prices would have to rise at no less than an exponential rate before any solution of equation (16) would estimate prices with reasonable accuracy, unless perhaps there were continual changes in expectations. Even in the last part of the Russian hyperinflation, although the rate of change in prices climbed steadily, it was nowhere near exponential. In view of the actual price rises that occurred, therefore, none of the hyperinflations appears to have been self-generating.

Does it also follow that self-generating inflations are somehow im-

26. In such a situation the inflation is self-generating in the sense that diminishing real cash balances create a continual rise in prices, which in turn leads to a continual fall in the balances. It is possible to prescribe values of the parameters so that, according to the model, even certain rates of *decrease* in the quantity of money will not stop the inflation once it gets under way. But we should not expect this solution of the model to apply. In the light of the sharp rise in the balances when a reform in the currency approaches, any diminution in the rate at which notes were issued would likely alter the prevailing expectation of a certain rate of future inflation to one of a less rapid rate, whether the reaction index were greater than unity or not. If so, the balances would rise at once if the policies of the note-issuing authorities justified more confidence in the future value of the currency. These sudden revisions in expectations cannot be accounted for in a model that predicts future prices on the basis of past changes in prices or money alone.

possible? There seems to be no reason why they could not occur; so far they have just not been observed. The world has seen inflations that go on for decades but do not develop self-generating characteristics. This evidence, combined with that from these seven relatively brief hyperinflations, suggests that price increases would become self-generating only after a prolonged period of hyperinflation. Even when the reaction index exceeded unity, if the percentage increase in the money supply were less than exponential, expectations would probably not sustain a percentage increase in prices at an exponential rate for very long. Prices would more likely exhibit a high degree of instability, with the percentage change in real cash balances alternately falling and rising at exponential rates depending on whether the increase in money in the immediate future were expected to accelerate or taper off. Under these circumstances it seems likely that reform of the currency would become a political and economic necessity. This could be the reason why self-generating price increases have never been observed—hyperinflation that otherwise proceeded to the stage where they began would not last long enough after to permit their detection.

VI. A NOTE ON LAGS

We have seen that, if the lag in expectations in the model is too short, inflation becomes self-generating. When the coefficient of expectation is quite large, which means that expected price changes follow the actual changes without a perceptible lag, the reaction index exceeds unity. Then, once the money supply increases, the logarithm of prices begins to rise at no less than an exponential rate. Subsequent increases in the money supply only add to the rate of rise in prices;[27] a reduced rate of increase in the supply will not make the rate of price rise less than exponential, except perhaps through indirect effects on expectations. The condition for stable moving equilibrium given in Section V confirms this statement by showing that a reaction index greater than unity creates unstable conditions.

Actually, any function that relates real cash balances to the rate of change in prices without a lag violates the condition for stability. For, given such a function,

$$f\left(\frac{M}{P}\right) = \frac{d \log P}{dt}, \tag{18}$$

the condition for the stable moving equilibrium of prices requires that

$$\frac{\partial \left(\frac{d \log P}{dt}\right)}{\partial P} = \left(\frac{-M}{P^2}\right) f' \tag{19}$$

27. Subject to the conditions set forth in n. 24.

be less than zero, provided that M is independent of P. Since real cash balances generally fall in response to a rise in the rate of change in prices, f' is usually negative; hence this partial derivative is positive, implying instability. An increase in the rate of change in prices occurs whenever they rise. The inflation will thus continue under its own momentum, as it were.

Certainly no mild inflation exhibits the properties of instability, and the seven hyperinflations do not appear to have them either. Therefore, some lag (or other restraint on changes) affects the dependence of real cash balances on the rate of change in prices to a significant degree. The lag in expectations, which conforms to the data in most months of the seven hyperinflations exceptionally well, appears to be unusually long. Estimates of its average length (see Tables 2 and 3) range from three to twenty months. On the other hand, a lag associated with another variable in the model—the desired level of the balances—is assumed to be extremely short.[28] This section points out that these two lags cannot be empirically distinguished. The extreme length estimated for the first lag may thus result from the additional effects of the second, as well as from those of a third, also discussed below, which concerns the expected duration of any rate of rise in prices. These three seem to be the main lags that require consideration in a monetary analysis of hyperinflation.

To begin with, what can we say about a lag in the balances?[29] Suppose that the actual levels of real cash balances were not always equal to desired levels but were adjusted at a rate proportional to the difference in their logarithms:

$$\frac{d \log \frac{M}{P}}{dt} = \pi \left(\log \frac{M^d}{P} - \log \frac{M}{P} \right), \tag{20}$$

where the superscript d denotes desired levels, and π is a positive constant. This assumption is analogous to the one used to describe how the unobserved expected price changes adjust to the actual changes, except that here the actual level of real cash balances adjusts to the unobserved desired level. Suppose further that expectations involve no lag and that the desired balances depend on the actual change in prices as follows:

$$\log \frac{M^d}{P} = - \alpha \frac{d \log P}{dt}. \tag{21}$$

28. See above, n. 2.

29. The argument that follows has benefited from discussions I have had with Marc Nerlove.

Combining equations (20) and (21), we get

$$\frac{d \log \frac{M}{P}}{dt} + \pi \log \frac{M}{P} = - \alpha\pi \frac{d \log P}{dt}. \qquad (12a)$$

This is identical to the reduced equation for the model derived in preceding sections, which used a lag in expectations instead. Compare equation (12a) with (12). The only difference is the substitution of π for β. When we treat (12a) as a differential equation and solve for $\log (M/P)$ in terms of $(d \log P)/(dt)$, the result is identical to the combination of equations (2) and (8), which underlies the regression function (11). The two lags thus imply the same relation between prices and money.

This equivalence of the two lags is perfectly reasonable. Individuals may well behave with only one or the other lag, but we cannot observe which one it is. Indeed, the behavior of two individuals who differed completely in this respect has identical effects on the data. One might adjust his expectations to current price changes rapidly but only slowly bring his cash balances in line with the amount desired. Another might tardily adjust his expectations but quickly change his cash balances. For both, we would observe a certain lag of changes in cash balances behind current price changes, and unless we assumed that the two lags affected the data differently,[30] we would not be able to distinguish between them.

The model can be viewed as an approximation, therefore, to a more general model involving both lags. By attaching the superscript d to real cash balances in (12a) and combining that equation with (20), we get the following second-order differential equation:

$$\frac{1}{(\beta + \pi)} \frac{d^2 \log \frac{M}{P}}{dt^2} + \frac{d \log \frac{M}{P}}{dt} + \left(\frac{\beta\pi}{\beta + \pi}\right) \log \frac{M}{P} \qquad (22)$$

$$= - \alpha \left(\frac{\beta\pi}{\beta + \pi}\right) \frac{d \log P}{dt}.$$

This, too, confounds the two lags. Interchanging β and π does not alter the equation in any way.

The model that was used is equivalent to this equation except for the first term, and what I have previously called the "coefficient of expectation" here approximates $(\beta\pi)/(\beta + \pi)$, an amalgam of two lags.[31] If

30. Suppose eq. (1) in n. 2 had $-d \log P/dt$ for its left-hand side. It would then be similar to (20) but would give a lag in the balances with implications that are not all equivalent to a lag in expectations.

31. Under the original assumption made in Sec. II that π is very large, this expression is only slightly less than β. For, as π increases, $(\beta\pi)/(\beta + \pi)$ approaches the value of β from below.

$\beta + \pi$ is fairly large or the second derivative fairly low, the first term contributes little to the relation. That the contribution of this term was fairly small in the seven hyperinflations is suggested by the good results obtained with the model used. The model describes most months quite well,[32] even though it ignores the first term. Of course, the above equation, incorporating both lags, would probably fit the data better than the model, though whether much better is questionable. Because of the many statistical difficulties as well as extensive computations involved, however, a fit using this equation has not been attempted.

Even though the coefficient of expectation in the model must be interpreted as a mixture of two lags that cannot be distinguished, it hardly seems possible that the lag in the balances could be more than a fraction as long as the lag in expectations. Once a person decides on the desired level of his balances, he can easily adjust his actual balances by spending them or by selling other assets for cash. The time required is negligible, because he adjusts his balances not so much by changing the level of his consumption over a period of time as by altering the form in which he holds his wealth. In forming his expectations, however, he may very well look far back in time in order to assess the current trend of prices. Nevertheless, there is no direct evidence on the relative importance of the two lags, and it should be understood that to some extent the estimates of the coefficient of expectation also reflect a lag in the balances and are to that extent too low as a measure of the lag in expectations alone. For simplicity of exposition, I have referred throughout only to the lag in expectations.

The estimates of α, on the other hand, are not subject to any such ambiguity, and the elasticity of demand defined by equation (4) does represent, as was intended, the percentage change in desired real cash balances with respect to changes in the expected rate of increase in prices.

Another kind of expectation that may be important, although it was not explicitly taken into account, concerns the expected duration of a rate of price change. It affects the desired level of the balances. A rate of price rise of 50 per cent per month may be entirely ignored if the rate is expected to last only one day; but balances will be considerably reduced if the rate is thought likely to continue for six months. Expected duration might follow rumors and conjectures about the future level of prices instantly without regard to the past. Then it would tend to produce erratic and unpredictable changes in desired real cash balances. But, if it depended primarily on the extent and duration of inflation in the recent

32. Moreover, neither lag accounts for the high levels of the balances in the ending months of hyperinflation (see n. 13).

past, it would behave much like the expected price change. Since the model describes most months of hyperinflation fairly well even though the effects of expected duration on the balances were not explicitly taken into account, quite likely the model implicitly incorporates these effects. Thus the exponentially weighted average of the rates of change in prices probably represents not the expected rate for the immediate future, as was assumed, but the average rate that is expected to last long enough to justify the trouble and expense of reducing cash balances. This rate could fall far short of the rate that might be expected to prevail in the coming weeks or months and thus could explain why the estimated values of the coefficient of expectation are so low. An average lag as long as twenty months may reflect not so much a failure to revise expected rates (or to adjust cash balances) rapidly as an unwillingness to incur the costs of low cash balances before the continued tendency for prices to rise is viewed as relatively permanent. Throughout the hyperinflations the expected duration of the price rise seems to have exercised considerable restraint on reductions in desired real cash balances.

Other factors than the past performance of prices undoubtedly influenced the expected duration at certain times. The balances rose near the end of all but two of the seven hyperinflations, while the model predicts they should have fallen (see Sec. IV). Prospects for the probable end of currency depreciation apparently made the public willing to hold larger balances immediately. Before the beginning months, too, the expected duration of inflation apparently underwent a sudden rise (see Sec. IV). The sharp decline in the balances following their long rise in the months preceding hyperinflation seems to reflect a sudden realization by the public that greater price increases lay ahead. The precise timing of such shifts in expectations appears incapable of prediction by economic variables, even though we may be certain such shifts will eventually occur under the circumstances. But, when the shifts are absent, expectations of price changes depend closely on past events.

VII. The Tax on Cash Balances

The analysis so far has linked the large price increases during hyperinflation to large increases in the quantity of money. But there is still the question, "Why did the quantity of money increase and by so large an amount?" The answer is twofold: (1) printing money was a convenient way to provide the government with real resources, though it tended to preclude other methods; and (2) the effectiveness of this method declined over time and so required ever larger issues.

In the unsettled conditions following the two world wars, governments were too weak to enact adequate tax programs and to administer them effectively. Issuing money was a method of raising revenue by a special kind of tax—a tax on cash balances. This tax is often appealing because it does not require detailed legislation and can be administered very simply. All that is required is to spend newly printed notes. The resulting inflation automatically imposes a tax on cash balances by depreciating the value of money.

The base of the tax is the level of real cash balances; the rate of the tax is the rate of depreciation in the real value of money, which is equal to the rate of rise in prices. Revenue (in real terms) from the tax is the product of the base and the rate,

$$\frac{M}{P} \left(\frac{dP}{dt} \frac{1}{P} \right).$$

The note-issuing authorities "collect" all the revenue; however, when prices rise in greater proportion than the quantity of money, that is, when real cash balances decline, part of the revenue goes to reduce the real value of the outstanding money supply.[33] Thus total revenue per period of time is the sum of two parts: first, the real value of new money issued per period of time,

$$\frac{dM}{dt} \frac{1}{P};$$

and, second, the reduction in outstanding monetary liabilities, equal to the decline per period of time in the real value of cash balances,

$$\frac{d\left(\dfrac{M}{P} \right)}{dt}.$$

This is demonstrated by the following identity:

$$\frac{dM}{dt} \frac{1}{P} - \frac{d\left(\dfrac{M}{P} \right)}{dt} \equiv \frac{M}{P} \left(\frac{dP}{dt} \frac{1}{P} \right). \tag{23}$$

The note-issuing authorities do not set the tax rate directly. They set the rate at which they increase the money supply, and this rate determines the tax rate through the process described in preceding sections.

Typically, institutions other than the government also have the authority to issue money. In so far as they exercise this authority, they

33. Inflation also reduces the real value of the principal and interest charges of debt fixed in nominal terms. However, amortization of debt cannot have required a very large fraction of government expenditures once hyperinflation began.

receive some of the revenue from the tax, even though the initiating factor is government creation of money. In the hyperinflations, as government issues swelled the reserves of private commercial banks, an expansion of bank credit could and did take place. Banks largely dissipated the revenue from their share of the tax by making loans at nominal rates of interest that did not take full account of the subsequent rise in prices, so that the real rate of interest received was on the average below the real return that could be obtained on capital. The revenue dissipated by the banks went to their borrowers.[34]

The revenue received by the government thus depends on the tax rate and on the fraction of the revenue that goes to banks and their borrowers. In addition, it depends on the tax base, that is, the level of real cash balances. A higher tax rate will not yield a proportionately higher revenue, because the balances will decline in response to the higher rate. Indeed, the balances may ultimately decline more than in proportion to the rise in the rate, so that a higher rate may yield less revenue. This will not be so immediately, however, because of the lag in expectations.[35] It takes time for expected price changes to adjust to the actual changes. Consequently, a rise in the tax rate, that is, in the rate of change in prices, will at least initially increase the revenue from the tax.

This fact helps to explain why a similar time pattern of revenue emerged in all the seven hyperinflations. The revenue was high at the start, when the expected rate of price increase was still low; tended to decline in the middle, as the expected rate started to rise considerably; and rose near the end, when the rate of new issues skyrocketed.[36] The

34. The government's share of total revenue depends on the proportion of money issued by governmental agencies. If this proportion is not the same for the quantity of money outstanding as for the amount currently issued, the government's share of the two parts of total revenue will differ. To compute the government's share of the total, we must multiply each part in (23) by separate fractions. For the first part, the appropriate fraction is the ratio of money currently issued by the government to total issues in a period of time; for the second, the fraction is the ratio of outstanding government issues to the total money supply.

35. This follows from the relation

$$\frac{d \log \dfrac{M}{P}}{dt} = - \alpha\beta \, (C - E) \,,$$

derived from equations (2) and (5), and from the condition that $\alpha\beta < 1$, found to hold for all the hyperinflations (see Sec. V).

36. Part of this rise in revenue resulted from the failure of real cash balances to make further declines in the final months, apparently because the end of hyperinflation appeared imminent (see Sec. IV).

note-issuing authorities in all the hyperinflations evidently responded to the belated decline in the balances in much the same manner. In the beginning months, when the quantity of money rose at rates much higher than those previously attained, the revenue was also much higher than before. Because of the lag in expectations, many months passed before real cash balances declined very much. When the balances finally began to decline by substantial amounts, the revenue decreased from the high level of the beginning months. The revenue could be enlarged, as for a short time it was, only by inflating at successively higher rates. Rates were quickly reached, however, that completely disrupted the economy, and they could not be long continued. The attempt to enlarge the revenue in the closing months thus produced the characteristic pattern of the hyperinflations: price increases did not peter out; they exploded.

The time pattern aside, the productivity of the tax can be analyzed most simply by comparing the revenue that was actually raised in the seven hyperinflations with the revenue that could have been raised if the quantity of money had risen at a constant rate. Under the latter condition, the actual and expected rate of rise in prices would eventually become practically equal to this constant rate,[37] and C can replace E in equation (3), the demand function for real cash balances. This substitution gives

$$\frac{M}{P} = e^{-aC-\gamma}. \tag{24}$$

Since total revenue, R, equals the rate of rise in prices times real cash balances, we have, substituting (24),

$$R = C e^{-aC-\gamma}. \tag{25}$$

Total revenue is a maximum when the derivative of this expression with respect to C is zero and the second derivative is negative, namely:

$$\frac{dR}{dC} = (1 - aC)\ e^{-aC-\gamma} = 0,$$

$$\frac{d^2R}{dC^2} = (a^2C - 2a)\ e^{-aC-\gamma} < 0. \tag{26}$$

These conditions are satisfied when $(1 - aC)$ equals zero. Therefore, the rate of tax on cash balances, that is, the rate of inflation, that yields the maximum revenue in (25) is $1/a$. At this rate of tax, the demand for real

37. We can then refer to these three rates simply as "the rate of inflation." Their equality follows from the constancy of real cash balances, which in turn follows from equation (15), given the constant rate of increase in money.

cash balances has an elasticity of -1. Table 9 shows this rate for the seven hyperinflations. It must be emphasized that the rates in columns 1 and 2 yield the maximum revenue only in the special sense of the revenue that can be maintained indefinitely. When the tax is first imposed, that is, at the beginning of inflation, there is no maximum yield; the higher the rate, the higher the yield, thanks to the delayed adjustment in the balances produced by the lag in expectations.

TABLE 9

RATE OF INFLATION THAT MAXIMIZES THE ULTIMATE
REVENUE FROM A TAX ON CASH BALANCES*

COUNTRY	RISE IN PRICES AND QUANTITY OF MONEY THAT MAXIMIZES ULTIMATE REVENUE		AVERAGE ACTUAL RATE OF RISE IN PRICES (PER CENT PER MONTH)
	Rate per Month Compounded Continuously $(1/\alpha)$ (1)	Per Cent per Month $[(e^{1/\alpha}-1)100]$ (2)	(3)
Austria..................	.117	12	47
Germany.................	.183	20	322
Greece...................	.244	28	365
Hungary (after World War I)	.115	12	46
Hungary (after World War II)	.236	32	19,800
Poland..................	.435	54	81
Russia..................	.327	39	57

* Rate of change in quantity of money is assumed constant. The values of α used are the estimated values shown in Table 3. Column 3 is reproduced from Table 1, row 7.

The table also lists for comparison the average rates of rise in prices that actually prevailed. The actual rates were well above the constant rates that would have maximized the ultimate revenue. With Table 10 we can compare the yield of the actual rates with the ultimate yield that could have been attained with a constant rate.

Table 10 presents various measures of the average revenue. The closing months of some of the hyperinflations were omitted (see note * to Table 10). To make comparisons among the countries, it is necessary to express the revenue relative to some standard of reference. Two alternative standards were used for Table 10. The first is the level of real cash balances in the beginning month of hyperinflation. Its use allows for differences in the base of the tax. The second is national income in a "normal" year. Its use allows for differences in economic resources.

TABLE 10

REVENUE FROM THE TAX ON CASH BALANCES

COUNTRY AND PERIOD*	RATIO OF GOVERNMENT MONEY TO TOTAL QUANTITY†	AVERAGE MONTHLY REVENUE AS A PERCENTAGE OF‡				
		Real Cash Balances in Beginning Month of Hyperinflation			National Income in a Base Year	
	Ultimate Maximum for a Constant Rate of Increase in Quantity of Money	Total $\left(\dfrac{M}{P}\dfrac{dP}{dt}\dfrac{1}{P}\right)$	From Issues of New Money $\left(\dfrac{dM}{dt}/P\right)$	From Issues of New Money $\left(\dfrac{dM}{dt}/P\right)$	From Issues of Government Money (Cols. [1] × [5])
	(1)	(2)	(3)	(4)	(5)	(6)
Austria						
Oct., 1921—Aug., 1922.	.30	9	24	18	26	8
Germany						
Aug., 1922—July, 1923.	.46–.59	30	30	25	12	6–7
Greece						
Nov., 1943—Aug., 1944	(.50)	22	30	22	(11)§	(6)§
Hungary						
Mar., 1923—Feb., 1924.	.66–.95	19	25	21	20	13–19
Hungary						
Aug., 1945—Feb., 1946.	.83–.93	18	32	21	7	7‖
Poland						
Jan.—Nov., 1923	.65–.75	36	36	31	4	3
Russia						
Dec., 1921—Jan., 1924.	1.00	41	41	41	0.5	0.5

* The period of the averages in cols. 3–6 is from the beginning month of hyperinflation to the last month included in the calculation of the regression lines (see Tables 1 and 3). For two reasons this period was not carried to the end of all the hyperinflations, shown in Table 1. First, the closing months frequently had extreme fluctuations in real cash balances. Using the end-of-month level of the balances would provide a poor approximation to their average level during the months. Second, in the closing months the level of the balances was sometimes unaccountably high in view of the large expected change in prices (see Sec. IV). These high levels very likely resulted from an expectation that hyperinflation would soon end. They temporarily made the revenue from the tax much higher than in the preceding months.

† "Government money" comprises notes issued by governmental agencies and deposits held by the public in the national bank and postal savings accounts. The total quantity of money comprises all notes and bank deposits held by the public. With one exception the ratios are rough approximations, since they were built up from annual figures for deposits that lack complete coverage. The exception refers to Hungary after World War II, for which fairly complete monthly data were used. Owing to the unavailability of Greek deposit figures during the war, the figure for Greece refers to 1941 and is apt to be a poor estimate for the hyperinflationary period, but it is the only one obtainable. For sources see Appendix B.

‡ Column 2: Product of the rate of change in prices shown in col. 1 of Table 9 and the index of real cash balances (with appropriate change of base) corresponding to this rate on the regression lines in Figs. 8–15.

Column 3: Average product for the period covered of the rate of change in prices ($\log_e P_t - \log_e P_{t-1}$) from the beginning to the end of the month and an end-of-month index of the real value of notes. Since the index tended to fall over most months, the use of its value at the end of the month makes this average an understatement of an average based on daily figures.

Column 4: The total revenue less the average change in real cash balances per month (see eq. [23]). This average change is equivalent to the difference between an index of the real value of notes at the beginning and at the end of the period, divided by the number of months covered.

Column 5:

$$(\text{Col. 4}) \times \left(\frac{\begin{array}{c}\text{Index of real cash balances in beginning}\\ \text{month of hyperinflation}\end{array}}{\text{Index in earlier months}}\right) \times \left(\frac{\begin{array}{c}\text{Quantity of money in the}\\ \text{normal year}\end{array}}{\begin{array}{c}\text{Average monthly national}\\ \text{income in the normal year}\end{array}}\right)$$

Though desirable, using months from the normal year in the third factor for the earlier months in the second factor would involve difficulties and was not attempted. The earlier months used, except for Hungary I and Poland, were prewar months to which the index of real cash balances could be readily extended. The normal years were later years for which reasonably reliable data on national income were available. The above product assumes that the third factor holds for the earlier months used in the second factor. This assumption is likely to be approximately correct, because the earlier months and the normal year had relatively stable prices. The normal year and earlier months used, respectively, were for Austria, 1929 and all of 1914; Germany, 1927 and all of 1913; Greece, 1949–52 and June, 1941; Hungary I, 1936 and July, 1921; Hungary II, 1936 and August–December, 1939; Poland, 1929 and January, 1921; and Russia, 1926–29 and December, 1913. The ratios of money to income in the normal years were calculated by Martin J. Bailey (see his "The Welfare Cost of Inflationary Finance," *Journal of Political Economy*, Vol. LXIV [April, 1956], Table 2

Column 3 gives the actual total revenue. It is the average product of the monthly rate of change in prices and an end-of-month index of real cash balances. Column 4 gives the amount of total revenue collected by banks and the government from spending new money. The total revenue in column 3 exceeds this amount by the average reduction in real cash balances per month. Column 2 shows the maximum ultimate revenue under the restriction that the rate of inflation is held constant, which is equivalent to the condition that the balances eventually remain constant. A comparison of columns 4 and 2 indicates that, in all countries except Austria, a constant rate of inflation could have yielded a revenue as large, on the average, as the amount actually collected.

This outcome seems surprising in view of the high and rising tax rates that were imposed. No purpose was served by such high rates unless the authorities intended to take advantage of the lag in expectations to collect more revenue than could ultimately be obtained with a constant rate. They could succeed in this intention by a policy of inflating at increasing rates and so repeatedly take advantage of this lag. The authorities successfully pursued this policy in the beginning and ending months and in much of the period preceding hyperinflation. The policy was temporarily abandoned in the middle months of all the hyperinflations, when the rate of price increase stopped rising and even fell somewhat. The average revenue exceeds the maximum amount in column 2 if most of the middle months are excluded. It is not clear why the authorities allowed the revenue to decline during these months. Perhaps they hesitated to continue a policy that promised to destroy the monetary system, and they hoped to restore some of the public's confidence in the currency. Apparently the need for revenue soon overrode whatever considerations prompted them to let the revenue decline, for the cumulative process of inflating at increasing rates was resumed in the closing months.

On this interpretation, the actual rate of rise in prices depended pri-

---

col. 5). These ratios do not apply to years as close to the periods of hyperinflation as the data sometimes permit, but they seem adequate for use in the above estimates.

Columns 3, 4, and 5 were derived from changes in figures for notes (except for Hungary II) that were used to approximate changes in notes and deposits combined. This derivation involves the assumption that notes and deposits increased at equal rates. The assumption is obviously not precisely true, since the ratio of notes to deposits varied (see Appendix B). Moreover, relatively small variations in this ratio imply large differences in their rates of increase. Where notes rose faster than deposits (Germany and Hungary I), the percentages in cols. 3 and 4 are somewhat overstated; and, where notes rose less rapidly (Poland), the percentages are understated.

Column 6: This gives the revenue from new issues collected by the government; private banks received the remaining revenue from new issues. These figures use changes in notes to approximate changes in government money, which was composed almost entirely of all the notes in circulation. Consequently, the figures are almost wholly free from the error to which cols. 3–5 are subject, discussed above.

§ The figures for Greece are inclosed in parentheses to emphasize their unknown reliability. Their derivation involves the assumption that the ratio of notes to total money given for 1941 holds for the later hyperinflationary period without alteration.

‖ Monthly data on deposits were used for the later Hungarian hyperinflation, and its revenue was multiplied by the ratio of government money to the total supply for each month before taking the average. Column 1 indicates the range of these monthly ratios for this hyperinflation.

marily on the revenue needs of the governments. We cannot measure these needs directly. But it will facilitate judging the outcome in terms of need to express the actual revenue as a percentage of national income rather than of initial real cash balances.

Rough estimates of this percentage are given in columns 5 and 6 of Table 10. Because data on national income are not available for the periods of hyperinflation, it was necessary to assume that the ratio of the quantity of money to national income in a later "normal" year, for which data on income are available, was the same as in earlier months, to which the index of real cash balances can be readily extended (see note to Table 10 for column 5). This assumption allowed a conversion of column 4 into percentages of national income. These percentages are shown in column 5. In so far as output during the hyperinflations fell below its level in the normal year, revenue as a percentage of contemporaneous national income would be somewhat higher. The government's share of this revenue was found by multiplying column 5 by the ratio of government money to the total supply. Unfortunately, this ratio cannot be estimated very closely, except for Hungary after World War II. Monthly data on deposits are unavailable for the other hyperinflations. Ratios based on annual data only, shown in column 1, were used. Column 6, which is the product of columns 1 and 5, shows the revenue going to the governments as percentages of normal-year national income. These percentages are not subject to one main error affecting those in columns 3–5 (see next to last paragraph of note ‡ to Table 10) and, while rough, are probably reasonably accurate.

In printing money to provide revenue, the governments of these countries collected on the average less than 10 per cent of normal levels of income. Hungary after World War I was the only exception.[38] Even a figure of 10 per cent seems low for ordinary governmental needs, which, as indicated by the little evidence available, probably ranged at the lowest from 10 to 20 per cent of national income. Germany, for example, collected 12 per cent of national income from all taxes in 1925, the second year after the hyperinflation. These results are consistent with the assumption made above that the authorities imposed increasing tax rates in the attempt

38. The range given for its revenue in that period may be too high, because the calculation of this range involved a comparison with the postwar year 1921, when real cash balances were probably somewhat below normal levels.

This qualification applies to the figures for Poland also, but any tendency for them to be too high was counteracted by the unusually low level to which real cash balances had fallen in the beginning month relative to their level in the year 1921 used for comparison. This fall reflects the high rate of inflation there during and after the war (see Table 7).

to collect somewhat more revenue than could be obtained with a constant rate. Other taxes yielded some revenue, of course, though presumably an amount insufficient for desired total expenditures. As the rate of price increase rose, however, the real value of whatever funds were raised by other taxes undoubtedly diminished, and during the later stages of hyperinflation these funds must have become nearly worthless owing to delays in collecting them.[39] Then the only recourse of the government for procuring all the funds needed immediately was to increase the tax on cash balances.

The results of this tax as recorded by the percentages in column 6 are remarkably similar in outcome, except for Russia,[40] despite the greater possible differences due to errors in the data. Certainly the differences are very much smaller than the corresponding differences in the behavior of prices. If, as these results suggest, the different countries sought and, by and large, collected from this tax a percentage of national income roughly of the same order of magnitude, the differences among the hyperinflations in the rate of increase in the quantity of money can be explained by corresponding differences in the factors affecting the amount of revenue. The rate of new issues required for a given revenue is larger when a higher fraction of the revenue goes to banks and when the tax base is smaller; and conversely. Variations in the tax base, namely, real cash balances, are

39. In 1945 Hungary instituted a scheme, which was only temporarily successful, for collecting taxes in a money of constant purchasing power (see Bertrand Nogaro, "Hungary's Recent Monetary Crisis and Its Theoretical Meaning," *American Economic Review*, XXXVIII [September, 1948], 530 ff.).

40. Its low percentage reflects the unusually low level of real cash balances already reached in 1921 before hyperinflation began, and the low ratio of the balances to national income relative to that of the other countries in the later years used for comparison. The low level of the balances in 1921 was undoubtedly due to the social upheaval in that country during 1914–21, which along with war reduced output to about one-half of prewar levels and shook the public's confidence in the currency. In the other countries the balances declined over this period but not to the same extent. The low ratio for Russia in the later years may possibly reflect special circumstances and may be too low as an estimate of prewar levels. The implication is that Russia's revenue was low because the yield of the tax for any feasible rates was exceptionally low. To a great extent this was undoubtedly true. But very likely the revenue the government wished to collect with this tax was also fairly low. The Russian currency reform, unlike those bringing the other hyperinflations to a close, was accomplished gradually. Between the end of 1922 and March 10, 1924, when the depreciating rubles were completely abandoned, the Russian government issued a stable-valued currency, the chervonets, which gradually replaced the old rubles. In so far as the government collected its regular taxes in chervontsi, the revenue did not lose value in the process of collection, and these taxes retained their productivity.

determined in turn by the reaction index and past rates of change in the quantity of money.

The model implies that there is no limit to the revenue that can be collected if the rate of increase in money can be raised to any level. Whether this implication holds for *any* rate, no matter how high, is an interesting but largely irrelevant question, for the rate cannot in fact be raised to any level, except perhaps momentarily. The disruption of the economy caused by extreme rates would arouse political pressures on a scale that would quickly force the government to curtail its issues. The most spectacular of all recorded hyperinflations, that in Hungary after World War II, did not last long. Price increases quickly built up to rates that must have made it impossible for the economy to function effectively. All rates of price increase in the other hyperinflations much above even 150 per cent per month came in the final months preceding a currency reform. In varying degrees all the hyperinflations showed that rising rates imposed in an attempt to collect a larger revenue than can be obtained with a constant rate very soon reach such tremendous heights that the monetary system verges on chaos, and a return to orthodox taxing methods becomes an economic and political necessity.

VIII. Summary of Findings: The Theory of Hyperinflation

This study set out to explain the monetary characteristics of hyperinflation as displayed by seven such episodes following the two world wars. These characteristics are summarized by the pattern of time series for money and prices: (1) the ratio of the quantity of money to the price level—real cash balances—tended to fall during hyperinflation as a whole but fluctuated drastically from month to month and (2) the rates at which money and prices rose tended to increase and in the final months preceding currency reform reached tremendous heights. This second pattern supplies the identifying characteristic of hyperinflation, but the explanation of the first holds the key to an explanation of the second and logically comes first in order of presentation.

1. FLUCTUATIONS IN REAL CASH BALANCES

The evidence given in the preceding sections verifies the hypothesis that these fluctuations result from changes in the variables that determine the demand for real cash balances. With a change in demand, individuals cannot alter the nominal amount of money in circulation, but they can alter the real value of their collective cash balances by spending or hoarding money, and so bid prices up or down, respectively. Only one of the variables that determine this demand has an amplitude of fluctuation during hyperinflation as large as that of the balances and could possibly account for large changes in the demand. That variable is the cost of holding money, which during hyperinflation is for all practical purposes the rate of depreciation in the real value of money or, equivalently, the rate of rise in prices.

To relate the rate of price rise to the demand for the balances, it is necessary to allow for lags. There are two lags that could delay the effect of a change in this rate on the demand. First, there will be a lag between the expected and the actual rate of price rise; it may take some time after a change in the actual rate before individuals expect the new rate to continue long enough to make adjustments in their balances worthwhile. Second, there will be a lag between the desired and the actual level of the balances; it may take some time after individuals decide to change the actual level before they achieve the desired level. The method used to take account of these lags relates actual real cash balances to an average of past rates of price change, weighted by an exponential curve, so that price changes more recent in time are given greater importance. The weights never fall to zero, but past price changes sufficiently distant in time receive too small a weight to have any influence on the weighted average. The steepness of the weighting pattern indicates the length of period over which most of the weight is distributed. This method of allowing for the two lags does not distinguish between them. However, the period of time required for adjusting the balances to desired levels seems negligible compared with the past period of time normally reviewed in forming expectations. For this reason I have assumed that the actual level of real cash balances always equals desired levels and that the weighted average of past rates of price change measures only the "expected rate of price change." But there is no direct evidence on the relative importance of the two lags, and the name given to the weighted average may be lacking somewhat in descriptive accuracy.

The specific form of the hypothesis, restated to allow for lags, asserts that variations in the expected rate of price change account for variations in real cash balances during hyperinflation, where the expected rate is an exponentially weighted average of past rates. The hypothesis was tested by fitting a least-squares regression to time series for the balances and the expected rate. The regression fits the data for most months of the seven hyperinflations with a high degree of accuracy, and thus the statistical results strongly support the hypothesis.

The regression functions derived from these fits provide good approximations to the demand function for the balances and so reveal certain characteristics of this demand during hyperinflation. The elasticity of demand with respect to the expected rate of price change increases in absolute value as this expected rate rises. This contradicts the often stated view that the degree to which individuals can reduce their holdings of a depreciating currency has a limit. The demand elasticity indicates that they reduce their holdings by an increasing proportion of each successive rise in the expected rate. Indeed, the reason why issuing money on a grand scale does not almost immediately lead to extreme flight from the currency is not due to inelasticity in the demand for it but to individuals' lingering confidence in its future value. Their confidence maintains the lag in expectations, whereby the expected rates of price change do not at first keep pace with the rapidly rising actual rates. However, the weighting pattern for the lag appears to become much steeper in the later months, indicating that the lag in the expected behind the actual rates tends to shorten in response to continual inflation.

Thus the large changes in the balances during hyperinflation correspond to large changes in the rate of price change with some delay, not simultaneously. The demand function that expresses this correspondence can be interpreted to represent a dynamic process in which the course of prices through time is determined by the current quantity of money and an exponentially weighted average of past rates of change in this quantity. The process implies that past and current changes in the quantity of money cause the hyperinflation of prices. This link between changes in prices and money is only broken when the absolute value of the slope of the demand function is especially high or the lag in expectations is especially short. In that event price increases become self-generating. What this means is that the rise in prices immediately produces a proportionately greater decline in real cash balances. Then the effect of percentage changes in prices and the balances on each other does not diminish, as a stable moving equilibrium of prices requires, but grows. Such a process sends up the *percentage* change in prices at no less than an exponential rate, even if the quantity of money remains constant. Apparently the demand slope and the lag never reached the critical level in the seven hyperinflations, for none had self-generating price increases. Instead of running away on their own, price increases remained closely linked to past and current changes in the quantity of money and could have been stopped at any time, as they finally were, by tapering off the issue of new money.

2. THE TREMENDOUS INCREASE IN MONEY AND PRICES

If in fact price increases were not self-generating, what accounted for their tremendous size? The above explanation of their behavior in terms of large increases in the quantity of money only raises the further question, "Why did this quantity increase so much?" Clearly, issuing money on a large scale serves as a major source of funds for government expenditures. The inflation resulting from new issues places a tax on cash balances by depreciating the value of money. The revenue in real terms raised by this tax is the product of the rate of rise in prices (the tax rate) and real cash balances (the tax base). By setting the rate of increase in the quantity of money, the note-issuing authorities indirectly determine the rate of tax through the process implied by the demand function. The simplicity of administering this tax undoubtedly explains why governments resorted to continual issues of money in the difficult periods after the two world wars. An explanation of why those issues became so large, however, is found in the response of the tax base to the tax rate.

If the tax rate remains constant, the tax base and, therefore, the revenue ultimately become constant. Among all constant rates, there is one that yields a maximum ultimate revenue. With a tax rate that increases rapidly enough, however, the revenue forever exceeds this maximum amount for a constant rate because of delays in adjusting the tax base produced by the lag in expectations. In the beginning and closing months of the seven hyperinflations, the authorities successfully pursued a policy of inflating at increasing tax rates to take advantage of this lag and collected more revenue thereby than they could have obtained with any constant rate. This policy led to actual rates far above the constant rate that would have maximized ultimate revenue and produced the tremendous increases in money and prices characteristic of hyperinflation.

In the middle months the rate of increase in the money supply tapered off, for what reason it is not entirely clear, and the revenue temporarily decreased. As a result, the revenue collected with the actual tax rates was not greater on the average than the amount that could have been obtained with a constant rate. The resumption of increasing rates in the closing months restored the revenue to amounts at least as large as those in the beginning months. In order to compensate for the low level to which the tax base fell after many months of hyperinflation, the tax rates rose to astronomical heights. This explosion of the rates in the final months completely disrupted the economy and forced the government to substitute a traditional tax program for a policy of printing money.

In Section I it was suggested that the seven hyperinflations represent the same economic process because of the similarity in the ratios of the average change in prices to the average change in the quantity of money (row 9 in Table 1). The model of hyperinflation described above depicts the nature of this process. But these ratios of averages cover up an extraordinary dissimilarity. Rows 13 and 15 also present ratios involving

prices and the quantity of money but not averages, and they differ widely. The model shows that these differences originate, not in the differing
responses of the public to a depreciating currency, but in the varying
rates at which money was issued. The average share of national income
that these new issues procured for the different governments was 3 to
about 15 per cent, except in Russia, which had the unusually low percentage of 0.5. The differences in these percentages are not large when compared with the very much larger differences between the hyperinflations
in the rates at which money rose. To some extent the governments may
have collected less revenue than was planned. But, in so far as the actual
collections met budgetary plans, the rates required to procure the intended amount in any month roughly equal the actual rates. The differences between the hyperinflations in the required rates that can be derived from the model thus account to a great extent for the corresponding
differences in the actual rates at which money rose.

The model used has definite limitations: it only applies accurately to
large price increases, and it fails to describe the closing months in four of
the hyperinflations. In the closing months real cash balances sometimes
rose when the model indicates they should have fallen. This limitation
likely results from expectations that current price increases would not
last very long. Such expectations are not related in any direct or obvious way to past changes in prices. To take account of this limitation of the
model does not seem to require revisions that would contradict the
premise of this study that domestic monetary factors alone explain hyperinflations.

Many prevailing theories of economic disturbances emphasize external
monetary factors like the foreign-exchange rate, as well as real factors
like the level of employment and real income, the structure of trade union-
ism, the rate and extent of capital formation, and so on. These factors are
prominent primarily in discussions of depression. Yet they also enter into
discussions of inflation. The theory of the cost-price spiral, which borrows
its concepts and framework from theories of income and employment
common in discussions of depression, has been applied to inflation with
the suggestion, sometimes explicit, that it applies to hyperinflation as
well. Closely related and often identical to the theory of the cost-price
spiral is the explanation of hyperinflation in terms of the depreciation of
the foreign-exchange rate.[41]

41. References to discussions of the cost-price spiral are too extensive to give even a
partial list here. The most explicit application of this theory to hyperinflation that I

These theories postulate that a rise in prices results from increases in wages or prices of imported goods and precedes increases in the quantity of money. This study points to the opposite sequence and indicates that an extreme rise in prices depends almost entirely on changes in the quantity of money. By implication, the rise in wages and the depreciation of the foreign-exchange rate in hyperinflations are effects of the rise in prices. Extreme changes in a short period of time in exchange rates will primarily reflect variations in the real value of the currency. It is quite true that the public might well expect depreciation of the currency to show up more accurately in depreciation of exchange rates than in any set of readily available commodity prices and so follow these rates in adjusting their balances. Circumstances are easy to imagine in which *for a short time* the exchanges might depreciate faster than prices rise and so appear to move in advance of prices. But this result would not mean that the rise in prices had become the effect rather than the cause of exchange depreciation. Real cash balances would be related to this depreciation only so long as it remained a good indicator of price changes.

The model suggests in addition that the spiral theory places emphasis on the wrong factors. *Hyper*inflation at least can be explained almost entirely in terms of the demand for money. This explanation places crucial importance on the supply of money. While the monetary authorities might capitulate to pressures for sustaining wage increases, as the spiral theory presumes, they will typically attend to many other considerations. The most important of these in hyperinflation is the revenue raised by issuing money, which was analyzed above. More precise analysis than this of the determinants of the money supply goes beyond a mechanistic account of the inflationary process and involves the motives of governments, with whom the authority to open and close the spigot of note issues ultimately lies.

---

have found is by Mrs. Joan Robinson in "Review of Bresciani-Turroni's *The Economics of Inflation*," *Economic Journal*, XLVIII (September, 1938), 507.

To my knowledge no one has argued that depreciation of the foreign-exchange rate alone is sufficient to explain hyperinflations, but it is often considered to be a causal factor. The attempts to find statistical confirmation of this view are inadequate and unconvincing. Probably the best attempt is that by James Harvey Rogers (see his *The Process of Inflation in France* [New York: Columbia University Press, 1929], chap. vii), on which Frank Graham based his interpretation of the German episode (see his *Exchange, Prices, and Production in Hyper-inflation: Germany, 1920–23* [Princeton, N.J.: Princeton University Press, 1930], esp. p. 172).

APPENDIX A
STATISTICAL METHODS

Equations (2) and (9) were combined to give the regression function (11), which has the form,

$$Y_t + aE_t + \gamma = \epsilon_t , \qquad (27)$$

where Y_t stands for $\log_e (M/P)_t$ and ϵ_t is a random variable. The method of computing E_t was given in note 6. The variance of the random variable is estimated by

$$V (\epsilon) = \frac{\Sigma (Y + aE + \gamma)^2}{N} . \qquad (28)$$

For simplicity the subscripts have been dropped with the understanding that the summation is over the values of Y and E that refer to the same period of time. N is the number of observations in the summation.

The parameters a and β can be estimated by the method of least squares. The estimates of a and β are those values that make (28) a minimum for all values of γ. The estimates in Table 3 were computed by maximizing the total correlation coefficient after making a substitution for a and γ, a procedure that is equivalent to minimizing (28). The total correlation coefficient, R, is defined as

$$R^2 = 1 - \frac{\Sigma (Y + aE + \gamma)^2}{\Sigma Y^2 - N \bar{Y}^2} , \qquad (29)$$

where the bar indicates the average value of the variable.

The values of γ and a that make R^2 a maximum for given values of β are $\hat{\gamma}$ and $\hat{a}$ and are found as follows:

$$\frac{\partial R^2}{\partial \gamma} = \frac{- 2\gamma N - 2 N \bar{Y} - 2 a N \bar{E}}{\Sigma Y^2 - N \bar{Y}^2} = 0 ,$$

$$\hat{\gamma} = - \bar{Y} - a \bar{E} , \qquad (30)$$

$$\frac{\partial R^2}{\partial a} = \frac{- 2 a \Sigma E^2 - 2 \Sigma YE - 2\gamma N \bar{E}}{\Sigma Y^2 - N \bar{Y}^2} = 0 ,$$

and, if $\hat{\gamma}$ is substituted for γ,

$$- \hat{a} = \frac{\Sigma YE - N \bar{E} \bar{Y}}{\Sigma E^2 - N \bar{E}^2} . \qquad (31)$$

R^2 is derived as a function of β by inserting (30) and (31) in (29).

$$R^2 (\beta) = \frac{(\Sigma YE - N \bar{Y} \bar{E})^2}{(\Sigma E^2 - N \bar{E}^2) (\Sigma Y^2 - N \bar{Y}^2)} . \qquad (32)$$

The value of β, $\hat{\beta}$, that makes $R^2(\beta)$ a maximum can be found by trying successive values of β that differ by .05 in (32). Given $\hat{\beta}$, $\hat{a}$ is computed from (31). This was the procedure used to calculate the estimates in Tables 3 and 5. It gives the same estimates as would minimizing (28), because the substitutions for a and γ, $\hat{\gamma}$ in (30) and $\hat{a}$ in (31), give, for every β, the maximum of R^2 for all γ and a. The maximum of $R^2(\beta)$ for all β gives the maximum with respect to all the variables, which is equivalent to the minimum of (28).

The reason for choosing a β that gives the maximum value of $R^2(\beta)$, instead of directly solving for the values that set to zero the partial derivatives of (28) with respect to each of the three variables, was one of computational efficiency. The length of the weighted average for computing E is determined by the value of β and can be fixed only by first assuming a value for β, which was the procedure that was followed. But, in the method of solving the partial derivatives simultaneously, the value of β remains to be determined, and therefore the minimum number of items that the accumulated product (9) should include to satisfy (10) (shown in Sec. III) cannot be fixed beforehand. This procedure would in this respect result in more computations than would be strictly necessary. Also, the method of finding the value of β that maximizes $R^2(\beta)$ gives as a byproduct the values of $R^2(\beta)$ for different values of β, which are necessary for calculating confidence intervals for the estimates. One further advantage to the method used is that, by knowing many values of $R^2(\beta)$ over a wide range, we are sure that there is a unique maximum for all positive values of β. As β becomes large, E approaches C, and $R^2(\beta)$ quickly approaches a limit.

A method of finding confidence intervals for the estimates of a and β that utilizes information gained in estimating the two parameters is afforded by the likelihood ratio. If the residuals from the regression function (27) are assumed to be independent and normally distributed with mean zero and variance σ^2, the likelihood function, L, is defined as

$$L = \left(\frac{1}{\sqrt{2\pi}\,\sigma}\right)^N \exp\left\{\frac{-1}{2\sigma^2}\sum_1^N (Y + aE + \gamma)^2\right\}. \qquad (33)$$

The likelihood ratio is then defined by

$$\lambda = \frac{L(\hat{w})}{L(\hat{\Omega})}, \qquad (34)$$

where $L(\hat{w})$ is the maximum of L over the region w of the null hypothesis, and $L(\hat{\Omega})$ is the maximum of L over the region Ω of all alternative hypotheses. As N becomes large, the distribution of $-2 \log_e \lambda$ approaches $\chi^2(r)$, where r is the number of restrictions on the values of the parameters specified in the null hypothesis.[42]

To find confidence intervals for the estimates of β, the values of σ, γ, and a that maximize L are inserted in (33). These values are found by partial differentiation of $\log L$.

$$\frac{\partial \log L}{\partial \sigma} = \frac{-N}{\sigma} + \frac{1}{\sigma^3} \Sigma (Y + aE + \gamma)^2 = 0 .$$

The maximum likelihood estimate of σ is

$$\hat{\sigma}^2 = \frac{\Sigma (Y + aE + \gamma)^2}{N} ,$$

which, by (29), can be written as

$$\hat{\sigma}^2 = (1 - R^2) \Sigma (Y - \bar{Y})^2 . \tag{35}$$

The values of γ and a that maximize L are $\hat{\gamma}$ and $\hat{a}$, as given by (30) and (31). The value of β that maximizes L is the same as the estimated value, $\hat{\beta}$, which was found to an accuracy of $\pm .05$. The components of the likelihood ratio are therefore expressed as follows:

$$\log L (\hat{w}) = \log L (\hat{\sigma}_0^2, \hat{\gamma}, \hat{a}, \beta_0) =$$

$$-\frac{N}{2} \log 2\pi - \frac{N}{2} \log \hat{\sigma}_0^2 - \frac{1}{2\hat{\sigma}_0^2} \Sigma [Y + \hat{a}E (\beta_0) + \hat{\gamma}]^2 , \tag{36}$$

where $\hat{\sigma}_0^2$ is computed using $\hat{\gamma}$, $\hat{a}$, and β_0; and $E(\beta_0)$ is computed using β_0.

$$\log L (\hat{\Omega}) = \log L (\hat{\sigma}^2, \hat{\gamma}, \hat{a}, \hat{\beta}) =$$

$$-\frac{N}{2} \log 2\pi - \frac{N}{2} \log \hat{\sigma}^2 - \frac{1}{2\hat{\sigma}^2} \Sigma [Y + \hat{a}E (\hat{\beta}) + \hat{\gamma}]^2 , \tag{37}$$

where $\hat{\sigma}^2$ is computed using $\hat{\gamma}$, $\hat{a}$, and $\hat{\beta}$; and $E(\hat{\beta})$ is computed using $\hat{\beta}$. Consequently,

$$-2 \log \lambda = N \log \hat{\sigma}_0^2 - N \log \hat{\sigma}^2 , \quad \text{or}$$

$$-2 \log \lambda = N \log [1 - R^2 (\beta_0)] - N \log [1 - R^2 (\hat{\beta})] , \tag{38}$$

which is distributed as $\chi^2(1)$. Only the right-hand tail of the chi-square distribution should be used in this test.

Confidence intervals for β in Table 3 were computed by inserting numbers that differed by .05 for β_0 in (38). The lowest and highest values,

42. S. S. Wilks, *Mathematical Statistics* (Princeton, N.J.: Princeton University Press, 1950), p. 151.

β_L and β_U, that just make (38) significant at the .10 level are the bounds of the confidence interval. This gives a confidence coefficient of .90.

Confidence intervals for estimates of a were found in a similar manner from the likelihood ratio. $L(\hat{w})$ is the maximum of L for given values of a. The lowest and highest values, a_L and a_U, that make the likelihood ratio significant at the .10 level are the bounds of the confidence interval. Since the value of β that maximizes L for given a cannot be found directly, a trial-and-error procedure was followed using values of β that differed by .05.

The confidence intervals for the estimates of $a\beta$ in Table 8, $(a\beta)_L$ and $(a\beta)_U$, are based on the likelihood ratio. $L(\hat{w})$ is the maximum of L under the one restriction that $a\beta = (a\beta)_0$. $(a\beta)_L$ and $(a\beta)_U$ are the extreme values of $a\beta$ that make the likelihood ratio significant at the .10 level. It turns out that $(a\beta)_L = a_U\beta_L$ and $(a\beta)_U = a_L\beta_U$. Computations by trial and error for each hyperinflation verified that they are the extreme values at the .10 level of significance for all β that differ by .05.

The significance tests summarized in Table 4 and described in note 9 are based on the likelihood ratio and its asymptotic properties. The likelihood function of this ratio for the tests is defined as

$$L = \sum_{i=1}^{7} \left(\frac{1}{\sqrt{2\pi}\sigma_i}\right)^{n_i} \exp\left\{\frac{-1}{2\sigma_i^2} \sum_{j=1}^{n_i} (Y + a_i E(\beta_i) + \gamma_i)_j^2\right\}. \quad (39)$$

The major summation is over the seven hyperinflations. The number of observations from each hyperinflation is given by n_i. The total number of observations from all seven hyperinflations is

$$\sum_{1}^{7} n_i = 149.$$

The likelihood ratio, (34), for the tests is defined as follows: The denominator, $L(\hat{\Omega})$, is the same in all the tests. It is the unrestricted maximum of the likelihood function. The values of a_i, β_i, and γ_i, which determine σ_i from (35), are those estimated from the observations of each hyperinflation separately. In the test of significance used for Table 4, the numerator of the likelihood ratio, $L(\hat{w})$, is the maximum of the likelihood function under the twelve restrictions that for all seven hyperinflations a_i is the same and β_i is the same. Here the appropriate number of degrees of freedom for chi square is twelve. In the tests of significance for the two fits described in note 9, $L(\hat{w})$ is the maximum of the likelihood function under six restrictions, which makes six the appropriate number of degrees of freedom to use in finding the significance level of the chi-square distribution. For the first fit the restrictions are that β_i is the same for all seven hyperinflations. For the second fit the six restrictions are that a_i is the same for all seven hyperinflations.

Finding the values of a, β, and γ that maximize the likelihood function under these various restrictions is equivalent to finding the values that minimize the following sum of squares under the given restrictions:

$$\sum_{i=1}^{7} \left\{ \sum_{j=1}^{n_i} (Y + a_i E(\beta_i) + \gamma_i)_j^2 \right\}. \tag{40}$$

There is no direct way to minimize the above relation, and the procedure followed was to approximate the minimum for values of β that differ by .05. The minimum is particularly difficult to compute under the six restrictions that all a_i are the same. Consequently, for these six restrictions the minimum of (40) was only shown to lie above a certain number. Greater accuracy was not necessary to prove that the appropriate likelihood ratio based on these restrictions is significant at the .005 level.

APPENDIX B

DATA AND SOURCES

This appendix contains the following three monthly time series for each hyperinflation:

1. *Logarithm of real cash balances.*—In the tables this series is shown as $\log_{10}(P/M)$, where P and M are indexes of prices and the quantity of authorized hand-to-hand currency.[43] This logarithm, when multiplied by $-1/\log_{10}e$, becomes $\log_e(M/P)$, which appears in equation (11). This series, as well as those described below, was computed more easily in its present form, and it could be used for all the statistical work of this study without conversion into natural logarithmic form. The values of the parameters a and β are independent of the base of the logarithms in the equations.

2. *Rate of change in prices per month.*—In the tables this series is shown as $\log_{10}(P_i/P_{i-1})$, where P_{i-1} and P_i are successive values of an index of the price level, the latter on the date opposite the item of the series and the former on the preceding date.[44] Multiplication of this series by $1/\log_{10}e$

43. Counterfeiting was widespread in all the countries during hyperinflation (see J. van Walré de Bordes, *The Austrian Crown* [London: P. S. King & Son, Ltd., 1924], Annex III), but it does not seem unreasonable to assume that the amount of counterfeit notes was negligible compared with the tremendous quantities of legal notes issued.

44. When this period between the two dates differs appreciably from thirty days, the logarithm is multiplied, unless otherwise noted, by the appropriate factor to make the figure a rate per thirty days. Where no earlier date is shown after the last item in the column, the period between the values of the price index used for this item is one month.

gives $\log_e(P_i/P_{i-1})$, which is the form of the series used in the equations. This series measures the average rate of change in prices during each month. When the rate is fairly steady, the series is a good approximation to the daily rate throughout the month; but, when the rate rises considerably, this series represents the daily rate at the end of the month more closely than it does the rate at the middle of the month.

3. *Expected rate of change in prices per month, $E(\beta)$.*—The derivation of this series is presented in Section III, and methods for its computation are given in note 6. The value of β used for each hyperinflation is the estimated value shown in Table 3. This series is shown in logarithms to the base 10. To convert to natural logarithms, multiply by $1/\log_{10} e$.

The tables of these series start with the final month of hyperinflation and carry back in time to include all the observations used in the regressions. The series of the rate of change in prices are carried back even further to include all the rates used to compute all the values of E that are included in the regressions.

Notes on sources and comments on the comprehensiveness and reliability of the data accompany each table. Series on deposits and real output are included along with supporting notes.

NOTES ON AUSTRIAN DATA

For 1919 and 1920 P is an index of the cost of living. Rents are excluded, since they were controlled and would bias the index downward compared with an index of the general price level. For 1921 and 1922 P is a different index of the cost of living that excludes rents but includes many prices not included in the earlier index.[45] The earlier index is linked to the later one by a factor that expresses the ratio of the averages of the indexes over the six-month period in which they overlap.

The rate of change in prices for the period preceding January 15, 1919, was found by assuming that the price index was unity on December 30, 1914. If, however, it was unity on June 30, 1914, the last rate in the second series should be changed to .0024, a difference that would have a negligible effect on the series for E. It is not clear whether the base for P in 1914 should be June or December of that year.

M is an index of the quantity of bank notes in circulation.[46] For the base year 1914 the quantity was taken as five hundred million crowns, a figure that Walré de Bordes considers slightly too low.[47] The bank notes were those of the Austro-Hungarian National Bank and were stamped by

45. Walré de Bordes, *op. cit.*, pp. 88 ff.
46. *Ibid.*, pp. 48 ff.
47. *Ibid.*, pp. 38, 64.

the Austrian government. Unstamped bank notes also circulated, but they disappeared gradually, probably completely by June, 1920.[48]

Table B2 gives figures on deposits less bank reserves (since reserves are included in M above) and the ratio of an index of bank notes to an

TABLE B1

TIME SERIES FOR AUSTRIA

Date	$\log_{10}(P/M)$ (1914=1) (1)	$\log_{10}(P_i/P_{i-1})$ (Per Month) (2)	$E(.05)$ (Per Month) (3)
1922			
Aug. 31	1.5988	.3699	.0885
July 31	1.4654	.2842	.0740
June 30	1.3365	.1247	.0633
May 31	1.3522	.1492	.0601
Apr. 30	1.2625	.0648	.0555
Mar. 31	1.2553	.0117	.0550
Feb. 28	1.3118	.0557	.0573
Jan. 31	1.3139	.1550	.0573
1921			
Dec. 31	1.2742	.1630	.0523
Nov. 30	1.2718	.2511	.0467
Oct. 31	1.1430	.2154	.0362
Sept. 30	1.0414	.1230	.0270
Aug. 31	.9956	.1193	.0221
July 31	.9085	−.0467	.0171
June 30	.9956	.0604	.0204
May 31	.9731	.0025	.0183
Apr. 30	.9731	.0187	.0191
Mar. 31	.9956	.0296	.0191
Feb. 28	.9956	.0611	.0186
Jan. 31	.9777	.0261	.0166
1920			
Dec. 31		.0427	
Oct. 15		.0127	
July 15		.0126	
Apr. 15		.0248	
Jan. 15		.0334	
1919			
July 15		.0065	
Jan. 15		.0027	
1914			
Dec. 30			

index of bank notes plus deposits in circulation for Austria. The deposit figures include postal savings, deposits in savings banks, sight liabilities of the national bank, and an estimate of deposits in commercial banks. Cash reserves are those in commercial banks.

The figures for the post office include savings but not current accounts

48. *Ibid.*, p. 45.

(i.e., sight deposits),[49] the amounts of which are unavailable. In 1923 the total debits of current accounts in the post office were 25 per cent of the debits of current accounts in the national bank.[50] If the amount of these accounts in the post office were also roughly 25 per cent of their amount in the national bank in the preceding years, the deposits in the post office that are excluded were a negligible proportion of total bank deposits, because all deposits in the national bank were a small proportion of the total.

The deposits of savings banks included above comprise all but about 1 per cent of the total deposits in such banks.[51]

Sight liabilities of the national bank[52] were held by the public and are properly included.[53]

TABLE B2

DEPOSIT DATA FOR AUSTRIA

End of Year	Bank Deposits *less* Cash Reserves (Million Kronen)	Ratio of Index of Bank Notes to Index of Bank Notes *plus* Deposits in Circulation
1913.........	7,423.1	1.00
1920.........	71,371.0	4.75
1921.........	494,914	4.12
1922.........	9,475,665	4.77

Figures for deposits held by the public less cash reserves in commercial banks for the years 1920–22 are based on the deposits and cash-reserve ratios of seven large Vienna banks.[54] To estimate deposits in commercial banks, the deposits in these seven banks were increased by 78.85 per cent, the percentage by which they fell short of the deposits (current, savings, and *Giro* accounts) of twenty-seven Vienna banks in 1920.[55] These twenty-

49. League of Nations, *Memorandum on Currency and Central Banks, 1913–1925* (Geneva: Publications Department of the League of Nations, 1926), II, 61.

50. B. H. Beckhart and H. Parker Willis, *Foreign Banking Systems* (New York: Henry Holt & Co., 1929), chap. ii.

51. League of Nations, *op. cit.*, p. 61.

52. Walré de Bordes, *op. cit.*, p. 53.

53. See Beckhart and Willis, *op. cit.*, pp. 133–34, and League of Nations, *Memorandum on Central Banks, 1913 and 1918–1923* (Geneva: Publications Department of the League of Nations, 1924), pp. 83, 91.

54. League of Nations, *Memorandum on Commercial Banks, 1913–1929* (Geneva: Publications Department of the League of Nations, 1931), pp. 62 ff.

55. Walré de Bordes, *op. cit.*, p. 56.

seven Vienna banks constituted almost the whole body of commercial banking proper within Austrian territory at the time. A great number of new banks established during the hyperinflation remained small.[56]

The above figures of bank deposits exclude deposits in the following institutions:[57]

1. Wiener Giro- und Cassen-Verein and Soldierungs-Verein, which were engaged in clearing transactions. The former's business was large, but most of its activities involved stock-exchange transactions. Before 1924 the latter's deposits can probably be considered negligible, since its debits were only 10 per cent of deposit debits for the national bank in 1923.

2. Provincial mortgage institutions, credit associations, and agricultural credit associations, which held savings deposits and greatly declined in importance during hyperinflation.[58]

Even though the coverage of bank deposits in the above figures is fairly comprehensive, the inadequacy of the data for commercial banks means that the figures in Table B2 must be taken as rough approximations.

Changes in real income in Austria during the hyperinflation were apparently not great.[59] Unemployment figures available show a rise in 1922, but there is no evidence that the relative amount of unemployment became important.[60]

NOTES ON GERMAN DATA

P is an index of wholesale prices compiled by the Statistisches Reichsamt.[61] For the months before 1923 P is the average monthly level of prices and is used to approximate the level of prices at the middle of the month. For the first half of 1923 P is the level of prices on a particular day and is available for ten-day intervals. For the second half of 1923 it refers to a particular day at weekly intervals. Where the period covered by the rate of change in prices in 1923 differs from thirty days, the figures were adjusted to give the rate per thirty days. In computing E, each rate of change in prices was treated as though it pertained to the fifteenth of the month. Adjusting the exponential weights to take account of observations not falling on the fifteenth would have involved an unnecessary complication.

5o. League of Nations, *Memorandum on Commercial Banks, 1913–1929*, p. 66.

57. Beckhart and Willis, *op. cit.*, chap. ii.

58. *Ibid.*, p. 169.

59. Walré de Bordes, *op. cit.*, p. 158.

60. Statistisches Reichsamt, *Statistisches Jahrbuch für das Deutsche Reich* (Berlin: Reimar Hobbing, 1925), Vol. XLIV: *1924–25*, International Section, Table 12.

61. Sonderhefte zur Wirtschaft und Statistik, *Zahlen zur Geldentwertung in Deutschland 1914 bis 1923* (Berlin: R. Hobbing, 1925), pp. 33 ff.

M is an index of the quantity of authorized bank notes in circulation.[62] For the months before 1923 the quantity of these bank notes is available for the end of the month, and linear interpolations of these figures were used to estimate M for the middle of the month. For 1923 the gold value of the quantity of bank notes is available weekly. These figures were converted to marks by multiplying by the dollar-exchange rate and by 4.198 (the number of gold marks that equaled one dollar before November, 1923). Weekly figures for the quantity of bank notes were interpolated to estimate M for the same day in each month in 1923 to which P refers. By that time the quantity of bank notes was increasing so rapidly that ordinary arithmetic interpolation would have been subject to large errors. Therefore, interpolations for 1923 were linear between the logarithms of the quantity of bank notes up to June and were linear between second logarithms thereafter. These interpolations are probably in error by negligible amounts for the months preceding September.

Illegal currencies issued in Germany in 1923 were estimated not to have exceeded 192 quintillion marks.[63] These currencies comprised over two-thirds of the outstanding legal bank notes on November 15, 1923, though a rapidly diminishing fraction thereafter. There is some reason to believe that the circulation of the illegal currencies was somewhat localized and that most of them were issued when the so-called needs for currency became acute, which occurred at the peaks of hyperinflation and would imply that they were issued at a rate roughly in proportion to that of the authorized bank notes. In so far as failure to take account of illegal currencies has made the figures for real cash balances for Germany in 1923 too low, the estimate of the parameter a is too high. While similar sources of upward bias in the estimates of a may exist for the other countries, there seems to be no indication that substantial amounts of illegal currencies were issued. Apparently, only in Germany were unauthorized currencies issued by local governments and private organizations.

Table B4 gives figures on deposits less bank reserves (M above includes these reserves) and the ratio of an index of bank notes to an index of bank notes plus deposits in circulation for Germany. The figures include deposits in the post office, savings banks, the Reichsbank, and a rough estimate of deposits in all commercial banks. Cash reserves are those of commercial banks.

The amount of deposits with the post office[64] are available for the years

62. *Ibid.*, pp. 45 ff.

63. German Government, *Germany's Economy, Currency and Finance* (Berlin: Zentral-Verlag G.m.b.H., 1924), p. 67.

64. Statistisches Reichsamt, *op. cit.*, p. 314.

TABLE B3

TIME SERIES FOR GERMANY

Date (Middle of Month unless Otherwise Noted)	$\log_{10}(P/M)$ (1913=1) (1)	$\log_{10}(P_i/P_{i-1})$ (Per Month) (2)	$E(.20)$ (Per Month) (3)
1923			
Nov. 13*	1.9445	2.5560	1.1155
Oct. 16	2.6263	1.5881	.7965
Sept. 18	2.6415	1.6259	.6212
Aug. 14	2.5717	1.1385	.3987
July 17	2.1303	.4842	.2349
June 15	1.9868	.3789	.1797
May 15	1.7782	.1542	.1356
Apr. 14	1.7076	.0155	.1315
Mar. 15	1.8261	− .0587	.1571
Feb. 15	2.0755	.3899	.2049
Jan. 15	1.9445	.1546	.1640
1922			
Dec.	1.9381	.1066	.1661
Nov.	2.0481	.3094	.1792
Oct.	1.9247	.2949	.1503
Sept.	1.7747	.1746	.1183
Aug.	1.7084	.2807	.1058
July	1.5024	.1556	.0671
June	1.3955	.0369	.0476
May	1.3983	.0070	.0501
Apr.	1.4231	.0681	.0597
Mar.	1.3886	.1219	.0579
Feb.	1.2934	.0490	.0438
Jan.	1.2550	.0218	.0427
1921			
Dec.	1.2608	.0088	.0473
Nov.	1.2975	.1426	.0559
Oct.	1.1855	.0756	.0367
Sept.	1.1351	.0327	.0281
Aug.	1.1225	.1279	.0271
July	1.0043	.0192	.0048
June	.9978	.0189	.0017
May	.9886	− .0059	− .0021
Apr.	.9983	− .0040	− .0013
Mar.	1.0056	− .0121	− .0007
Feb.	1.0220	− .0195	.0018
Jan.	1.0370	− .0003	.0065
1920			
Dec.	1.0410	− .0203	.0081
Nov.	1.0730	.0126	.0144
Oct.	1.0652	− .0094	.0148
Sept.	1.0884	.0141	.0202

* Prices still rose sharply but at diminishing rates until November 20, 1923, when the mark exchange rate with the dollar was officially fixed and prices became relatively stable.

Date (Middle of Month unless Otherwise Noted)	$\log_{10}(P/M)$ (1913 = 1) (1)	$\log_{10}(P_i/P_{i-1})$ (Per Month) (2)	$E(.20)$ (Per Month) (3)
1920—*Continued*			
Aug............	....	.0256	....
July............	....	− .0047	....
June............	....	− .0379	....
May............	....	− .0167	....
Apr............	....	− .0376	....
Mar............	....	.0061	....
Feb............	....	.1276	....
Jan............	....	.1943	....
1919			
Dec............	....	.0735	....
Nov............	....	.0815	....
Oct............	....	.0569	....
Sept............	....	.0675	....
Aug............	....	.0951	....
July............	....	.0416	....
June............	....	.0158	....
May............	....	.0164	....
Apr............	....	.0186	....
Mar............	....	.0064	....
Feb............	....	.0131	....
Jan............	....	.0291	....
1918			
Dec............	....	.0200	....
Nov............	....	.0000	....
Oct............	....	.0075	....
Sept............	....	− .0094	....
Aug............	....	.0530	....
July............	....	.0020	....
June............	....	.0126	....
May............	....	− .0021	....
Apr............	....	.0129	....
Mar............	....	.0000	....
Feb............	....	− .0129	....
Jan............	....	.0021	....
1917			
Dec............	....	.0000	....
Nov............	....	.0043	....
Oct............	....	.0043	....
Sept............	....	− .0086	....
Aug............	....	.0720	....
July............	....	.0180	....
June............	....	.0053	....

1913–22 but not for 1923. The magnitude of these deposits was relatively small before 1923, and their slow growth up to 1923 suggests that their magnitude in that year was insignificant.

The figures for savings banks include all deposits of almost all such banks.[65]

The figures for deposits with the Reichsbank cover private (non-government) current accounts.[66] They are not separated in the figures from government current accounts for the years before 1921, however. For 1913 and 1919 this item is omitted from the estimate of deposits. This understates the estimate by probably no more than 5 per cent for

TABLE B4

DEPOSIT DATA FOR GERMANY

End of Year	Bank Deposits *less* Cash Reserves (Million Marks)	Ratio of Index of Bank Notes to Index of Bank Notes *plus* Deposits in Circulation
1913.........	29,640	1.00
1919.........	93,340	2.09
1920.........	138,261	2.22
1921.........	197,800	2.29
1922.........	272,220	1.93
1923.........	$1,959 \times 10^{12}$	3.33

1919 and by even less for 1913, since the total of all Reichsbank deposits was less than 15 per cent of all bank deposits at the end of 1919. Furthermore, cash reserves of commercial banks, included in the figures for these two years, were mostly balances in the Reichsbank and account for over one-half of its private accounts.

Private accounts in the Reichsbank for 1920 were estimated by the figure for January, 1921, since the private accounts seem to have been stable during this period. Even if this January figure is not applicable to the preceding month, the greatest amount by which it could differ from the actual figure for the end of 1920 would not greatly bias the estimate of bank deposits.

Commercial bank deposits held by the public less cash reserves were

65. League of Nations, *Memorandum on Commercial Banks, 1913–1929*, p. 135.

66. League of Nations, *Memorandum on Central Banks, 1913 and 1918–1923*, p. 199.

extrapolated from figures for almost all commercial banks.[67] Benchmarks for the estimates were provided by complete figures for all commercial banks for the end of 1913 and 1923.[68] The figures for the two years 1921 and 1922 were estimated by a linear interpolation of the second logarithms of the figures for December 30, 1920, and January 1, 1924, including an adjustment for deviations from the same kind of trend in the deposits of the eight major Berlin banks. These estimates could have a substantial error but probably not enough to create the relative fall in the ratio of bank notes to deposits in 1922.

Data on deposits in mortgage, public, and co-operative banks are not available for the relevant years, but their position in 1913 and 1924 indi-

TABLE B5

INDEX OF OUTPUT FOR GERMANY

Year	Index of Output (1913 = 100)	Year	Index of Output (1913 = 100)
1914.	82	1920.	66
1915.	74	1921.	73
1916.	69	1922.	80
1917.	67	1923.	61
1918.	66	1923 (Sept.–Dec.).	42
1919.	55		

cates that they declined greatly during the hyperinflation.[69] Their deposits in 1923 were probably less than 10 per cent of those of commercial banks alone.

Table B5 gives an index of output for Germany that is a simple average of indexes of industrial production, agricultural output, and commercial transportation figures. The index portrays in a general way changes in real income.[70]

The index of output for the last part of 1923 is the midpoint of an interval estimate of the aggregate real income of German industrial workers. It is likely to be an understatement of total real income. The

67. League of Nations, *Memorandum on Commercial Banks, 1913–1929*, pp. 129 ff., and P. Barret Whale, *Joint Stock Banking in Germany* (London: Macmillan & Co., Ltd., 1930), p. 191.

68. League of Nations, *Memorandum on Commercial Banks, 1913–1929*, pp. 129 ff.

69. *Ibid.*

70. Graham, *op. cit.*, p. 316.

figures in Table B5 take into account territorial changes resulting from the loss of Upper Silesia to Poland on October 12, 1921. However, the German marks in that area continued to circulate in fixed number along with the Polish marks, which were introduced in March, 1923. By the time the Polish mark was made sole legal tender in November of that year, the value of the German marks had depreciated to nothing.[71]

NOTES ON GREEK DATA

P is an index of the cost of food in Athens.[72] The rate of change in prices for the period before 1941 is based on the fact that prices rose no more than threefold over the entire period 1938–41.[73] In computing E, however, the rate for the period June, 1938, to December, 1940, was taken to be zero. If the rate was actually as high as .0145 for this entire period, the error in E for any of the months would be no greater than .0005.

M is an index of the quantity of bank notes issued by the Bank of Greece.[74] The circulation of these bank notes was largely limited to the area near Athens,[75] which provides some justification for having confidence in a price index of food in Athens only. Nevertheless, little stock can be placed in figures of such limited coverage. Furthermore, data on deposits and changes in real income are apparently nonexistent. Bank deposits should not be dismissed as entirely insignificant, though their effects in the other hyperinflations were minor, because deposits in Greece were as large in value as the quantity of bank notes in circulation during the hyperinflation.[76]

The series are not shown for dates later than November 10, 1944. On this date the country made a second attempt at currency stabilization, which was not entirely successful. Prices continued to rise afterward, though at rates far below those that prevailed before November, 1944.

71. League of Nations, *Memorandum on Currency and Central Banks, 1913–1924* (Geneva: Publications Department of the League of Nations, 1925), II, 128.

72. William C. Cleveland and Dimitrios Delivanis, *Greek Monetary Developments, 1939–1948* ("Indiana University Publications, Social Science Series," No. 6 [Bloomington: Indiana University, 1949]), Appendix.

73. Vera Lutz, "The Record of Inflation: European Experience since 1939," chap. iii of preliminary draft for "The American Assembly" (Graduate School of Business, Columbia University, n.d.), p. 86. (Mimeographed.)

74. Cleveland and Delivanis, *op. cit.*

75. *Ibid.*, p. 99.

76. Lutz, *op. cit.*, p. 96.

TABLE B6

TIME SERIES FOR GREECE

Date	$\log_{10}(P/M)$ (June, 1941 = 1) (1)	$\log_{10}(P_i/P_{i-1})$ (Per Month) (2)	$E(.15)$ (Per Month) (3)
1944			
Nov. 10	3.5580	5.9320	.9095
Oct. 31	2.5369	1.9540	.6694
Sept. 30	2.5310	1.3030	.4615
Aug. 31	2.3491	.6524	.3253
July 31	2.3213	.6077	.2724
June 30	2.0752	.2040	.2181
May 31	2.1626	.4120	.2204
Apr. 30	2.0192	.3022	.1894
Mar. 31	2.0554	.2800	.1712
Feb. 29	1.9499	.1832	.1536
Jan. 31	1.8791	.3884	.1488
1943			
Dec. 31	1.5867	.1294	.1101
Nov. 30	1.5999	.2790	.1069
Oct. 31	1.4442	.1687	.0791
Sept. 30	1.4002	.1331	.0646
Aug. 31	1.3553	.0590	.0535
July 31	1.3835	.1278	.0526
June 30	1.3419	.0465	.0405
May 31	1.3538	.0268	.0395
Apr. 30	1.3732	.1224	.0415
Mar. 31	1.3310	.0446	.0284
Feb. 28	1.3505	− .0514	.0258
Jan. 31	1.4402	− .0704	.0383
1942			
Dec. 31	. . . .	− .1268	. . . .
Nov. 30	. . . .	− .0590	. . . .
Oct. 31	. . . .	.1730	. . . .
Sept. 30	. . . .	.0887	. . . .
Aug. 31	. . . .	.1030	. . . .
July 31	. . . .	.1065	. . . .
June 30	. . . .	.1414	. . . .
May 31	. . . .	.0577	. . . .
Apr. 30	. . . .	.1190	. . . .
Mar. 31	. . . .	.1231	. . . .
Feb. 28	. . . .	.0630	. . . .
Jan. 31	. . . .	.0328	. . . .
1941			
Dec. 31	. . . .	.1696	. . . .
Nov. 30	. . . .	.1472	. . . .
Oct. 31	. . . .	.1569	. . . .
Sept. 30	. . . .	.1200	. . . .
Aug. 31	. . . .	.1012	. . . .
July 31	. . . .	.1776	. . . .
June 30	. . . .	.1396	. . . .
May 31	. . . .	.0969	. . . .
Apr. 30	. . . .	.0000	. . . .
Mar. 31	. . . .	.0215	. . . .
1940			
Dec. 31	. . . .	.0145	. . . .
1938			
June 30	. . . .	. . . .	. . . .

NOTES ON HUNGARIAN DATA FOR AFTER WORLD WAR I

For the years before December, 1923, P is an index of retail prices based on the year 1913. Thereafter, P is an index of wholesale prices based on the year 1914. The two indexes were linked together on the assumption that prices changed very little between the two base years.[77]

TABLE B7

TIME SERIES FOR HUNGARY FOLLOWING WORLD WAR I

Date (End of Month)	$\log_{10}(P/M)$ (July, 1921=1) (1)	$\log_{10}(P_i/P_{i-1})$ (Per Month) (2)	$E(.10)$ (Per Month) (3)
1924			
Feb............	1.7332	.2536	.1086
Jan............	1.5514	.1124	.0934
1923			
Dec............	1.5051	.0958	.0914
Nov...........	1.4472	.0340	.0909
Oct............	1.4728	.0253	.0969
Sept..........	1.5490	.0784	.1044
Aug...........	1.6385	.2086	.1072
July..........	1.6776	.2966	.0965
June..........	1.5453	.1867	.0755
May..........	1.4713	.0514	.0638
Apr...........	1.4969	.1022	.0651
Mar..........	1.4800	.1983	.0611
Feb...........	1.3201	.0357	.0463
Jan...........	1.2923	.0618	.0479
1922			
Dec...........	1.2201	.0105	.0464
Nov..........	1.2304	$-.0040$	.0502
Oct...........	1.2480	.0923	.0559
Sept..........	1.2330	.0945	.0520
Aug...........	1.2405	.0898	.0476
July..........	1.2330	.1300	.0432
June..........	....	.0691	....
May..........	....	.0099	....
Apr...........	....	.0359	....
Mar..........	....	.0662	....
Feb...........	....	.0209	....
Jan...........	....	$-.0078$	....
1921			
Dec...........	....	$-.0026$	....
Nov..........	....	.0898	....
Oct...........	....	.0334	....
Sept..........	....	.0634	....
Aug..........	....	.1092	....
July.........	....	.0193	....
1914			
July.........	....	....	....

77. John Parke Young, *European Currency and Finance* (Commission of Gold and Silver Inquiry, U.S. Senate, Serial 9 [Washington, D.C.: Government Printing Office, 1925]), II, 322.

M is an index of the quantity of notes issued by the State Note Institute.[78] These figures neglect issues of *bons de caisse* in 1923, which apparently circulated as a media of exchange. However, they remained below about 3 per cent of the number of notes in circulation.[79]

Table B8 gives figures on deposits less bank reserves (M above includes reserves) and the ratio of an index of notes to an index of notes plus deposits in circulation for Hungary for the years after World War I. The figures include deposits of all the important commercial banks, current accounts (excluding checking and savings deposits) of the post office, and deposits in savings banks.[80] Cash reserves are those of commercial banks.

TABLE B8

DEPOSIT DATA FOR HUNGARY FOLLOWING
WORLD WAR I

End of Year	Bank Deposits *less* Cash Reserves (Million Kronen)	Ratio of Index of Notes to Index of Notes *plus* Deposits in Circulation
1920.	18,398	1.00
1921.	28,496	1.07
1922.	53,038	1.35
1923.	159,958	1.95
1924.	5,201,805	1.06

Current accounts in the State Note Institute are excluded, because the Institute served mainly as a bankers' bank.[81] Even if these accounts are included in the totals, the pattern of the ratios in Table B8 still retains the peak in 1923. The same kinds of deposits as are included in the figures in the table accounted for 83 per cent of total bank deposits held by the public in 1925.[82] Besides figures on checking and savings deposits in the post office and deposits in small commercial banks, such figures on deposits in municipal savings banks and co-operative credit societies are also excluded, because they are unavailable. These last two institutions probably lost business during the hyperinflation, in which case the coverage of deposits in Table B8 would be nearly complete.

78. *Ibid.*, p. 321.

79. League of Nations, *Memorandum on Currency and Central Banks, 1913–1924*, I, 123.

80. League of Nations, *Memorandum on Currency and Central Banks, 1913–1925*, II, 65, 85.

81. League of Nations, *Memorandum on Currency and Central Banks, 1913–1924*, II, 92.

82. League of Nations, *Memorandum on Commercial Banks, 1913–1929*, p. 170.

An unusual aspect of deposits for this period in Hungary was the phenomenal growth of current accounts in the post office. They increased over a thousand times from 1920 to 1924. Deposits in commercial banks, which seem to account for most of the growth in deposits during other hyperinflations, increased only a little over two hundred times. Data on output for Hungary after World War I are apparently unavailable.

NOTES ON HUNGARIAN DATA FOR AFTER WORLD WAR II

For the months after July, 1945, P is an index of prices compiled by Professor Varga.[83] For the earlier period P is an index of the cost of living in Budapest.[84] The rates of change in prices based on the cost-of-living index differ in level from those given in the second column of Table B9

TABLE B9

TIME SERIES FOR HUNGARY FOLLOWING WORLD WAR II

Date (End of Month)	$\log_{10}(P/M)$ (Dec., 1939=1) (1)	$\log_{10}(P_i/P_{i-1})$ (Per Month) (2)	$E(.15)$ (Per Month) (3)
1946			
July...........	4.5879	14.6226	3.2211
June...........	2.9782	4.9264	1.3758
May...........	3.1740	2.4992	.8011
Apr...........	3.0255	1.2821	.5263
Mar...........	2.9761	.6323	.4040
Feb...........	3.2040	.7804	.3670
Jan...........	2.9718	.2411	.3001
1945			
Dec...........	3.0655	.5041	.3097
Nov...........	2.8954	.7283	.2783
Oct...........	2.6866	.8070	.2055
Sept...........	2.2630	.3456	.1081
Aug...........	2.1359	.2118	.0696
July...........	2.0825	.1352	.0466
June...........	....	.0003	....
May...........	....	.0004	....
Apr...........	....	.0520	....
1944			
June...........	....	.0077	....
1943			
June...........	....	.0056	....
1942			
June...........	....	....	....

83. Stefan Varga, "Zerfall und Stabilisierung der ungarischen Währung," *Neue Zürcher Zeitung*, January 7, 1947, p. 4.

84. Statistical Office of the United Nations, *Monthly Bulletin of Statistics*, June, 1947, No. 6, p. 120.

for the final months of the hyperinflation; however, the former rates do not show a materially different pattern from the rates in the table.

M is an index of the quantity of bank notes issued by the National Bank of Hungary and the quantity of deposits in the thirty major commercial and savings banks.[85] The ratio of deposits to bank notes rose astronomically during the hyperinflation. In view of the fact that this ratio ordinarily declined in the other hyperinflations, a breakdown of deposits into various kinds would be desirable, because deposits in a new unit of currency, which was stable in real value when it was first introduced, appeared in January, 1946.[86] Deposits of this new currency should be excluded from the figures as long as the currency had a stable value. Presumably they are excluded from the published figures,[87] but, since the data on deposits are not broken down, this presumption cannot be verified.

Output in Hungary seems to have been stable during the hyperinflation following World War II, though the evidence is spotty. Production figures on basic raw materials do not decline, and unemployment figures only increase after the date of the reform in the currency.[88] Undoubtedly real income was much below prewar levels.

NOTES ON POLISH DATA

For the months before September, 1921, *P* is an index of the retail prices of foods only. Thereafter it is a geometric average of fifty-seven commodity prices at wholesale.[89] The two indexes were linked together.

M is the quantity of bank notes issued by the Bank of Poland.[90] The Polish mark was introduced into Upper Silesia on March 1, 1923, and was made legal tender in November of that year. It gradually replaced the German mark during this period.[91] One result of transferring this territory to Poland from Germany was that the former's currency was given a larger area within which to circulate, and more Polish marks could be issued without affecting the Polish price level. The ratio of *M* to *P* could

85. *Ibid.*, pp. 54, 106.

86. Nogaro, *op. cit.* (The tables in Nogaro's article contain some errors. Original sources were used.)

87. L'Office Central Hongrois de Statistique, *Revue hongroise de statistique*, October–December, 1946, Nos. 10–12, p. 154.

88. Statistical Office of the United Nations, *op. cit.*, esp. p. 20.

89. League of Nations, *Memorandum on Currency and Central Banks, 1913–1924*, II, 298, and Young, *op. cit.*, p. 349.

90. Young, *op. cit.*, p. 347.

91. League of Nations, *Memorandum on Currency and Central Banks, 1913–1924*, II, 128.

thus rise, even if real cash balances within the original borders were constant. This no doubt partly explains the slight rise that occurred in real cash balances in October and November, 1923, above the level at which the expected rate of change in prices suggests they should have been.

TABLE B10

TIME SERIES FOR POLAND

Date (End of Month)	$\log_{10}(P/M)$ (Jan., 1921 = 1) (1)	$\log_{10}(P_i/P_{i-1})$ (Per Month) (2)	$E(.30)$ (Per Month) (3)
1924			
Jan............	2.2279	.2309	.2860
1923			
Dec............	2.3962	.3211	.3053
Nov...........	2.4472	.3947	.2997
Oct...........	2.4150	.5740	.2665
Sept..........	2.1553	.1396	.1590
Aug...........	2.2279	.2367	.1657
July..........	2.1761	.2127	.1409
June..........	2.0645	.2232	.1158
May..........	1.9542	.0264	.0782
Apr...........	1.9956	.0299	.0963
Mar..........	2.0719	.0609	.1196
Feb...........	2.2041	.1979	.1401
Jan...........	2.1173	.1966	.1199
1922			
Dec...........	1.9823	.0992	.0930
Nov..........	1.9590	.1364	.0908
Oct..........	1.8808	.1210	.0749
Sept..........	1.8573	.0501	.0588
Aug...........	1.8865	.1260	.0618
July..........	1.8195	.0639	.0394
June..........	1.8062	.0473	.0308
May..........	1.7924	.0199	.0250
Apr...........	1.7993	.0097	.0268
Mar..........	....	.0636	....
Feb..........	....	.0299	....
Jan..........	....	.0164	....
1921			
Dec..........	....	.0115	....
Nov..........	....	− .0488	....
Oct..........	....	.0368	....
Sept..........	....	.0526	....
Aug..........	....	.0676	....
July..........	....	.1105	....
June..........	....	.0353	....
May..........	....	.0126	....
Apr..........	....	− .0159	....
Mar..........	....	.0142	....
Feb..........	....	.1024	....
Jan..........	....	.0304	....
1914			
June..........	....	....	....

Table B11 gives figures on deposits less bank reserves (M above includes reserves) and the ratio of an index of bank notes to an index of bank notes plus deposits in circulation for Poland. The figures include deposits held by the public in the Bank of Poland,[92] in the post office (savings deposits only),[93] and in almost all commercial banks.[94] Cash reserves are those of commercial banks.

Non-government deposits in the Bank of Poland were held by banks, businesses, and individuals.[95] The part held by banks was largely excluded by deducting that part of commercial banks' cash reserves that includes balances with the national bank. However, the portion of total deposits in the Bank of Poland not held by the government in 1920 and

TABLE B11

DEPOSIT DATA FOR POLAND

End of Year	Bank Deposits *less* Cash Reserves (Million Marks)	Ratio of Index of Bank Notes to Index of Bank Notes *plus* Deposits in Circulation
1920........	12,094	1.00
1921........	47,857	1.03
1922........	224,290	0.97
1923........	64,229,000	0.94

1923 had to be estimated, because it is not differentiated from government deposits for those two years. The estimates for 1920 and 1923 are based on the proportion of non-government to government deposits in the Bank of Poland at the end of 1921 and in September, 1923, respectively. Since deposits in the Bank of Poland not held by the government were large compared with total bank deposits in Poland at the time, the figure for total bank deposits in the table depends heavily on the accuracy of these estimates. Their accuracy will be only fair at best, because they are based on ratios that were not necessarily constant.

Furthermore, figures on deposits in commercial banks for 1923 are unavailable and had to be estimated from deposits in the sixteen major

92. League of Nations, *Memorandum on Central Banks, 1913 and 1918–1923*, p. 285.

93. League of Nations, *Memorandum on Currency and Central Banks, 1913–1925*, II, 86.

94. League of Nations, *Memorandum on Commercial Banks, 1913–1925* (Geneva: Publications Department of the League of Nations, 1931), p. 230.

95. League of Nations, *Memorandum on Central Banks, 1913 and 1918–1923*, p. 292.

commercial banks.[96] The deposits in these sixteen banks at the end of 1923 were increased by 91 per cent to serve as an estimate of total commercial-bank deposits in that year. Ninety-one is the percentage by which deposits in the sixteen banks at the end of January, 1923, fell short of deposits in all commercial banks at the end of 1922. The 91 is a slightly low percentage to use, because it would have been desirable to use a figure for deposits in the sixteen banks for the first of January, 1923, rather than for the end of that month. Deposits at the first of that month were undoubtedly somewhat smaller than deposits at the end, but a figure for the ending date is not available. The cash-reserve ratio of commercial banks at the end of 1923 is taken to be 40 per cent, the approximate ratio that it had been at the end of the previous four years.

The figures in Table B11 exclude deposits in the National Economic Bank and the State Land Bank. At the end of 1925 the kinds of deposits included in the table were 65 per cent of the total deposits in all forms not held by the government in Poland.[97] Even under the assumption that the banks whose deposits are included in the above table gained relatively to the smaller non-commercial banks whose deposits were excluded, the estimates of total deposits cannot be considered very comprehensive. Yet, since the figures cover a large proportion of total deposits, the ratios in the table reflect to some extent the major movements in total deposits relative to bank notes.

The only evidence available related to real income is figures on unemployment. These show a decline for the period from 1922 to August, 1923, except for a short rise in the early part of 1923. Unemployment seems not to have risen until after the first of 1924.[98]

NOTES ON RUSSIAN DATA

P is an index of retail prices for all of Russia published by the Central Bureau of Labor Statistics.[99] Two other available indexes, one of retail prices and the other of wholesale prices, agree substantially with the index used.[100]

M is an index of the quantity of paper rubles in circulation.[101] The total circulation of paper money and coins at the beginning of 1914 is estimated

96. League of Nations, *Memorandum on Currency and Central Banks, 1913–1925*, II, 86.

97. League of Nations, *Memorandum on Commercial Banks, 1913–1929*, pp. 230 ff.

98. Statistisches Reichsamt, *op. cit.*, Table 13.

99. Young, *op. cit.*, Table 81, p. 360.

100. League of Nations, *Memorandum on Currency and Central Banks, 1913–1924*, I, 199, and Young, *op. cit.*, p. 360.

101. Young, *op. cit.*, p. 359.

at 2,512 million rubles.[102] All coins had disappeared from circulation by 1916. The figures for 1923 are given in either chervontsi or chervonets gold rubles. The procedure for converting these units into those that apply to the rubles in circulation before 1923 is as follows: Convert ten chervonets gold rubles into one chervonets. Then convert chervontsi into

TABLE B12

TIME SERIES FOR RUSSIA

Date (First of Month)	$\log_{10}(P/M)$ (1913=1) (1)	$\log_{10}(P_i/P_{i-1})$ (Per Month) (2)	$E(.35)$ (Per Month) (3)
1924			
Feb..............	3.1106	.4958	.3478
Jan..............	2.8854	.3728	.2858
1923			
Dec.	2.7694	.3226	.2493
Nov.............	2.7126	.2224	.2186
Oct.............	2.8633	.2938	.2170
Sept............	2.7033	.2360	.1848
Aug.............	2.5944	.2192	.1633
July............	2.5145	.1677	.1399
June............	2.4548	.1644	.1283
May.............	2.3541	.1443	.1131
Apr.............	2.3424	.1012	.1000
Mar.............	2.3820	.0503	.0996
Feb.............	2.4183	.1153	.1202
Jan.............	2.4281	.0975	.1223
1922			
Dec.............	2.4594	.1667	.1327
Nov.............	2.4232	.1972	.1185
Oct.............	2.3365	.0880	.0855
Sept............	2.3345	.0305	.0844
Aug.............	2.4713	−.0158	.1070
July............	2.6571	.0566	.1585
June............	2.7767	.0872	.2011
May.............	2.9079	.2172	.2489
Apr.............	2.8949	.3403	.2622
Mar.............	2.7767	.3254	.2295
Feb.............	2.6656	.2770	.1894
Jan.............	2.6160	.3195	.1527

old paper rubles according to the official daily rate of exchange.[103] (One new ruble, issued in 1923, equaled one hundred 1922 rubles and one million pre-1922 rubles.) The official daily exchange rates were based on the free-market rates. The difference between the two quotations was rarely more than $3\frac{1}{2}$ per cent in Moscow, though it sometimes reached as high as

102. League of Nations, *Memorandum on Currency and Central Banks, 1913–1924*, II, 140.

103. S. S. Katzenellenbaum, *Russian Currency and Banking, 1914–1924* (London: P. S. King & Son, Ltd., 1925), p. 111.

20 per cent in the provinces.[104] Gold treasury bonds (certificates of the *centrocassa* of the Commissioner of Finance) were not included in M, because they circulated mainly among state enterprises and institutions.[105]

In December, 1922, the government began to issue a separate currency called the chervonets ruble, which was not increased in such quantities as to depreciate much in value. The two currencies circulated together and exchanged according to free-market rates, as noted above. An index of wholesale prices in chervontsi is available.[106] The chervontsi were perfect

TABLE B13

TIME SERIES FOR RUSSIA

Date (First of Month)	$\log_{10}(P_i/P_{i-1})$ (Per Month)	Date (First of Month)	$\log_{10}(P_i/P_{i-1})$ (Per Month)
1921		Sept............	.0076
Dec............	.1599	Aug............	.0470
Nov............	.0667	July...........	.0930
Oct............	.0302	June...........	.0557
Sept...........	−.0216	May...........	.0834
Aug............	−.0022	Apr............	.0976
July...........	.1145	Mar............	.0909
June...........	.1620	Feb............	.1062
May...........	.0777	Jan............	.1309
Apr............	.1118	1919	
Mar............	.1064	Dec............	.1194
Feb............	.1092	Nov............	.1683
Jan............	.1461	Oct............	.0546
1920			
Dec............	.0580		
Nov............	.0380		
Oct............	.0180		

substitutes for the depreciating rubles. The amount outstanding of the former is not included in M, which comprises rubles only, because only prices quoted in rubles were undergoing hyperinflation. The fact that such a perfect substitute for rubles existed undoubtedly contributed to the speed at which the rubles declined in value.

All forms of private bank credit soon disappeared after the nationalization of Russian banking in December, 1917. At the beginning of 1914 deposits of all commercial banks totaled 2,545 million rubles; by 1920 deposits of the public were virtually extinct.[107] Credit was extended by the

104. *Ibid.*, pp. 120–21.

105. League of Nations, *Memorandum on Currency and Central Banks, 1913–1924*, II, 143.

106. Statistisches Reichsamt, *op. cit.*, Table 14.

107. Katzenellenbaum, *op. cit.*, pp. 150, 152.

new State Bank established in 1922, but very few of its deposits were held by the public.[108] With the establishment of the State Bank, private banking was also allowed, but it did not develop to any degree until 1923. By 1923 all banking was conducted in relatively stable chervontsi rather than in regular rubles.[109] Consequently, if state enterprises are considered to be a part of the government, deposits held by the public were small enough to neglect.

The currency reform that finally resulted in the complete abandonment of the ruble was begun in February, 1924. It was completed on March 10, 1924, when 1 chervonets officially exchanged for 500,000 1923

TABLE B14

INDEXES OF OUTPUT FOR RUSSIA

YEAR	INDEX OF (1913 = 100)	
	Industrial Production	Agricultural Output
1920.	. . . .	65
1921.	13	55
1922.	24	69
1923.	35	76
1924.	49	69

rubles or 500 billion old (pre-1922) rubles. Russian data during these years are based on the Julian calendar. Add thirteen days to the above dates to convert to the Gregorian calendar.

Table B14 gives an index of industrial production and an index of agricultural output.[110] On the supposition that agricultural output dominated the total product of the economy, the movement in its index suggests that total real income rose until sometime in 1923 or 1924 and then fell. Another index of real income for the fiscal years 1922–23 and 1924–25 is 58 and 77 per cent, respectively, of the 1913 level.[111]

108. *Ibid.*, p. 159.

109. *Ibid.*, pp. 183 ff.

110. Jean Dessirier, "Indices comparés de la production industrielle et de la production agricole en divers pays de 1870 à 1928," *Bulletin de la statistique générale de la France*, XVIII, Sec. 1 (October–December, 1928), 104.

111. Serge N. Prokopovicz, *Histoire économique de l'U.R.S.S.* (Paris: Chez Flammarion, 1952), p. 567.

III

German Money and Prices, 1932–44

JOHN J. KLEIN

German Money and Prices, 1932–44[1]

Fʀᴏᴍ 1932 to 1944 the German wholesale-price index increased 22 per cent. During the same period the average quantity of money increased 437 per cent. The purpose of this study is to explain the divergence between these two figures.

Section I of this paper illustrates the magnitude of the problem by presenting summary and comparative data on the German, Italian, British, and American economies for the period under study. Sections II and III describe the problems involved in determining the increase in German money and prices from 1932 to 1944. Section IV discusses the level of real cash balances and income velocity through the period. Section V describes some of the economic policies of Germany which may explain the divergence between the increases in the stock of money and the price level that remains after adjusting the stock of money and prices. Section VI summarizes the major conclusions of the preceding sections.

I. Pʀɪᴄᴇs, Mᴏɴᴇʏ, ᴀɴᴅ Iɴᴄᴏᴍᴇ ɪɴ Gᴇʀᴍᴀɴʏ, Iᴛᴀʟʏ, ᴛʜᴇ Uɴɪᴛᴇᴅ Kɪɴɢᴅᴏᴍ, ᴀɴᴅ ᴛʜᴇ Uɴɪᴛᴇᴅ Sᴛᴀᴛᴇs, 1932–44

A. GERMANY

Columns 1, 2, and 3 of Table 1 give indexes of wholesale prices, the stock of money, and real cash balances from 1932 to 1944 for old Germany. The year 1932 is throughout taken as equal to 100. These indexes are based on 1932, because it represents the trough of the German depression. When not otherwise mentioned, the figures given in this section are yearly averages. The figures for money and prices are plotted in Figure 1.

According to these figures, changes in German wholesale prices and the quantity of money roughly correspond from 1932 through 1935. From 1936 on, however, the stock of money pulls away from the price level. Real cash balances in 1936 were 106 per cent of their 1932 level. By late 1936, the change in the stock of money from the 1932 depression levels was considerably larger than the change in the price level. For example, the quantity of hand-to-hand currency in circulation on December 31, 1936, was 120 per cent of the 1932 average. The wholesale-price index was then 108.

1. This paper is based on the author's "German Monetary Development, 1932–44" (unpublished doctoral dissertation, University of Chicago, June, 1955).

121

In the light of the problem confronting us—explaining divergent movements in German prices and money—late 1936 is rather important, because by then Germany was close to, if not already at, full employment. The average number of unemployed workers reported by the German employment offices decreased from 5,602,700 in 1932 to 1,592,700 in 1936. The 1929 unemployment figures had been 1,391,000. In October, 1936, there were 1,076,500 unemployed. One year later the number was scarcely a half-million.[2] Hence, one might not expect any substantial rise in prices

TABLE 1*

INDEXES OF GERMAN WHOLESALE PRICES, STOCK OF MONEY, REAL CASH
BALANCES, NATIONAL INCOME, AND INCOME VELOCITY, 1932–44

Year	Official Wholesale- Price Index (1)	Adjusted Stock of Money (2)	Real Cash Balances (Col. [2]÷ Col. [1]) (3)	National Income† (Billion Reichsmarks) (4)	Income Velocity† (5)
1932........	100.0	100.0	100.0	45.2	1.35
1933........	96.7	96.2	99.5	46.5	1.44
1934........	102.0	99.6	97.6	52.7	1.58
1935........	105.5	106.2	100.7	58.6	1.65
1936........	107.9	114.0	105.7	65.8	1.73
1937........	109.7	124.0	113.0	73.8	1.78
1938........	109.5	139.4	127.3	82.1	1.76
1939........	110.8	160.6	144.9	89.8	1.67
1940........	114.0	196.9	172.7	92.5	1.41
1941........	116.4	257.4	221.1	97.8	1.14
1942........	118.5	333.4	281.4	98	.88
1943........	120.4	424.9	352.9	99	.70
1944........	121.9	536.6	440.2	90	.50

* Source: Column 1: 1932–41, Statistisches Reichsamt, *Statistisches Jahrbuch für das Deutsche Reich* (Berlin, 1930–41/42), Vols. L–LIX; 1942–44; Länderrat des Amerikanischen Besatzungsgebiets, *Statistisches Handbuch von Deutschland, 1928–1944* (München, 1949), p. 460. (I have changed the figures from a 1913 to a 1932 base.)
    Column 2: See Sec. II.
    Column 4: 1932–41, Statistisches Reichsamt, *op. cit.*, Vols. L–LIX; 1942–41, Deutsches Institut für Wirtschaftsforschung, *Die deutsche Wirtschaft zwei Jahre nach dem Zusammenbruch* (Berlin, 1947), pp. 268–69.
    † National income divided by the average stock of money.

before late 1936 because of unemployed men and resources in the economy. But certainly after that one would anticipate rising prices. This expectation, however, is not borne out by Table 1.

Late 1936 is important for another reason—the "General Price Stop" was enacted. Labor shortages as well as material shortages had already begun to appear in various sectors of the economy in 1935, particularly in the building trades. In Germany, then, at approximately the same time,

2. Statistisches Reichsamt, *Statistisches Jahrbuch für das Deutsche Reich* (Berlin, 1930–41/42), Vols. L–LIX (hereinafter cited as "*Jahrbuch*").

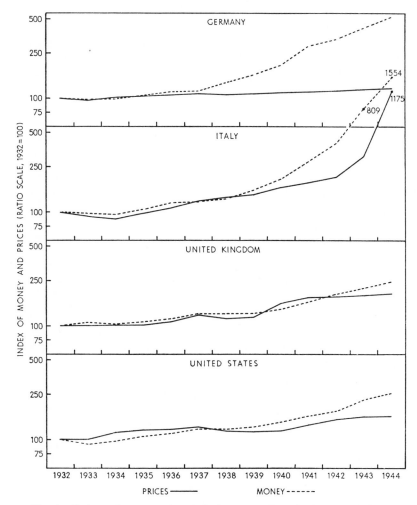

Fig. 1.—Indexes of money and prices in Germany, Italy, the United Kingdom, and the United States, 1932–44. These indexes are annual averages of monthly figures. Prices are those of commodities at wholesale. Money comprises the following items: for Germany, hand-to-hand currency *plus* "other" and savings deposits; for Italy, hand-to-hand currency; for the United Kingdom, notes in circulation *plus* net deposits of clearing banks; and for the United States, currency outside banks *plus* adjusted demand and time deposits.

Sources: Columns 1 and 2 of Tables 1, 2, 3, and 4.

(a) the increase in the stock of money caught up with and passed both the rate of increase and the total increase over 1932 of the price level; (b) full employment of resources was reached; and (c) a general price ceiling was put into effect. For these reasons it has been contended that 1936 marks the beginning of Germany's repressed inflation.[3]

National income figures, however, do not support this conclusion. The national income of Germany increased from 45.2 billion reichsmarks in 1932 to 65.8 billion reichsmarks in 1936 and to 82.1 billion reichsmarks in 1938, as is shown in Table 1. Dividing national income by the stock of money, we find that German income velocity increased from 1.35 in 1932 to 1.73 in 1936. This increased velocity is what one would expect with greater business activity. Thus, over the period 1932–36 there were (a) an increase in money supply; (b) a rising national income; (c) a rising price level; (d) an increased income velocity; and (e), with national income rising more than prices, a rising real income. From 1936 to 1938 income velocity remained relatively constant, rising slightly from 1.73 in 1936 to 1.78 in 1937 and falling to 1.76 in 1938. In this period (a) the stock of money increased; (b) national income increased; (c) the price level rose slightly; (d) income velocity remained relatively constant; and (e) real income rose.

Although full employment was reached by late 1936, there was enough slack yet left in the economy in the form of women not in the labor market, a less-than-forty-hour week, idle machine capacity, etc., to permit an increase in real production through most of 1938. The absorption of this supply of productive factors into the economy accounts for the indicated rise in real income. Thus, on the basis of national income data, I should be inclined to consider late 1938 rather than late 1936 as the beginning of repressed inflation in Germany.[4] By 1939 the wholesale-price index was 111, and the stock of money 161, per cent of 1932. Further, from 1939 on, income velocity decreased rapidly. During the same period prices remained relatively constant, money in circulation rose greatly, and national income rose slightly. For example, in 1944 prices were 122, and the stock of money 537, per cent of 1932.

The large increase in the stock of money might be expected to produce rising prices when all resources are employed. This did not occur in Ger-

3. Walter Eucken, *This Unsuccessful Age* (New York, 1952), p. 71, and "On the Theory of the Centrally Administered Economy: An Analysis of the German Experiment," *Economica*, XV (1948), 79–100, 173–93.

4. Repressed inflation is characterized by (a) full employment; (b) a stable price index; (c) a rising stock of money; (d) a national income which is increasing at a slower rate than the stock of money; and (e) price, wage, demand, production, etc., controls.

many. To combat the inflationary potential of its increase in money supply, Germany had controls over prices, wages, demand, production, consumption, etc., all concomitants of repressed inflation. Yet, other nations had such controls and did not manage to avoid inflation.

B. ITALY

As Table 2 and Figure 1 show, from 1932 through 1938 the movement in the Italian wholesale-price index roughly parallels the movement in Italian hand-to-hand currency (notes and coin).[5] From 1939 through 1942

TABLE 2*

INDEXES OF ITALIAN WHOLESALE PRICES, HAND-TO-
HAND CURRENCY, AND REAL CASH
BALANCES, 1932–44

Year	Wholesale Prices (1)	Hand-to-Hand Currency (2)	Real Cash Balances (Col. [2]÷ Col. [1]) (3)
1932...........	100.0	100.0	100.0
1933...........	91.1	96.8	106.3
1934...........	89.1	95.1	106.7
1935...........	98.0	106.6	108.8
1936...........	109.8	120.9	110.1
1937...........	128.0	125.3	97.9
1938...........	136.9	133.4	97.4
1939...........	142.8	158.3	110.9
1940...........	166.7	198.3	119.0
1941...........	186.0	280.1	150.6
1942...........	208.9	416.6	199.4
1943...........	313.4	809.1	258.2
1944...........	1,175.2	1,554.1	132.2

* Source: Instituto Centrale di Statistica Repubblica Italiana, *Annuario statistico italiano, 1944–1948*, Series V, Vol. I.

Italy presents the same type of increase in real cash balances which began in 1936 in Germany and continued through the war. In 1932, 1938, 1939, and 1942 real cash balances were 100, 97, 111, and 199, respectively. The

5. My discussion of Italy will be limited to a treatment of the wholesale-price level and hand-to-hand currency. The Italian current and time accounts are omitted from discussion because (*a*) the number of institutions varied over the period (it was not until 1943 that comprehensive figures covering 365 institutions holding about 99 per cent of all bank deposits became available) and (*b*) "the inflation potential of bank money was weakened . . . because of the strong contraction of trade and the habit now become general of paying in cash rather than checks of *giro conto*" (Guilio Pietranera, "Considerations on the Dynamics of the Italian Inflation," *Banca Nazionale del Lavoro Quarterly Review*, I [1947–48], 27).

years from 1941 to early 1943 were a period of heavy military preparations. Under these conditions the slowly rising price level suggests a state of repressed inflation. It should be noted, however, that "in the first war years the wholesale price index numbers were compiled on the basis of official prices and therefore only partially reflected the real market situation."[6] Presumably, therefore, a more satisfactory index of wholesale prices would parallel the movement in the stock of money (i.e., hand-to-hand currency) more closely than the index in Table 2.

In 1943, when the price index more accurately reflected the market situation, the Italian wholesale-price index moved sharply upward, although not so sharply as hand-to-hand currency. In 1944 prices rose much more rapidly than the monetary circulation. Thus real cash balances declined markedly. True, real cash balances were still 132 per cent of their 1932 level, but this level was much lower than German real cash balances in 1944, which were 440 per cent of their 1932 level. Thus, over the whole period 1932–44 the Italian wholesale-price index and the stock of money are fairly well correlated, contrary to the German figures.

Italy, like Germany and most of the other warring powers, had a full set of policies designed to suppress any potential inflation. It had exchange controls, a blocked investment policy, and price controls. How successful were these policies? The indexes show their lack of effectiveness.[7]

C. THE UNITED KINGDOM

In general, Britain presents a picture somewhat similar to the German situation. There is this difference, however: the range between the stock-of-money index and the wholesale-price index is much greater in Germany than in the United Kingdom.

Table 3 and Figure 1 show that British prices and the stock of money moved together through the period 1932–39. In 1939 real cash balances were 108 per cent of their 1932 level. They dropped to 89 per cent in 1940. This was a result of the British inflation from late 1939 through 1940.

Owing to inflation, Britain imposed economic controls. They were, however, only gradually introduced into the economy of Great Britain. For example, in late 1939 gasoline, coal, gas, and electricity were the only important commodities being rationed. By early 1940 direct rationing

6. Marcello Mancini, "Bank Credits in Italy Classified by Business Branches and Bank Groups (1936–1946)," *Banco Nazionale del Lavoro Quarterly Review*, I (1947–48), 184, n. 1.

7. Italian national income has not been discussed in this section, because I have not seen in any original Italian sources a continuous and comparable series on Italian national income.

was used to restrict the consumption of dairy and meat products, tobacco, tea, and textiles. Bread, cereals, and potatoes were unrationed.germany had no such piecemeal system. According to a decree of August 24, 1939, and others which followed over a period of weeks, Germany imposed rationing on practically all articles popularly consumed: food, clothing, fuel, etc. Furthermore, since late 1936 Germany had tried to combat the effects of expanded purchasing power upon prices by means of a general

TABLE 3*

INDEXES OF BRITISH WHOLESALE PRICES, STOCK OF MONEY, REAL
CASH BALANCES, NATIONAL INCOME, AND INCOME
VELOCITY, 1932–47

Year	Wholesale Prices	Stock of Money†	Real Cash Balances (Col. [2] ÷ Col. [1])	National Income (Millions of Pounds)	Income Velocity‡
	(1)	(2)	(3)	(4)	(5)
1932........	100.0	100.0	100.0	3,969	1.92
1933........	100.1	108.3	108.2	4,068	1.82
1934........	103.0	105.0	101.9	4,369	2.01
1935........	103.9	111.4	107.2	4,650	2.02
1936........	110.2	119.9	108.8	4,955	2.00
1937........	127.0	130.6	102.8	5,197	1.93
1938........	118.5	130.5	110.1	5,327	1.97
1939........	120.1	129.8	108.1	5,714	2.13
1940........	159.5	142.2	89.2	6,824	2.32
1941........	178.3	169.8	95.2	8,047	2.29
1942........	186.1	191.3	102.8	8,894	2.25
1943........	190.0	218.2	114.8	9,490	2.10
1944........	194.0	248.9	128.3	9,624	1.87
1945........	197.5	281.8	142.7	9,605	1.65
1946........	204.6	303.8	148.5	9,362	1.61
1947........	224.0	330.9	147.7	10,159	1.49

* Source: Columns 1 and 2, London and Cambridge Economic Service, *Bulletin I*, XXVIII (1950), 32–33. The figures are based upon monthly averages.
   Column 4, Colin Clark, *Conditions of Economic Progress* (London, 1951), p. 63. These figures are for national income at market prices.
   † Notes in circulation and clearing-bank net deposits.
   ‡ National income divided by the average stock of money.

price ceiling. Britain did not follow the German method of price controls to combat inflation. It resorted first in late 1939 to a system of subsidies to producers of articles contained in the cost-of-living index.

In 1941 the United Kingdom began to experience repressed inflation. British control policies seemed to take effect, and the rate of increase in the price level declined perceptibly through the remaining war years. Real cash balances rose from 95 per cent of 1932 in 1941 to 128 per cent in 1944. The stock of money and the wholesale-price index increased from

170 and 178 per cent of 1932 in 1941 to 249 and 194 per cent in 1944, respectively.

These figures suggest that Britain had better success than Germany in restricting the increase in the stock of money but was less successful than Germany in holding down the price index. This analysis, however, may be deceptive, because repressed inflation began in 1938 in Germany and in 1941 in the United Kingdom—there having been a lag in both countries from the time of the enactment of controls to the beginning of repressed inflation. In the three years from 1941 to 1944, the stock of money, wholesale prices, and real cash balances in Britain rose 47, 9, and 35 per cent, respectively. In Germany from 1938 to 1941 these same indexes rose 85, 6, and 74 per cent, respectively. These figures indicate that Great Britain was nearly as successful as Germany in holding down the price index and that Britain in 1944 had less to fear than Germany from the potential effects of repressed inflation because of both the slower rate of growth in the stock of money and the shorter period of time during which the British economy had been restricted.

What happens if the periods are made more nearly comparable by extending the British figures to 1947 and the German figures to 1944? The length of time covered in each instance is then seven years. British real cash balances in 1945 were 150 per cent of their 1941 level. They then stabilized and were 154 and 155 per cent in 1946 and 1947, respectively. This was a period in which Britain still had extensive economic controls. German real cash balances in 1944, on the other hand, were 346 per cent of their 1938 level. At no time during repressed inflation, therefore, did British prices and the stock of money diverge as much as German prices and the stock of money.

A study of the national income of Great Britain leads to substantially the same conclusions. Column 5 of Table 3 gives British income velocity from 1932 to 1947. Following the depression of the late 1930's, income velocity increased from a low of 1.93 in 1938 to a high of 2.32 in 1940. After this, it declined gradually, reaching a low of 1.87 in 1944. Thereafter, income velocity continued to decline, falling to 1.49 in 1947. British income velocity in 1947 was 65 per cent of its 1941 value. German income velocity in 1944, on the other hand, was 28 per cent of its 1938 value.

D. THE UNITED STATES

In what respects are Germany and the United States similar? Table 4 and Figure 1 show that in 1941 prices in the United States were 135 per cent, the stock of money 163 per cent, and real cash balances 121 per cent of the 1932 level. By 1944 real cash balances were 162 per cent of the

1932 level. In Germany they were 440 per cent. The situation in the United States is only slightly closer to that of Germany than in Great Britain and Italy.

How do the differing circumstances in the economies of the United States and Germany affect this conclusion? From 1932 to 1941 the United States tried to get out of depression. It devalued the dollar, and banking

TABLE 4*

INDEXES OF AMERICAN WHOLESALE PRICES, STOCK OF MONEY, REAL CASH BALANCES, NATIONAL INCOME, AND INCOME VELOCITY, 1932–46

Year	Wholesale Prices (1)	Stock of Money† (2)	Real Cash Balances (Col. [2]÷ Col. [1]) (3)	National Income (Millions of Dollars) (4)	Income Velocity‡ (5)
1932.........	100.0	100.0	100.0	41,690	.93
1933.........	101.7	90.7	89.2	39,584	.97
1934.........	115.7	98.3	85.0	48,613	1.10
1935.........	123.5	109.1	88.3	56,789	1.16
1936.........	124.7	119.8	96.1	64,719	1.20
1937.........	133.3	125.8	94.4	73,627	1.30
1938.........	121.4	124.4	102.5	67,375	1.30
1939.........	119.0	133.7	112.4	72,532	1.21
1940.........	121.4	147.0	121.1	81,347	1.23
1941.........	134.9	163.1	120.9	103,834	1.41
1942.........	152.5	178.1	116.8	137,119	1.71
1943.........	159.1	226.9	142.6	169,686	1.66
1944.........	160.6	259.3	161.5	183,838	1.58
1945.........	163.4	307.6	188.2	182,691	1.32
1946.........	186.9	350.7	187.6	180,286	1.14

* Source: Columns 1 and 2, various issues of the *Federal Reserve Bulletin;* col. 4, United States Department of Commerce, *National Income and Product of the United States, 1929–1950* (Washington, D.C., 1951), Table 1, p. 150.

† End of June currency outside banks, adjusted demand deposits, and time deposits.

‡ National income divided by the average stock of money.

conditions improved by 1935. As a result there was an increase in demand deposits and hence in the stock of money. Yet, in spite of vast public works, deficit finance, increased prices, and an increased stock of money, the United States did not achieve full employment of the labor force until early 1942. Only then did it reach a position comparable to that reached by Germany in 1936.[8] Price control and rationing systems similar to those in Germany were introduced. Hence, to make the observations more nearly comparable, I shall use 1942 as a base of 100 for the United States and 1938 as the base of 100 for Germany.

8. The United States and Germany were not comparable in many ways. Enforcement was less arbitrary and rigid in the United States.

In the United States real cash balances in 1944 were 138 per cent of their 1942 level. In 1940, the third year of repressed inflation in Germany, real cash balances were 136 per cent of their 1938 level. Hence, the magnitude of the divergence between the price index and stock-of-money movements in the United States were almost identical for three years of repressed inflation. It is likely, however, that there is considerable bias in the price index for the United States during the war years due to the evasion of price controls and to increased consumption of both luxury and substandard items. Thus the United States and Germany present roughly the same type of problem—lack of correspondence between price and stock-of-money movements—for a period of three years.

What happens if the data for the United States are extended beyond 1944? Real cash balances for 1945 and 1946 become 161.2 and 160.7 per cent of their 1942 level, respectively. German real cash balances, on the other hand, in 1941 and 1942 were 174 and 221 per cent, respectively, of their 1938 level. Thus the situations in the United States and Germany become dissimilar.

Income-velocity figures for the United States tell essentially the same story as the real-cash-balance figures. Income velocity reflects the recovery from the depression of the early 1930's, the recession of 1938, the recovery from 1939 to 1941, and, finally, with repressed inflation, the accumulation of cash balances. Income velocity rose from 0.93 in 1932 to 1.30 in 1937, fell to 1.23 in 1940, rose to 1.71 in 1942, and then fell to 1.58 in 1944. By 1946 it had fallen to 1.14, or 66 per cent of its 1942 level. In Germany after four years of repressed inflation income velocity was 50 per cent of its 1938 level.

E. SUMMARY

This comparative analysis has at least three contributions to make to a study of German money and prices. First, it shows that, for the countries discussed, prices and the stock-of-money movements were more dissimilar in Germany than in Italy, the United Kingdom, or the United States. The cases of Germany and the United States may seem comparable. But one hesitates to treat them as such because of dissimilar economic situations and the short period of time in which their respective economic situations were comparable. On the whole, the situation presented by the four countries is that of a continuum, with Germany and Italy being the extremes. The difference between the price level and the stock of money in 1944 was greatest in Germany, with the United States, the United Kingdom, and Italy following in that order.

Second, it raises the question, "Is the apparently different result in

Germany to be attributed to a more effective set of controls or to a biased official German price index?" This possibility will be discussed in Section III.

And, third, it shows that the lack of price inflation and the existence of effective economic controls may be related when there is full employment.

II. The German Stock of Money, 1932-44

The German stock-of-money figures, as presented in this study, include hand-to-hand currency, *Giroguthaben*, demand deposits, and time deposits. The purpose of this section is threefold: (1) to estimate and describe these components of the stock of money; (2) to trace their development through the period 1932-44; and (3) to determine their relative importance.

A. DESCRIPTION OF THE COMPONENTS OF THE STOCK OF MONEY

1. *Hand-to-hand currency.*—The unit of German currency is the reichsmark, which is divisible into 100 reichspfennigs. Hand-to-hand currency during the period under study consisted of (1) Reichsbank notes; (2) Rentenbank notes; (3) private bank notes; and (4) small coin. Soldier's money, consisting of *Reichskreditkassen* notes and *Wehrmachtsbehilfsgeld*, is not included in this study, because it was not to be used within the borders of Germany except for canteen purposes.

Of the four types of hand-to-hand currency listed, only Reichsbank notes were legal tender for unlimited payments. Gold coins which had been legal tender were not considered legal tender after August 16, 1938, and all gold coins had to be sold to the Reichsbank by September 1, 1938.[9] Reichsbank notes were available in denominations of 1, 2, 5, 10, 20, 50, 100, and 1,000 reichsmarks.

There was no effective reserve requirement for Reichsbank notes after 1933. Before that they had a backing of 40 per cent—30 per cent gold and 10 per cent foreign exchange—but the Reichsbank law was amended on October 27, 1933, to provide that this requirement could be rescinded upon a vote of the Reichsbank directors. This they proceeded to do. There was, however, statutory coverage for the notes. This coverage consisted chiefly of (*a*) three-month treasury bills of the Reich; (*b*) three-month, three-name commercial paper; (*c*) securities on the stock exchange and treasury certificates falling due one year from purchase; (*d*) balances at call; (*e*) bills of exchange; and (*f*) bonds at three-quarters of their market value.

---

9. *Reichsgesetzblatt* (Berlin: Reichsverlagsamt, 1938), I, 901.

Rentenbank notes were a holdover from the 1923 hyperinflation. Their issue has been generally credited with stopping the 1923 hyperinflation.[10] They were not legal tender, and their lawful use was limited to acceptance by governmental offices. They did, however, circulate freely. Rentenbank notes were available in denominations of 1, 2, 10, 50, 100, and 1,000 rentenmarks.

The private bank-note-issuing privileges of the state banks were repealed, and in 1935 their notes were withdrawn from circulation.[11] Hence, private bank notes were not important in the period under study.

Subsidiary coin was available in denominations of 1, 2, 5, 10, and 50 reichspfennigs, as well as in 1, 2, and 5 reichsmarks.

There were two main problems in determining the average hand-to-hand currency in Germany from 1932 to 1944. These were (1) ascertaining vault cash and (2) adjusting for a changing German monetary area.

First, no adjustment for vault cash has been made in the figures for hand-to-hand currency. Most German balance sheets which give a cash-reserve figure do not distinguish between vault cash, credits at the central bank, foreign moneys, and dividend coupons. The figures for the circulation of hand-to-hand currency are, however, net of the Reichsbank note and coin holdings.

Second is the problem of a changing German monetary area. One of the factors which caused the increase in the circulation of hand-to-hand currency in Germany was the increased area in which the reichsmark became legal tender.

The reichsmark was made legal tender in Austria in April, 1938; in Sudentenland in October, 1938; in Memel territory in March, 1939; in the Free City of Danzig in September, 1939; in East Upper Silesia in September, 1939; in the Annexed Eastern Provinces in November, 1939; in Eupen, Malmedy, and Moresnet in June, 1940; in Luxemburg in February, 1941; in Alsace and Lorraine in March, 1941; in Carinthia, Carniola, and Lower Styria in June, 1941; and in Bialystock in January, 1942. The above areas were directly incorporated into the Reich. The reichsmark was also made legal tender in the Protectorate of Bohemia-Moravia concurrently with the Czech koruna.

To what extent does this extension of the area in which the reichsmark was made legal tender lessen the actual increase in the stock of money in old Germany? For the purposes of this study it has been assumed that the amount of money issued for the newly annexed areas was the same per-

10. See, e.g., C. W. Guillebaud, *The Economic Recovery of Germany from 1933 to the Incorporation of Austria in March 1938* (London, 1939), chap. i.

11. *Reichsgesetzblatt* (1933), II, 1034.

centage of total hand-to-hand currency as the population of their areas was of the new total population; this assumption is then used to estimate the stock of money in the territory of 1937 Germany.

How accurate is this assumption? In 1938 the number of Reichsbank notes increased by 1,125 million reichsmarks due to the currency conversion in Austria and the Sudetenland. This increase amounted to 13.7 per cent of the average amount of hand-to-hand currency in 1938. In the middle of 1939 the new population of Germany, not including Memelland, was 79,375,000.[12] Thus old Germany, Austria, and the Sudetenland were the only areas included in these population estimates. Old Germany had a population of 69,286,000 in 1939. Thus the population of old Germany was 12.7 per cent less than new Germany. This indicates that, at least for old Germany, Austria, and the Sudetenland, the population increase arising from the annexation of new territories is a fairly close estimate of the increase in the stock of money arising from those annexations.

The importance of the territorial adjustment is indicated by the fact that unadjusted hand-to-hand currency gives a figure for 1944 which is 688 per cent of its 1932 level. Hand-to-hand currency that has been adjusted for territorial change was 489 per cent of the 1932 level.

2. *"Giroguthaben."*—In addition to checking accounts, German monetary institutions have developed a *Giro* transfer system—which is a cashless transfer system rather different from the systems found in other Western countries. Actually the use of checks proper in Germany through World War II was not extensively developed. Many individuals held checking accounts for the purpose of being able to withdraw cash quickly rather than for making payments by check.

In the *Giro* transfer system a receiver of a credit has no active role to play in the mechanics of a cashless transfer. Instead, another member of the system—the payer—writes to the checking office asking that his account be debited and that of the creditor be credited.

During the period under study there were three *Giro* systems which were of major importance. In order of importance these were: (1) the *Reichsbankverkehr;* (2) the *Postscheckverkehr;* and (3) the savings *Giroverkehr.* Only the balances of the *Postscheckverkehr* have been included in the *Giro* portion of the stock of money. They include holdings of individuals, merchants, small businessmen, etc. The balances of the Reichsbank system are omitted, because the balances of the Reich, other public bodies, large business firms, and banks are inadequately distinguished from one another. The savings bank *Giro* system balances are excluded, because they are included in savings bank sight deposits.

12. *Jahrbuch,* LIX, 22.

The problems involved in determining the average balances of the postal *Giro* system are similar to those of determining average hand-to-hand currency. The main problem was to adjust the data for territorial changes. The area served by this system expanded with the incorporation of new territories into Germany. The method of adjusting for these difficulties is the same as that used in determining the average hand-to-hand currency.

3. *Deposits.*—There are three categories into which German banking statistics usually classify deposits. These are (1) amounts due to other banks; (2) other deposits; and (3) savings deposits. In a further classification, groups (1) and (2) are combined, and then this sum is subdivided into two groups: (*a*) demand deposits and (*b*) time deposits. No breakdown is given, however, of "other" deposits into demand and time deposits. Both "other" and savings deposits are treated as components of the stock of money in this paper.[13]

It is difficult to get accurate deposit statistics, since most German banking institutions did some commercial banking. For example, commercial, public, mortgage, savings, co-operative credit, and postal savings banks all granted commercial credit or did mortgage financing.[14] Statistics on deposits are not available for all categories of banks, and thus various types of institutions have been omitted. The figures used in this study, however, do cover most German bank deposits.

The major problem involved in determining the amount of deposits in Germany was the lack of data after 1939 owing to the suspension of publication of official commercial banking statistics. It was possible to construct an estimate of deposits from the balance sheets of the large Berlin banks and of the savings banks. Few adjustments have been made for the expansion of the German boundaries as were done for hand-to-hand cur-

13. The question whether or not to consider savings deposits as money depends on the extent to which people view them as substitutes for *Giro* and checking accounts. German savings deposits subject to legal notice could be withdrawn on demand in amounts up to 1,000 reichsmarks. In this sense they were fairly close substitutes for cash up to amounts of 1,000 reichsmarks. Furthermore, withdrawals beyond this amount usually disregarded the three-month notice required. Omitting savings accounts would not take into consideration that, with the unavailability of goods through the war, as well as a lack of possible financial investment, individuals tended to accumulate savings deposits rather than the lower-interest-earning "sight" deposits.

14. It should perhaps be noted that there was no really effective reserve requirement in Germany for commercial banks. The credit supervisory board from time to time determined the cash-reserve requirement—cash in hand and deposits with the Reichsbank. The cash-reserve requirement could not be fixed any higher than 10 per cent. In 1936 cash reserves averaged less than 3.5 per cent of total deposits in commercial and public banks.

rency and postal *Giro* accounts. That this was not a major problem, however, was due, first, to the availability of alternate sets of figures and, second, to the fact that the business of the large Berlin banks did not substantially penetrate into the annexed regions.

Banks whose deposits are included in this study are: (1) the commercial and public banks—the big Berlin banks, provincial banks having branches, mortgage banks, special labor and buildings trade banks, state

TABLE 5*

THE GERMAN STOCK OF MONEY AND ITS COMPONENTS, 1932–44

(In Million Reichsmarks)

Year	Average Hand-to-Hand Currency† (1)	Average "Other" Deposits‡ (2)	Average Savings Deposits§ (3)	Average Stock of Money‖ (4)	Average Stock of Money (1932 = 100) (5)
1932.	5,802	13,113	14,527	33,442	100.0
1933.	5,359	12,193	14,626	32,178	96.2
1934.	5,477	12,290	15,525	33,292	99.6
1935.	5,761	12,777	16,974	35,512	106.2
1936.	6,174	13,475	18,490	38,139	114.0
1937.	6,686	14,718	20,078	41,482	124.0
1938.	7,479	16,634	22,517	46,630	139.4
1939.	8,992	19,474	25,242	53,708	160.6
1940.	10,485	24,692	30,657	65,834	196.9
1941.	12,716	32,307	41,062	86,065	257.4
1942.	16,445	38,739	56,319	111,503	333.4
1943.	20,983	45,623	75,498	142,104	424.9
1944.	28,375	56,473	94,601	179,449	536.6

* Source and derivation: John J. Klein, "German Monetary Development, 1932–44" (unpublished doctoral dissertation, University of Chicago, June, 1955), chap. ii, pp. 22–42, and Appendix II, pp. 99–102.

† Notes and coin.

‡ Of the *Postscheckverkehr*, commercial and public banks, savings banks, and rural and urban co-operative credit associations.

§ Of commercial and public banks, savings banks, and rural and urban co-operative credit associations.

‖ Columns 1, 2, and 3 added together.

banks, land banks, public land credit banks, rural landowner union banks, and municipal credit institutions; (2) savings banks; (3) urban co-operative credit associations; and (4) rural co-operative credit associations.

B. THE DEVELOPMENT OF THE GERMAN STOCK OF MONEY

RELATIVE IMPORTANCE OF THE COMPONENTS

Table 5 summarizes the data on the German stock of money. Hand-to-hand currency consists of notes and coin. "Other" deposits are those of the postal *Giro* system, commercial and public banks, savings banks, and rural and urban co-operative credit associations. They are exclusive of interbank deposits and for the most part consist of demand (i.e., *Giro* and sight) deposits. Savings deposits consist of the savings balances of commercial and public banks, savings banks, and rural and urban co-operative credit associations.

During the period under study hand-to-hand currency increased 4.9 times, "other" deposits 4.3 times, and savings deposits 6.5 times. The average monetary circulation as a whole increased 5.4 times. Total monetary circulation rose from 33.4 billion reichsmarks in 1932 to 179.4 billion reichsmarks in 1944.

The rate of rise in the average stock of money increased from 1934 through 1941, when the stock of money was 30.8 per cent higher than in the preceding year. Percentagewise, the years in which the stock of money experienced the greatest acceleration were 1934, 1940, and 1941. In those years the rates at which the rate of increase in the average monetary circulation was rising were 7.3, 7.4, and 8.2 per cent, respectively. In 1942, 1943, and 1944 the rate of increase decreased somewhat, but these decreases were so small that those years ranked second, third, and fourth, respectively, in percentage increases of the average monetary circulation. Thus it was in the war years, 1940–44, that the stock of money experienced its greatest increase.

Savings deposits contributed most to the increase in the stock of money over the period as a whole. From 1933 to 1936 and from 1941 to 1943 they rose faster than either "other" deposits or hand-to-hand currency. The increase in the earlier period can be attributed to the attempt of individuals to recoup their savings balances, which were seriously depleted by the depression of 1929–33. The later increase was due to a lack of investment outlets. *Giro* and sight deposit banking became more important in the increase in the stock of money from 1937 through 1940. This may have been due to the greater business activity that grew out of full employment of resources and to savings balances being at desired levels. Hand-to-hand currency contributed most to the rise in the total stock of money in 1939—the first year of World War II—and in 1944. Allied bombings, displaced persons, and disrupted transportation may have had a good deal to do with the rise in 1944. The increase in hand-to-hand currency was relatively more important than the increase in "other" deposits from 1934 to 1936—the period of employment creation —in 1939, and in the war years of 1942–44.

The ratio of hand-to-hand currency to "other" deposits changed from 44 per cent in 1932 to 50 per cent in 1944. The ratio of hand-to-hand currency to savings deposits, however, dropped from 40 per cent in 1932 to 30 per cent in 1944.

C. SUMMARY

This section shows, first, that the main problems involved in determining the stock of money for Germany are those of a lack of data and the necessity of adjusting downward the stock of money data for the period 1938–44 in order to take into account the expanded area of Germany. Second, this section indicates that savings deposits, hand-to-hand currency, and "other" deposits were first, second, and third, respectively, in order of importance in their contributions to the increase in the average stock of money. And, third, this section shows the importance of the war years in the increase in the average stock of money.

III. German Prices, 1932–44

A rise in prices need not follow an increase in the stock of money if there are unemployed resources available in the economy. However, once the factors of production are fully utilized, then, in the absence of counteractive measures, an increase in the stock of money will lead to a rise in prices. Assume that a government wishes to avoid such an increase in prices but that at the same time the political situation warrants the diversion of a larger share of the country's resources to government use. An increased spending policy ensues. Under such circumstances that government must either increase taxes—an unpopular measure at any time—or prevent the increased incomes from being fully spent.

Germany did not choose to pay for its increased expenditures by taxation.[15] To avoid a price boom, and simultaneously to have ready access to the credit market, the German government imposed economic controls. First wage, price, and credit controls and then rationing. Eventually Germany became a directed economy.

The objective of such controls is the restriction of spending on the part of individuals, so that individual spending will increase less rapidly than the quantity of money. Such a policy, if rigorously enforced, should restrain a rise in the price level. As indicated earlier, this policy appears to have been successful in Nazi Germany. The purpose of the present section is to examine this conclusion carefully. To do so, possible bias in the German wholesale-price index will be estimated, and new estimates of the price level will be derived.

A. BIAS IN THE GERMAN PRICE INDEX

1. *A description of the official German wholesale-price index and some of the problems which it raises.*—The official German wholesale-price index

---

15. Nor did it urge individuals to invest in government securities. It did, however, borrow heavily from the German banking system.

is a weighted price index. It is composed of four broad classes of goods: (1) agricultural goods; (2) colonial produce; (3) industrial raw materials and semifinished goods; and (4) manufactured commodities. Their weights in the combined wholesale goods price index are 35, 3, 38, and 24, respectively. Each of these four classes of goods is composed of other categories of goods that are given appropriate weights. In turn, these categories are composed of individual goods of certain sorts and qualities that are given weights and are priced according to the price of the given sort and quality of the goods in a specified market.

The preceding gives rise to the very important question whether, as the period progressed, the given weights remained appropriate.[16] The ones I list are based upon average per capita consumption of the selected commodities from 1908 to 1913 and for 1925. These per capita consumption figures were valued at representative 1913 prices. If, for example, the price of a good of a given quality remained the same under price controls, and its weight remained the same, to what extent would the price index be distorted if the particular good became unavailable and a higher-priced, better-quality good had to be purchased in its place? Possibly the better-quality good had not been used in the original composition of the index. Or then there may have been a deterioration in the quality of the original good. Either of the two preceding cases indicates that prices were actually higher than the official index showed. Likewise, if a greater proportion of raw materials were devoted to the production of war goods through the war years—as was the actual case—then the weights in the composition of the wholesale-price index would be further distorted.[17]

2. *Estimating bias in the official German wholesale-price index.*—One possible way of getting at bias in the price index is to construct an implicit price index and then compare it with the official index. A way of doing this is to compare over a period of years the value of the commodities produced in the economy with the quantity of goods produced. Dividing the former by the latter will give an implicit price index.

The logic for this method of analysis is based on the right-hand side of the equation of exchange, $MV = PQ$. If P represents the price index for a group of commodities and Q the quantity index for the same group of commodities, then their product is an index which represents the total value of that group of commodities. Let X be the symbol for this index.

16. A detailed breakdown of the weights will be found in Statistisches Reichsamt, *Vierteljahrshefte zur Statistik des Deutschen Reichs*, I (Berlin, 1937), 170.

17. For a discussion of the difficulties in German price indexes see F. Rompe, "Der Aussagewert der Preisindexziffern," *Jahrbücher für Nationalökonomie und Statistik*, CLVIII, (1943), 207–33.

If X and Q are known, then the implicit price index is P. That is to say, $P = X/Q$.

a) Implicit prices for all commodities.—A composite production index for all commodities and a value index for all commodities (current value) are needed to estimate the bias in the official wholesale-price index.

There is available the production index of the Deutsches Institut für Wirtschaftsforschung.[18] This index includes, first, industrial raw materials and semifinished production. Iron, metals, coal, gas, electricity, potash, chemicals, textiles, paper, etc., are among the commodities included in this category. Second, it includes finished goods—producers' as well as consumers' finished goods. Shoes, household articles, radios, etc., are some of the items in this group. These items are mainly included in Classes III and IV of the official wholesale-price index. Thus almost everything in the official index except for colonial produce and agricultural production are included in the Deutsches Institut index of production. In fact, in certain respects this index is broader, since it includes in its two classifications some foodstuffs and luxury goods. What needs to be done is to add agricultural production and colonial produce to manufactured and semi-finished goods.

One method is to (1) multiply the quantities produced of agricultural commodities covered by the official wholesale-price index by their prices in some given base year;[19] (2) sum the resulting products; (3) do this for the production of a succession of years—always using base-year prices; and (4) add the preceding results to the index of industrial production (appropriately weighted).[20] Colonial produce is omitted, since data are not available. Some of the colonial produce, however, is included in the index of industrial production. The results of this procedure are shown in column 1 of Table 6. This shows that production reached its highest level in 1939.

One source of possible error in this production index is that those commodities which are omitted due to the lack of production data may have had a change in production unlike that of the commodities included in the

18. *Die deutsche Wirtschaft zwei Jahre nach dem Zusammenbruch* (Berlin, 1947), pp. 264–65.

19. Prices in 1936 have been used in the construction of the index. This year was chosen as the base year so that the Deutsches Institut data for industrial production—which use 1936 as a base—could be used along with the index for agricultural production to derive the all-commodities production index.

20. The weighting method used assumes that the ratio of the volume of agricultural production to all production is the same as the ratio of farm income to total national income in 1936.

index.[21] Thus the constructed index may not be representative of all production. Increased production of a good may arise from changed physical, technical, and demand conditions. In the latter case the relative importance of the good has changed. When this happens, increased production may come as a result of the transfer of factors of production and their employment in the manufacture of the more desired commodity. In so far as the production of commodities omitted changed largely in the same degree as those items included in the index, the index accurately reflects the changed production of all commodities.

TABLE 6*

INDEXES OF THE VOLUME AND VALUE OF ALL PRODUCTION, THE
IMPLICIT PRICE LEVEL, AND THE OFFICIAL WHOLESALE-
PRICE LEVEL, 1932–44

Year	Volume of All Production (1)	Value of All Production (2)	Implicit Prices (Col. [2]÷ Col. [1]) (3)	Official Wholesale Prices (4)
1932.	100.0	100.0	100.0	100.0
1933.	110.3	111.1	100.7	96.7
1934.	138.3	143.6	103.8	102.0
1935.	157.6	168.3	106.8	105.5
1936.	175.0	191.3	109.3	107.9
1937.	191.9	219.5	114.4	109.7
1938.	202.9	234.6	115.6	109.5
1939.	203.1	244.6	120.4	110.8
1940.	182.4	259.2	142.1	114.0
1941.	181.2	282.8	156.1	116.5
1942.	179.8	281.5	156.6	118.5
1943.	178.8	282.0	157.7	120.4
1944.	161.3	252.7	156.7	121.9

* Source and derivation: Klein, *op. cit.*, chap. iii, pp. 43–55, and Appendix III, pp. 103–13.

Next, a value series for all production had to be derived. This was done by first adding the gross cash income of German agriculture to the value of farm products consumed on the farm, giving them an appropriate weight, and then adding the preceding to the value of industrial production (appropriately weighted).[22] Dividing the value series by the volume series gives rise to the implicit price index for all commodities. This is shown in Table 6.

21. Over all, 15 per cent of the commodities included in the official wholesale-price index have been omitted from the all-production index.

22. The weighting method assumes that the ratio of the value of agricultural production to the value of all production is the same as the ratio of farm income to total national income in 1936.

Table 6 shows that the volume and value indexes for all production are divergent. It follows from this that the German price level rose. The implicit price index for all commodities was 120, 142, 156, and 157 per cent of its 1932 level in 1939, 1940, 1941, and 1944, respectively. Thus the table shows an increase in the price level which is greater than that shown by the official wholesale-price index.

Increased prices for war goods, the production and sale of a different assortment of goods, and quality deterioration are all partly reflected in the implicit wholesale-price index for all commodities. The reasons for this are that the value and volume of production indexes include (1) not only commodities which were directly managed by the government but also some that were not under government control and (2) some commodities that are not included in the official price index. The indexes of the Deutsches Institut für Wirtschaftsforschung in particular cover commodities not included in the price index of the Statistisches Reichsamt.[23]

The index of prices developed thus far, however, is not comprehensive enough. If there were, for example, widespread sales in the black market, then the value of production as given in Table 6 is an underestimate of the actual value of production, because black-market sales naturally would not be reported to the government. Further, the real volume of production as given in Table 6 would also be an underestimate of actual production. Hence, both the value and the volume of German production have to be adjusted to take black-market activity into account.

Dr. Alfred Jacobs of the Statistisches Reichsamt has estimated the excess of black market sales over their legal value for food, beverages, and tobacco as follows: 1940—4 billion reichsmarks; 1941—3 billion reichsmarks; 1942—5 billion reichsmarks; 1943—9 billion reichsmarks; and 1944—14 billion reichsmarks. The considerable magnitude of these figures is more of high prices than of the quantities of goods involved. These were estimated to be only two per cent of legal market transactions in these commodities.[24]

These figures may be used to correct the implicit price index by assuming that (1) the sales of food, beverages, and tobacco in old Germany and in greater Germany, which includes Austria and the Sudetenland, bear the same relationship to each other as do the population of old and greater Germany; (2) black-market sales of industrial production were 62 per cent of all black-market sales—this assumes that black-market behavior

23. See Ferdinand Grünig, "Die Wirtschaftstätigkeit nach dem Zusammenbruch im Vergleich zur Vorkriegzeit," *Die deutsche Wirtschaft zwei Jahre nach dem Zusammenbruch* (Berlin, 1947), p. 62.

24. United States Strategic Bombing Survey, Overall Economic Effects Division, "The Gross National Product of Germany, 1936–1944," *Special Paper No. 1*, prepared by Wesley C. Haraldson and Edward F. Denison, p. 3.

was similar in all commodity groups;[25] (3) black-market activity increased the current value of production by the same percentage that it did total sales; and (4) the volume of all production is 2 per cent higher than shown in each of the years from 1940 to 1944.

Table 7 shows that, when black-market sales are taken into account, the implicit price level in Germany rose by some 52 per cent from 1938 to 1944. Without black-market sales, the implicit price index rose only by 35 per cent.

b) The average denomination of money as a measure of the price level.— Thus far the given estimates of price-level change in Germany have been

TABLE 7*

IMPLICIT GERMAN PRICE LEVEL BASED ON
BLACK-MARKET ACTIVITY, 1938–44

Year	Value of Production (1)	Volume of Production (2)	Implicit Price Level (Col. [1] ÷ Col. [2]) (3)
1938.........	100.0	100.0	100.0
1939.........	104.3	100.1	104.2
1940.........	114.8	91.7	125.2
1941.........	123.9	91.1	136.0
1942.........	125.7	90.4	139.0
1943.........	130.4	89.9	145.1
1944.........	123.4	81.1	152.2

* Source and derivation: Klein, *op. cit.*, chap. iii, pp. 62–65.

based on aggregate value and quantity comparisons. Another way of estimating German price changes is to observe the changes in the distribution of total hand-to-hand currency among various denominations of money. If prices become higher, then, since one has to pay more for his goods, he prefers to carry larger denominations of money with him for his purchases. Changes in the average denomination of money thus measure changes in the price level.

Table 8 shows the average denomination of currency in Germany from 1932 to 1943. In 1938 the average denomination of currency was 2.21 reichsmarks, while in 1932 it had been 2.42 reichsmarks. The decreases in the average denomination of currency in the years 1933 and 1934 can

25. In the official German wholesale-price index, food, beverages, and tobacco come under the categories of agricultural goods and colonial produce. These two categories have a weight of 38 per cent in the index. This leaves 62 per cent for industrial production.

probably be attributed to the dishoarding which took place in those years as German economic conditions improved relative to the depressed state of 1932. Dishoarding should not have affected the figures after 1934. Any of the succeeding years, therefore, could have been taken as a base. The year 1938, however, was selected as a base because it represents, as previously discussed, the beginning of repressed inflation in Germany.

TABLE 8*

AVERAGE DENOMINATION OF
CURRENCY, 1932–43

YEAR	AVERAGE DENOMINATION OF CURRENCY	
	In Reichsmarks†	1938=100
1932...........	2.42	109.5
1933...........	2.22	100.5
1934...........	2.12	95.9
1935...........	2.08	94.1
1936...........	2.08	94.1
1937...........	2.10	95.0
1938...........	2.21	100.0
1939...........	2.49	112.7
1940...........	2.66	120.4
1941...........	2.82	127.6
1942...........	3.41	154.3
1943...........	4.05	183.3

* Source: 1931–40, various issues of *Verwaltungsbericht der Deutschen Reichsbank* 1931 to 1941; 1941–43, Länderrat des Amerikanischen Besatzungsgebiets, *Statistisches Handbuch von Deutschland 1928–1944* (München, 1949).

† These figures were derived by adding the end of the preceding and current year total value of circulating currency figures and then dividing this by the sum of the end of the preceding and current year total pieces of money in circulation. They are unadjusted for territorial expansion of Germany. Thus, when they are used, it is assumed that the average denomination of money behaved in the same way in old Germany and greater Germany.

By 1943 the average denomination of currency was 183 per cent of its 1938 level. If it is assumed that denominations of currency are continuous, that there was no change in German real income from 1938 to 1943, and that the suppliers of currency were willing to supply the denominations demanded, then it may be said that actual prices in Germany increased by 83 per cent in this period. This price increase is, however, contingent upon the stated assumptions. What happens if the first two assumptions are relaxed?

First, the assumption that denominations of money are continuous is not realistic. What will happen to the average denomination of currency with a rise in prices, first with and then without this assumption?

Assuming that velocity, relative prices, and real income remain unchanged, then an increase in the stock of money will be matched by a corresponding increase in the price level. What happens to the average denomination of money? Consider the conditions (1) that the individual desires at least the same number of bills with a rise in prices—say, for example, 12—and (2) that he wants a given division (e.g., 50 per cent and 50 per cent) of the total value of currency among denominations of money bearing a certain relation to each other (e.g., 1:5). If the individual initially holds his money in 10- and 50-reichsmark notes and if there were 200 reichsmarks outstanding in total value, then the situation is that indicated in Case A:

CASE A: *Continuous Denominations before Price Rise*
50 Rm. (Value of individual notes) × 2 (No. of notes) = 100 Rm.
10 Rm. (Value of individual notes) × 10 (No. of notes) = 100 Rm.

Total value = 200 Rm.
Average denomination of currency = 16.6 Rm.

What happens when the price level doubles? Under the given assumptions the currency outstanding will double. The total value of currency will be 400 reichsmarks. Then the situation is represented by Case B.

CASE B: *Continuous Denominations after Price Doubling*
100 Rm. (Value of individual notes) × 2 (No. of notes) = 200 Rm.
20 Rm. (Value of individual notes) × 10 (No. of notes) = 200 Rm.

Total value = 400 Rm.
Average denomination of currency = 33.3 Rm.

Hence, the average denomination of currency will be 33.3 reichsmarks. Both the price level and the average denomination of currency have doubled.

Now drop the assumption that denominations are continuous and assume instead that they are discrete. Assume further that there are only 10- and 50-reichsmark notes. The two conditions listed cannot be satisfied. If condition (1) is satisfied, the average denomination of money will double. If condition (2) is satisfied, the 50-50 division of the value of currency remains the same, but the number of outstanding bills doubles. Thus the average denomination of currency will remain the same. Clearly, then, with discrete denominations the two given conditions are not compatible with each other. The most that can be said is that it is likely that the individual will hold more bills than before but not so many as to keep the average denomination of money the same as before the rise in the price level.

What relation, then, given discrete denominations, do the change in the price level and the change in the average denomination of money bear to each other? This is not determinate. One would expect that with the change in the price level individuals would at first hold only a few additional 50-mark notes. Here, then, the average denomination of currency lags behind the rise in the price level. Later, however, individuals, seeing the continuing price rise, may decide to shift out of their 10-reichsmark notes into 50-mark notes. Hence, if, for example, prices have risen twofold and individuals shift from 10- to 50-mark notes, it may be found that the average denomination of currency has increased more than twofold. In light of the preceding discussion, if one had statistics on actual price movements over short periods of time in addition to the available figures on the distribution of currency among the various denominations, it might be found that the average denomination of currency moves in a lag-and-spurt pattern relative to price-level changes.

What happens when the assumption of no change in real income is dropped? Assume continuous denominations of currency for the sake of simplicity. This eliminates the problem of a changed number and proportion of bills. Assume further that (1) there was no change in velocity and relative prices; (2) the price level was the same; and (3) prior to a change in real income the individual wants a given division of the total value of currency among denominations of money bearing a certain relation to each other. Now consider the case of a drop in real income.

Under the given assumptions, real income and the stock of outstanding currency will change proportionately. The average denomination of money, however, will not change proportionately. With a drop in real income the consumer's desired division of the total value of currency will change. Individuals will have to forego part of their consumption. The part which they will have to forego will probably consist of the more expensive durable and luxury items in their consumption pattern. The items which they will now purchase will cost less per item than those which they purchased previously. Hence individuals will tend to carry a greater proportion of their currency in the form of smaller bills than previously. In this case, then, the average denomination of currency will decrease when real income decreases. The reverse of the preceding would be true in the case of an increase in real income.[26]

If one combines a Case B price increase with a decrease in real income akin to that discussed in the preceding paragraph, then the average denomination of money cannot rise proportionately to the price level rise. Assume that, as the price index rises, real income decreases. Then on bal-

26. This assumes no problem of hoarding or dishoarding of notes.

ance the average denomination of currency has risen less than the price level. The value of estimating price level changes from average denomination of currency changes is thus lessened by real income changes.

Aside from the difficulties raised by varying territory, changed real income, and discrete denominations of currency, how much of the disparity between official prices and the increase in the stock of money is accounted for by this estimate of the actual price level in Germany? In 1943 official prices, average denomination of currency prices, and the stock of money were 110, 183, and 305 per cent of their 1938 levels, respectively. Thus, the average denomination of money estimate of price change considerably lessens the magnitude of the problem remaining to be explained.

B. SUMMARY

This section has presented the results of three ways of measuring the change in the German price level during the Nazi regime. All three methods indicate that the price level did in fact rise more than the official index shows. The first method resulted in an index of implicit prices for all commodities based on the value and volume of production from 1932 to 1944. Second, black-market sales and production were used to adjust the first estimate of prices. And, third, the average denomination of money was used as a measure of the price level. These methods show that German prices in 1943 were 136, 145, or 183 per cent, respectively, of their 1938 level depending upon which of the three alternative methods is referred to. Official prices, as previously indicated, were only 110 per cent of their 1938 level.

IV. REAL CASH BALANCES, NATIONAL INCOME, AND INCOME VELOCITY, 1938–44

The present section brings together the estimates of Sections II and III to see (1) if the analysis of data in those sections lessens the divergence between changes in the stock of money and the price level and (2) how the adjusted figures affect velocity and real income.

A. REAL CASH BALANCES

Official German wholesale prices in 1938 were 110 per cent of their 1932 level. On the other hand, average monetary circulation was 139 per cent of its 1932 level. Thus real cash balances in 1938 were 127 per cent of their 1932 level. This is not an unusual result. Germany was becoming increasingly prosperous through 1938, income velocity had increased through 1937 and then remained relatively stable in 1938, and unemployment no longer existed.

From 1939 on, however, real cash balances showed a much more marked increase. Official German wholesale prices in 1944 were 111 per cent of their 1938 level. Average monetary circulation was 385 per cent of its 1938 level. Thus real cash balances were 346 per cent of their 1938 level. This is an unusual result. During a period of war and inflation the increased cost of holding money would tend to produce a decline in real cash balances; the increased mobility of the population and increased uncertainty, to produce a rise. In the absence of other counteractive measures such as economic controls, therefore, either a moderate rise or

TABLE 9

REAL CASH BALANCES, 1938–44

Year	Unadjusted*	Stock of Money Adjusted†	Money and Prices Adjusted‡	Money and Prices Adjusted§
1938.........	100.0	100.0	100.0	100.0
1939.........	135.5	113.8	110.6	102.2
1940.........	172.6	135.6	112.8	117.3
1941.........	204.5	173.7	135.7	144.7
1942.........	259.8	221.0	172.0	155.0
1943.........	322.3	277.0	210.0	166.2
1944.........	435.8	345.7	252.8	200.1

* Unadjusted hand-to-hand currency divided by the official wholesale-price index.

† Adjusted average monetary circulation divided by the official wholesale-price index.

‡ Adjusted average monetary circulation divided by the black-market estimate of price-level change.

§ Adjusted average monetary circulation divided by the average denomination of money estimate of price-level change. The 1944 price figure used is the 1943 average denomination of currency-price estimate multiplied by the percentage (104.9) that 1944 black-market prices were of 1943 prices.

a fall in real cash balances would not be surprising. But none of the factors listed seems strong enough to produce as large a change as occurred in real cash balances.

If one expects real cash balances to remain approximately the same, how do the estimates of German money-stock and price-level change affect the level of real cash balances? Table 9 summarizes this material.

If unadjusted average hand-to-hand currency is used as the stock of money, then real cash balances in 1943 and 1944 were 322 and 436 per cent of their 1938 level, respectively, when the official wholesale-price index is used. Adjusting the stock of money to include average hand-to-hand currency, other deposits, and savings deposits—all adjusted for territorial expansion—reduces the over-all increase in real cash balances after 1938 by 15 per cent through 1943 and by 21 per cent through 1944.

If average monetary circulation is used as the stock of money, then real cash balances in 1943 were 166 or 210 per cent of their 1938 level, when average denomination of money or black-market price estimates, respectively, are used as prices. Therefore, these two estimates of price-level change through 1943 reduce by 40 and 24 per cent, respectively, the increase in real cash balances which remains after the stock of money has been adjusted. Through 1944 the average denomination of money and black-market price estimates reduced this remaining increase by 42 and 27 per cent, respectively.

This procedure of adjusting monetary circulation and constructing an estimate of the German price level has considerably lessened the problem of explaining the divergence between changes in the stock of money and the price level. Both procedures taken together account for 54 or 42 per cent of the increase in real cash balances, depending on whether average denomination of money prices or black-market prices are taken to represent the price level. Forty-six or 58 per cent, respectively, remain unexplained.

B. IMPLICIT PRICES AND REAL INCOME

What light do the implicit price indexes shed on the movements in German real income?

The official wholesale-price index shows that German real income increased through 1941. It remained fairly high through 1943. In 1944 it decreased to approximately its 1938 level. Official real income then was 98.5 per cent of the 1938 level.

When the factors of production are fully utilized, apart from the results of technical innovation, it is difficult to increase real national income. The results which the implicit price indexes give are more in keeping with the data on national income than the result of the official price index—only too much so. Dividing national income by the average denomination of money price-level estimate shows that German real income remained fairly close to its 1938 level through 1941 and then dropped sharply in 1942. It continued to drop through the remainder of the war, until in 1944 it was 57 per cent of the 1938 level. According to the black-market estimate, it was 72 per cent of the 1938 level.

The preceding results raise a question concerning the accuracy of the money income figures. It seems very unlikely that German real income dropped as severely as the figures indicate. If the implicit price indexes are reasonable—and it would appear so from the behavior of real cash balances—then the solution which is suggested is that actual money income increased more than published national income. Further, it seems reasonable that, having questioned the accuracy of the official price index, one should also question the accuracy of published national income. A larger money income would also help to explain the behavior of computed income velocity.

C. CORRECTED NATIONAL INCOME AND INCOME VELOCITY

It appears that three corrections need to be made in the figures on German national income.

First, the figures thus far used to represent old German income are from official sources through 1941. For the years 1942–44 the numbers used are estimates made by the Deutsches Institut für Wirtschaftsfor- schung, which estimated national income from total sales for the years 1942, 1943, and 1944. These were also the years in which both income velocity and national income decreased the most. This suggests that the Deutsches Institut figures may be inaccurate. Is there any other method of deriving national income estimates for those years?

Gross national product in Germany, Austria, and the Sudetenland for the period 1936–44 has been independently estimated by the United States Strategic Bombing Survey. Assuming the gross national product of this German area and the national income of old Germany to be closely related enables one to make an estimate of national income in Germany from 1942 to 1944. Doing this yields a substantially higher estimate of income in 1944.

Second, the German concept of national income does not include the pay of the armed forces. The pay of the armed forces became increasingly important through the war and hence should be added to national income.

Third, the Statistisches Reichsamt and the United States Strategic Bombing Survey did not correct their data for illegal black-market ac- tivity. As previously indicated, black-market sales figures are available after 1939. Thus for a more accurate estimate of national income the effects of black-market operations should be taken into account.

The results of these procedures are included in Table 10. These esti- mates of national income yield a money income in 1944 which was 166 per cent of its 1938 level. Income velocity was then 0.79.

The volume of production index of Table 7 may be used as a check on the preceding conclusions. It indicates that money income in 1944 was either 156 or 123 per cent of 1938, depending on whether real production (81 per cent of 1938) is multiplied by the average denomination of money or by the black-market price estimate. The latter figure is the same as the value of all production. Thus there is considerable divergence between the money income calculated in the preceding paragraph and that which is based on real production. For 1943 the money income based on real production and the implicit price series were 130 or 165 per cent of 1938, depending on which price index is used. The money income shown in Table 10 was 154 per cent of the 1938 level. The money income found by using average denomination of money prices thus comes closer to that calculated in the preceding table.

D. SUMMARY

This section shows, first, that the adjustment of the average monetary circulation and the construction of implicit price indexes reduces the increase in real cash balances by either 54 or 42 per cent from 1938 to 1944. Second, it indicates that money income increased 66 per cent from 1938

TABLE 10

ESTIMATES OF NATIONAL INCOME AND IN-
COME VELOCITY, 1938–44*

Year	Official National Income (1)	Adjusted National Income (2)	Income Velocity No. 1† (3)	Income Velocity No. 2† (4)
1938.........	100.0	100.0	1.76	1.83
1939.........	109.4	110.2	1.67	1.75
1940.........	112.7	120.4	1.41	1.56
1941.........	119.1	134.5	1.14	1.33
1942.........	119.4	141.0	0.88	1.08
1943.........	120.6	153.9	0.70	0.92
1944.........	109.6	165.7	0.50	0.79

* Source and derivation: Klein, *op. cit.*, chap. iv, pp. 72–75.
† The money incomes of columns 1 and 2, respectively, divided by the total average monetary circulation for each year.

to 1944. Third, it shows that income velocity in 1944 was 43 per cent of the 1938 level. And, fourth, it gives rise to confusing real income figures. Corrected money national income divided by the black-market estimate of prices in 1944 yields a real income figure which was 109 per cent of 1938. Dividing the same national income figures by the average denomination of money price estimate for 1944 yields a real income which was 86 per cent of its 1938 level. On the other hand, calculated real production was 81 per cent of its 1938 level.

V. GERMAN ECONOMIC POLICIES, 1932–44

The preceding sections have established that income velocity and real cash balances experienced great changes in the second World War. These changes in economic behavior were far more pronounced in Germany than similar changes in other belligerent countries. Thus Germany from 1939 on stands as a contradiction to the hypothesis that changes in cash balances are proportional to changes in income.

How can this be explained? The only remaining explanations after having adjusted the relevant money, price, and income statistics are (1) that transportation disruptions in 1943 and 1944 led to the holding of more cash balances and (2) that the German economic controls system was successful not only in restricting individual spending but also in inducing individuals to hold their accumulating assets in the form of cash. The purpose of the present section is to describe briefly the economic policies which may have led to the latter result.

A. FISCAL POLICY

German fiscal policy during the Hitler period can be divided into five intervals—four prior to the war and one during the war.

First, there is the period of the employment creation bills which in fact began with the pre-Hitler, Von Papen government. There had been a lack of lending ability in the economy. It was considered desirable to have a works program to alleviate the large amount of unemployment. Since the Reichsbank could discount commercial paper without limit, it was felt that it would be advantageous to have the type of works program that could be financed by paper that the Reichsbank was able to discount. Hence local governments were urged to place orders for roads, public buildings, houses, etc. These were to be financed by employment creation bills which arose in the following manner. The local body would place an order with a contractor. He drew a bill of exchange, had the local body indorse it, and presented it to either a commercial or a public bank. The bank in turn would accept it, treat it as a commercial bill, and discount it at the Reichsbank. Generally, a bank discounting an employment bill would use it to pay off obligations on past transactions. These bills had a nominal life of three months but could be prolonged indefinitely. Thus the credit structure changed to one representing current transactions in industry and trade. Liquidity in banking being restored, interest rates fell.

Second comes the period of the special bills from 1935 to 1938. In this phase capital funds for the government were still obtained by the above scheme, but there was more reliance on long-term Reich loans and treasury-bond issues. There was some change in the pattern of the above scheme. The bills were no longer called "employment creation bills" but rather "special bills." They now had a nominal life of six months and were discountable after three months. They were still renewable without limit, but their discount by commercial banks at the private rate, which had been lower than the Reichsbank rate, was discontinued. Most of the increase in bill holdings and credit came in the public and state banks.

Third is the period of financial change which began in April, 1938. The special bills were replaced by six-month delivery bills for payment of public contracts. They were not eligible for rediscount with the Reichsbank. This was an interim measure, since there was to be no more prefinancing by special bills. In addition, new $4\frac{1}{2}$ per cent Reich loans were issued in an increasing volume, so that there was an increase of long-term as well as short-term debt.

Fourth, in May, 1939, the period of the new financial plan began. Delivery bills were to be replaced by "(a) increased quantities of ordinary non-interest bearing treasury bonds, and (b) two new types of tax certificates."[27] The issue of the latter, however, was discontinued shortly after the outbreak of the war. Further, treasury bonds were no longer open to public subscription. They were to continue to be placed with insurance funds, savings banks, and local authorities. Savings which flowed into the capital market, if they were not taken up by the Reich loans, could be used to purchase industrial bonds and shares.

And, fifth, there is the period of war finance. During the war the Reich credit policy consisted for the most part of securing short-term credit in the form of treasury bills, treasury notes, and army promissory notes. The latter were used to make advance payment to war contractors. These notes could be sold to the banks by the contractor or used as collateral for loans. In addition, the Reich continued to receive its long-term funds in a manner similar to that of the preceding period. It placed bond issues with commercial banks, credit co-operatives, savings banks, insurance companies, social insurance funds, and other agencies.

During this entire period the German government was running a deficit. For example, in the fiscal year beginning April 1, 1943, receipts were 67.8 billion reichsmarks, while expenditures were 153 billion reichsmarks. Total Reich debt then mounted to 273.4 billion reichsmarks.[28] Increased government expenditures led to increased incomes. Thus there was inflationary pressure. Germany neither increased its tax rates nor had the public subscribe to bond issues in order to reduce this inflationary pressure. To accomplish this purpose, it relied solely on price, rationing, and capital-market controls.

27. Reichs-Kredit-Gesellschaft, *Economic Conditions in Germany in the Middle of the Year 1939* (Aktiengesellschaft Berlin, August, 1939), p. 44.

28. Edward Wolf, "Geld und Finanzprobleme der deutschen Nachkriegswirtschaft," *Die deutsche Wirtschaft zwei Jahre nach dem Zusammenbruch* (Berlin, 1947), pp. 198–99.

When the German public was unable to increase its purchases with its increased income, its "other" and savings deposit accounts rose. Cash balances were accordingly built up, and income velocity reduced. The government then obtained these funds through the issuance of securities that the banking system subscribed to—there being a lack of other interest-bearing assets available in which to invest their accumulated funds. With increased income, businesses and individuals paid off their debts to the banking system and had little need for more credit. German credit institutions thus seemed to be converted largely into intermediaries between the Reich treasury and the public.

B. PRICE POLICY

Price control has been regarded as the principal defense of the German economy against price inflation. This method came into existence early in the Hitler regime. Wages were the first prices stabilized. They were frozen in 1934 at 1933 levels. Agricultural prices also were controlled after 1933. They were regulated at every subsequent stage from production to the market.

With respect to other prices, a Reich commissioner for price control was appointed in November, 1934. He was to establish "normal prices" in various industries. His job was primarily to keep prices down. This was in accord with the policy of pre-Hitler regimes which took deflation as an alternative to devaluation because of the memories of the 1923 hyperinflation. The commissioner's control was at first over industrial prices alone, but he was shortly given control over all commodities. Through 1935, however, prices rose, and, because of this, an effort was made to decentralize price controls by assigning them to the economic ministries. This policy also was soon changed.

On November 26, 1936, a general price-stop decree was enacted, and provision made for a Reich commissioner for price formation. This price stop was comprehensive and applied to every price except wages, and capital, agricultural, and money market prices, which were controlled by other commissioners. There were elements of elasticity, however, in this price policy. The commissioner could grant price increases by way of exception to the general rule. He likewise could lower any price by decree. Generally, he looked at profit margins. He would refuse to grant a price increase if the profit margins of the firm were relatively high. Cost-plus-profit prices were introduced first in construction and electrical industries and then extended to all firms filling orders for the government.

During 1937 price decreases occurred in commodity sectors dominated by cartel and other price agreements. This affected prices which had remained relatively stable during the slump years. For example, price reductions were absorbed by manufacturers, retailers, and wholesalers in electrical equipment, chemical goods, clocks and watches, etc., ranging from 5 to 10 per cent.

With the beginning of the second World War the price-stop decrees of 1936 were extended. All price calculations were re-examined.

In 1940 and 1941 revision of regulations affecting price-fixing associations was undertaken. The emphasis here was

on approval by the price commissioner of price agreements, whether among producers or distributors in the same stage of production or distribution, resale price-maintenance agreements, or agreements regarding the calculation of cost on government contracts. Exempted from the terms of the ordinance were such price agreements as those made by producers to fix prices to wholesalers; moreover approval of the Price Commissioner was not required for joining a price fixing association.[29]

Cartels and syndicates, however, had to submit at the beginning of the business year a list of new members participating in price-fixing activity.

German price policy again changed in 1941. The Reich commissioner for price control announced that prices paid by the government for war supplies would be uniform prices based on the cost of "fair average" producers with medium costs rather than on the production-cost conditions of individual producers in the economy.

New principles were introduced into price controls in 1942: (1) multiple prices for the same product, designed to overcome the spread of cost among producers, and (2) granting of price rises with increasing cost.

In general, before November, 1936, Germany had selective price controls, and after that date it had a general price ceiling. Prices for government orders were by and large determined on the basis of the costs of "fair average" producers. Most other prices were more directly tied to the price ceiling that was set in 1936.

C. PRODUCTION CONTROL

Production control was introduced into the German economy early in the Nazi regime. The basis of this control was in the allocation of raw materials. According to a decree issued by the Minister of Economics on September 4, 1934, he was empowered to supervise the trade of commodities. He could issue rules concerning their purchase, distribution, storage, sale, and consumption.[30] His agents in this process were various supervisory

---

29. Sidney Merlin, "Trends in German Economic Control since 1933," *Quarterly Journal of Economics*, LVII (February, 1943), 189.

30. *Reichsgesetzblatt* (1934), I, 816.

boards. These boards had control over such commodities as tobacco, industrial fats, wool, cotton, hides, iron and steel, timber, coal, chemicals, paper, and non-precious metals. In addition, there existed the Reich Food Estate, which had control over agricultural production.

Near the outbreak of World War II, the laws concerning this supervision of commodities were strengthened. The activities of the boards were also extended to include the rationing of consumption goods. Rationing was imposed over practically all articles popularly consumed: food, clothing, coal, etc. Rationing cards were issued for regular needs and supply certificates for general needs. Thus there was rationing of both final consumption goods, and—through the quota system—raw materials.

The above production and consumption controls, impressive as they may appear to be, did little more than restrict civilian production and consumption to prewar levels through 1942. Most of the economy "was permitted to operate in a leisurely, semi-peace fashion under the loose supervision of Funk's Economic Ministry."[31] The boards under Funk were for the most part loosely organized. The Economic Ministry

expressed the general attitude that sacrifices of the civilian population should be kept at a minimum. It tried to equilibrate the divergent claims of the industrialists, the military, the gauleiters, and the equilibrium was by no means one of maximum output. On the contrary, it was an equilibrium of excess capacity, in which high cost firms were protected, production of superfluous civilian goods continued, and scarce materials allocated to nonessential programs.[32]

German authorities realized after the Battle of Stalingrad in December, 1942, that current economic policies were not resulting in the production of armaments sufficient to insure success in the new phase of the war. For this reason a new Ministry for War Production was created. Albert Speer as its head had almost unlimited control over the industrial resources of Germany. His assistants for the most part were young managers of efficient business enterprises.

At this late date industrial capacity could not be expanded. The only alternatives were either to restrict civilian consumption or to improve the use of existing industrial capacity. He took the latter course and achieved significant increases in armaments production.[33]

What were the results, then, of the German production and rationing policies? First, civilian consumption through 1942 was kept near the prewar levels. These, of course, were high relative to 1932. With increasing

31. United States Strategic Bombing Survey, Overall Economic Effects Division, *The Effects of Strategic Bombing on the German War Economy* (October 31, 1951), p. 24.

32. *Ibid.*

33. *Ibid.*, chap. viii, "German Armament Production."

incomes, price controls, and slightly decreasing supplies of goods, individuals tended to accumulate cash balances. Only in 1943 was civilian consumption more severely restricted. There were shortages in coal, housing, and clothing. Much of this restriction can be attributed, however, not to German controls but rather to allied bombings and transportation disruptions. This might tend further to increase cash balances. And, second, the production controls system through 1942 resulted in the misallocation of those resources that were devoted to armament production.

D. CAPITAL MARKET CONTROL

Capital market control in Germany took the form of restricting capital issue and of limiting dividends.

According to a resolution of May 31, 1933, capital stock could be issued only after approval by a special committee of the Reichsbank. This procedure resulted in a virtual ban of capital issue until 1936, when there was some relaxation of the ban. This relaxation continued through 1939, but, for the most part, firms were forced to finance expansion out of the internal accumulation of funds. The end of the restriction of capital issue, of course, was to encourage the banking system to invest in government rather than private securities.

By 1939 industry had accumulated sufficient reserves to be able to expand mostly out of its own funds. With the beginning of the war, manufacturers found it difficult to replace their inventories and machinery. Accordingly, they accumulated balances rather than invested internally. Firms did two things with their balances: they held them or they purchased shares on the stock market. Individuals were also purchasing shares with their excess cash balances. Because of this there was a stock-market inflation. Stock prices in 1941 were 145 per cent of their 1939 level.

The stock market was the only free and unregulated market in Germany. With the rise of stock prices the government took measures which brought it under regulation. Stocks bought since the war had to be registered. People who had bought securities were required to sell them to the Reich upon demand. Stock prices fell somewhat during the latter part of 1941 but revived a bit in 1942. Finally, share prices were frozen at the level of January 25, 1943. In June, 1943, stock prices were 154 per cent of their 1939 level.

Another part of the control of the capital market was the limitation of dividends. According to the Investment Law of March 29, 1934, the amount of cash distribution of dividends to stockholders was limited to 6 per cent.[34] Excess dividends above those of the preceding year were to

34. *Reichsgesetzblatt* (1934), I, 295.

be invested in government securities. This was later amended by a provision that excess earnings be handed over to the Gold Discount Bank for a period of three years for investment in government securities.[35] "The effect of the Act was insignificant because by the end of 1940 the accumulated balances amounted to only 108,000,000 marks."[36] In 1941 a new dividend limitation act progressively taxed dividends exceeding 6 per cent (in some cases 8 per cent). This act further provided that firms could increase their capital to a position commensurate with their asset position. This aimed at the capitalization of the large cash reserves of business and industry in order to lessen stock-market speculation. Thus outstanding stocks were revalued.

In general, then, there was no systematic control of the private capital market in Germany. Industrial expansion was largely left to the individual firm. The measures which were enacted resulted in the accumulation of liquid balances in the business sector of the economy. Without controls over share prices, individuals purchased stock as a hedge against inflation. Businesses also purchased stock. Thus, in the absence of any increased supply of shares, stock prices were driven up.[37] Later, when stock prices were controlled, the last free alternative to holding idle cash balances was closed.

E. SUMMARY

This section has briefly outlined some of the economic policies of the period 1932–44 which may have led to a drop in income velocity and to a rise in real cash balances. These policies were an inflationary fiscal policy and price, production, consumption, and capital market controls. All these controls combined to limit the ability of the public to spend its increased incomes after the stage of full employment was reached in 1938. In addition, other factors not discussed here may have also played an important role in reducing the effects of the stock of money upon the price level. Among these are (1) foreign trade controls; (2) allied bombings in 1943 and 1944 and consequent transportation disruptions;[38] (3) the

35. *Ibid.*, p. 1222.

36. "Civil Affairs Handbook: Germany, Section 2T: Government and Administration. 'Economic Controls in Nazi Germany,'" *Army Service Forces Manual M356-2T* (U.S. Army Service Forces, 1 February 1944), p. 164.

37. This indicates what might have happened to the official price level in the absence of price controls. All prices, however, might not have risen as much as stock prices actually did, because there would have been alternative investment outlets available.

38. "The attack on transportation beginning in September 1944 was the most important single cause of Germany's ultimate economic collapse" (see United States Strategic Bombing Survey, Overall Economic Effects Division, *The Effects of Strategic Bombing on the German War Economy*, p. 13).

stern punishment of price-ceiling violators—in some cases individuals were executed for selling goods at above-ceiling prices; and (4) the strong patriotism of the typical German.

VI. CONCLUSION

The purpose of this study as initially stated was to explain the divergent movements in the German stock of money and official price index from 1932 to 1944. A second way of stating the problem was that the decrease in German income velocity required explanation.

TABLE 11

SUMMARY OF RESULTS: STOCK OF MONEY, PRICES, REAL CASH BALANCES, REAL INCOME, MONEY INCOME, AND INCOME VELOCITY (OLD GERMANY) IN 1944 AS A PERCENTAGE OF 1938

Category	Stock of Money	Prices	Real Cash Balances	Real Income	Money Income	Income Velocity
Unadjusted figures..	485*	111†	436	98	110‡	23
Adjusted figures:						
a) Results not depending on prices	385§	....	....	....	166‖	43
b) At black-market prices..........	385	152	253	109	166	43
c) At average denomination of money prices....	385	192	200	86	166	43
Results using directly computed real income						
a) At black-market prices..........	385	152	253	81#	123	32
b) At average denomination of money prices....	385	192	200	81	156	41

* Unadjusted hand-to-hand currency.
† Official wholesale prices.
‡ Money income of the Deutsches Institut für Wirtschaftsforschung.
§ Adjusted average monetary circulation.
‖ Corrected Deutsches Institut national income further adjusted for pay of the armed forces and black-market operations.
From the volume of all production index shown in Table 7.

With an increasing monetary stock and price level, one expects an increase in velocity because of the desire to hold less money. The desire, however, for maintaining a given level of real cash balances provides a limit to the expansion of velocity. Germany behaved along these lines through 1938. After that, because of the full employment of resources, the war, and rising prices, one would have expected real cash balances to decline and income velocity to rise. This, however, did not happen.

Instead, real cash balances increased rapidly, while income velocity decreased sharply.

Other countries such as Italy, Great Britain, and the United States during similar periods also experienced rises in real cash balances and decreases in income velocity. In no case, however, were the increases in real cash balances nearly as great as those in Germany. Nor were the decreases in income velocity nearly as great as those in Germany. Was the German situation really different from the others?

Table 11 summarizes the results of this study. It shows that, before adjusting the data, German real cash balances and income velocity in 1944 were 436 and 23 per cent, respectively, of their 1938 level. After correcting the money, price, and income data, real cash balances were either 253 or 200 per cent, while income velocity becomes 43 per cent of the 1938 level. On the other hand, (1) real cash balances in Italy were 136 per cent of their 1938 level in 1944; (2) real cash balances and income velocity in Great Britain were 155 and 65 per cent, respectively, of their 1941 level in 1947; and (3) real cash balances and income velocity in the United States were 161 and 66 per cent, respectively, of their 1942 level in 1946. If 1942 over 1938 is used for Germany in order to make it comparable with the United States, one finds that real cash balances become either 172 or 155 per cent, while income velocity becomes 59 per cent of the 1938 level. Thus the United States and Germany become somewhat comparable for a short period of time. Over all, however, even after correcting the German data and leaving the price and income statistics of other countries untouched, one finds that the German situation still differs from that of other countries.

The correction of price, money, and income series lessens considerably the increase in German real cash balances and the decrease in income velocity. But it appears that German economic behavior did in fact change. The only apparent reasons for this change are that direct controls were partially effective and that in 1943 and 1944 transportation disruptions caused individuals to hold larger cash balances.

IV

Inflation in the Confederacy, 1861–65

EUGENE M. LERNER

Inflation in the Confederacy, 1861–65

THE worst inflation in American history since Revolutionary times plagued the South during the Civil War. For thirty-one consecutive months, from October, 1861, to March, 1864, the Confederate commodity price index rose at the average rate of 10 per cent per month. In April, 1865, when Lee surrendered and the Civil War ended, the index was ninety-two times its prewar base. Like all people living through rapid inflation, southerners directed their invective against the instrumentality through which the increase in prices occurred. They exhorted, threatened, vilified, and enacted legislation to regulate and control businessmen and farmers who sold goods at more than "fair" prices. Their Congress declared the capable Secretary of the Treasury, Christopher G. Memminger, unfit for public office; but prices continued to rise. Memminger resigned, but his successor was no more successful at stopping the rise of prices.

The rapid and continuous rise of the commodity-price level was caused by an ever expanding stock of money, a sharp rise in velocity, and a drop in real income. This paper deals with the behavior of these forces and analyzes their interrelationship.

I. Confederate Taxation

Many southerners expected an early and easy victory because Yankees were merchants and traders—not fighters. Furthermore, "Cotton was King." The British navy was expected to run the blockade and fight against the North in order to secure a steady supply of cotton. Without cotton, so the southerners believed, English textile mills must close, unemployment develop, and markets disappear. The victory at Bull Run in July, 1861, bolstered these hopeful Confederate anticipations of success. Northerners also expected a short and victorious war. Men were asked to volunteer for army service for only ninety days. The North had the raw materials, the factories, and the population. These resources, northerners felt, would prove overwhelming. Neither the South nor the North thought it necessary to enact drastic war measures to raise substantial amounts of revenue through taxation.

In May, 1861, Secretary Memminger recommended that a property tax be levied to provide no more than $15 million during the coming fiscal year. He further recommended that the President be authorized to reduce this tax if sufficient funds were raised through bond sales and custom duties. The southern states that seceded from the Union insisted upon preserving states' rights and were opposed to a powerful central government that taxed heavily. The Confederate Congress held that the administration's modest $15-million tax request was too high and wanted a program yielding no more than $10 million.[1] In August, 1861, the Congress passed its revenue bill. It taxed only property and personal possessions at the flat rate of one-half of 1 per cent.

The United States Congress raised import duties, levied a direct tax of $20 million, and, for the first time, enacted a 3 per cent tax on incomes over $800. These mild measures also came late and did not raise significant sums for the North during the first fiscal year of the war.

The Confederate government lacked the machinery to assess and collect the modest one-half of 1 per cent property tax. War broke out shortly after the Confederate government was formed. Virginia, Tennessee, Arkansas, and North Carolina did not join the Confederacy until Fort Sumpter was attacked and Lincoln called for troops. Substantial agencies of the government, like the Supreme Court, were unorganized; and important posts in the Confederate war and treasury departments were unfilled.

To avoid duplicating the individual state's tax-collecting machinery and to expedite the administration of the government's tax levy, Secretary Memminger hoped to utilize each state's assessment figures and collection facilities. The Congress invited the state's co-operation by conceding a 10 per cent reduction in the tax quota of each state assuming responsibility for raising the assessed amount of money.

A detailed questionnaire revealed that each state assessed property differently. Some, for example, levied a uniform poll tax upon slaves; others valued them and imposed *ad valorem* taxes. The lack of uniformity forced the Confederate government to reassess all property. Here difficulties were encountered. Some states prohibited the use of their officials by the Confederate government, and inexperienced assessors had to be hired. Tax forms arrived late because parts of the law were revised, large numbers of printers and binders joined the army, and paper was scarce. When finally the forms arrived, property was not uniformly valued. "Murmuring and discontent" followed.

Southern governors objected to using state facilities for collecting the Confederate government's property tax. Governor A. B. Moore, of Ala-

---

1. For a more complete description of this tax bill and other points of Confederate finance see Eugene M. Lerner, "The Monetary and Fiscal Programs of the Confederate Government, 1861–65," *Journal of Political Economy*, LXII (December, 1954), 506–22.

bama, spoke eloquently on this point. In addressing a joint meeting of the legislature of his state, he declared, "The collection of this tax by the State would be an onerous and unpleasant duty as it imposes upon the State the necessity of enforcing the laws of the Confederate Government against her own citizens."[2]

Each state wanted the 10 per cent discount, and all assumed the responsibility for raising the assessed amount. However, only South Carolina actually collected the money in taxes. Texas raised its quota by confiscating alien property. Other states floated bond issues to raise the money. Many of these securities were purchased by banks, and the stock of money expanded.[3] The first Confederate tax bill, therefore, had the unintended effect of increasing rather than reducing the stock of money. During the first year of the war $61 million entered the Treasury. Absolutely nothing came from the property tax. By September 30, 1863, $1.2 billion entered the Treasury. Only 1.7 per cent of this amount were the proceeds of the property tax.

Subsequent tax legislation was cumbersome and intricate; disappointment and delay were the inevitable results. As war continued, taxes became more difficult to assess and to collect. There was a growing shortage of forms and of trained men. Southern governors ordered Confederate tax-collectors out of their states. Tax-evading became a sport, and the invading Union forces completely disrupted the tax administration. Tax-collectors often dropped their work and abandoned their homes before the advancing Union troops. In Arkansas, for instance, a special treasury agent tried to transmit instructions to A. B. Greenwood, the state's permanent collector. The agent reported that "Mr. Greenwood fled with his property from the state to avoid capture by the enemy and has settled in Texas."[4] Up to October, 1864, less than 5 per cent of all revenue entering the Confederate Treasury came from taxes. In the North the tax program was more successful. From 1861 through 1865 almost 21 per cent of all United States government expenditures were met by taxes.

2. "A. B. Moore to Gentlemen of the Senate and House of Representatives, October 28, 1861," in the U.S. War Department, *The War of the Rebellion*, Series IV (Washington, D.C.: Government Printing Office, 1880–1901), I, 698.

3. If banks had not bought state bonds, comparable sums of money would not have been loaned to private persons. Loyalty to the state governments made bankers willing to lower their reserve ratios and buy state bonds. Furthermore, the risk on a loan to a private person in the South during the war was larger than the risk on a loan to the state government. The private person might be conscripted, his goods confiscated, or his property destroyed. Loans to private persons were therefore screened carefully.

4. Letter from Allen, chief clerk of the Confederate Treasury Department, to Secretary Memminger, in Raphael P. Thian (ed.), *Appendix* (Washington, D.C., 1878), II, 250.

II. Confederate Bonds

Anticipating small tax receipts, Secretary Memminger hoped to prevent a rapid rise of prices by selling large amounts of bonds to private people and non-banking corporations. Southern planters could not spare funds until after the harvest. War, however, broke out in April. Secretary Memminger therefore proposed the realistic plan of immediately securing pledges for bond purchases. When the crops were sold, planters were expected to redeem their pledges by purchasing the bonds.

In May, 1861, the Confederate Congress adopted the Secretary's plan and authorized a $50-million bond issue. Each legislator became a solicitor of pledges, and the public responded so enthusiastically that Secretary Memminger asked Congress to authorize another $50-million bond issue in order to cover all the pledges he received. "This large sum of money may be counted on with certainty," he told Congress, "if the sales of the produce can be effected."[5]

At harvest time in 1861 the market for exported goods was smaller than had been expected. Southern ports were blockaded, and trading with the enemy was discouraged. A grand design of forcing Europe to recognize the Confederacy was afoot, and southerners themselves prevented the export of King Cotton. Vigilante groups were formed to destroy cotton ready for shipment on the docks and to persuade patriots to hold back their supplies. Consequently, the price of cotton fell. By September, 1861, the price of cotton was almost 25 per cent below its June, 1861, value. During this period, the general price index for all commodities rose 27 cent. The real income of the cotton-planters fell sharply, and many who planned to buy bonds when they sold their crops became disgruntled. Instead of buying bonds, they demanded immediate government aid.

Planters proposed two support programs: the government might either buy the cotton crop outright or grant loans using the crop as collateral. Despite protests and pressure, Secretary Memminger completely rejected both alternatives. "Subsidizing cotton eliminated the incentive to change output," and the immediate need was for "measures to relieve the demand for provisions and grain."[6] Either subsidy would entail an expenditure of $100–$200 million. The increase in the stock of money would bring on a further rise in prices. It would make the first bond issue, like the first tax bill, have a net inflationary effect.

Secretary Memminger was widely attacked for failing to buy the cotton crop, both then and by present-day historians. He felt it necessary,

5. "Report of November 20, 1861" (*ibid.*, III, 17).
6. "Report of October 15, 1861" (*ibid.*, pp. 50–51).

however, to keep government expenditures as low as possible to restrain prices. To serve this end, he delayed paying Confederate troops; he urged purchasing agents to buy provisions with bonds instead of cash; and he withheld warrants for requisitions unless bonds were accepted by government suppliers. As a measure of economy, he also lowered the interest rate on bonds.

Confederate bonds issued in May, 1861, yielded 8 per cent. Succeeding issues yielded as low as 4 per cent. Undoubtedly some southerners continued to buy bonds with no thought of their return or capital value. War meant fighting, sacrificing, and buying bonds, whether they yielded 4 or 8 per cent. Others, however, were greatly concerned, and bond sales fell. The rise of commodity prices made the return on bonds negative and destroyed their value. Under the circumstances patriotism was the only motive for southerners to buy bonds.

To rebuild the sale of bonds in the face of rising prices, Secretary Memminger induced the Congress to enact legislation designed to "arrest the circulation of notes and lessen the volume of currency" by placing a time limit on the eligibility of certain currency issues to buy the higher-interest-yielding bonds. On March 23, 1863, Congress passed the requested law discriminating against specific currency issues. Notes that were issued before December 1, 1862, for example, were convertible into 8 per cent bonds until April 20, 1863. Between April 20 and August 1, 1863, they could be funded into 7 per cent bonds. Thereafter, these notes could no longer be used to purchase any bonds of the Confederate government.

The conditions of this act defeated the very ends the act was intended to serve. Limiting the right of certain notes to buy bonds penalized the holders of these notes. Instead of encouraging the purchase of bonds and "arresting the circulation of notes," the act discouraged a person from holding cash balances. The increase in velocity drove prices still higher.

Rising prices and falling yields discouraged bond purchases and made the Confederate bond program impotent. Up to October, 1864, less than 30 per cent of all the revenue entering the Confederate Treasury came from bonds.

III. CONFEDERATE MONEY

The extreme budgetary difficulties and the failure of the Confederate bond program caused unpaid bills to accumulate rapidly on Secretary Memminger's desk. Printing notes was the expedient way of meeting these obligations. On March 9, 1861, the Confederate Congress authorized issuing notes "for such sum or sums as the exigencies of the public service may require, but not to exceed at any one time one million of dollars." During the next four years the Treasury printed over fifteen hundred times this amount.

As early as November, 1861, Secretary Memminger reported that "daily requisitions exceed the supply of money by nearly 50 per cent."[7] He expanded the Treasury note-signing bureau from seventy-two employees in July, 1862, to two hundred and sixty-two in July, 1863. Even so, an insufficient amount of currency was issued. As war continued, paper, suitable engravings, and printers became harder to find. In desperation, Secretary Memminger recommended that the South resort to honoring counterfeits. Any person holding a bogus note should be able to exchange it for a 6 per cent call certificate. The counterfeits could then be stamped "valid" by the Treasury and reissued.

Currency continued to grow in quantity. Secretary Memminger warned Congress that "this increase causes a daily advance in prices . . . which if not arrested must result in consequences disastrous to the best interest of the country." But Congress had no alternative to issuing notes. The *Wilmington Journal* spoke for a wide audience in denouncing taxation:

> We of today are paying the price of our righteous war of defence in blood and wounds and death; in hearts wrung and anguished by the loss of fathers, sons, and brothers, and in every sort of personal privation and suffering, and it is but just and right that posterity should pay in money the price of that heritage of freedom, property, and glory which we will bequeath them. . . . Let our authorities then fearlessly task and stretch the public credit to the utmost, in order to carry on the war so that taxation may not crush to earth our already overburdened people.[8]

The public credit could not be stretched any further because investments in land, inventories, equipment, and other durable goods were more attractive than bonds. Under these circumstances, the Confederate Congress could not stop the printing presses.

As Union armies reduced the area of the South where Confederate notes were accepted as legal tender, southerners shipped their notes to those sections where it still passed as currency. In New Orleans the greenback price of "uncurrent Confederate Notes" was regularly quoted in the weekly newspaper long after the city fell to the North. These shipments increased the stock of money in the areas where Confederate notes were accepted, driving prices still higher.

7. "Report of November 10, 1861" (*ibid.*, p. 30).
8. April 9, 1863.

From July 1, 1861, to October 1, 1863, 68.6 per cent of all the revenue entering the Confederate Treasury came from the printing press. No one planned to finance the war this way. Because it was so financed, inflation became inevitable.

IV. BANK EXPANSION

The number of Confederate notes outstanding increased from $1 million in June, 1861, to more than $826 million in January, 1864. Many of these notes entered the Confederate banking system and added to re-

TABLE 1

TOTAL STOCK OF MONEY IN THE SOUTH
IN MILLIONS OF DOLLARS

Date	Bank Notes and Deposits*	Confederate Government Notes	Total	Index: January, 1861 = 100
1861:				
January........	$ 94.6	....	$ 94.6	100
April..........	121.8	....	121.8	130
June..........	119.3	$ 1.1	120.4	130
October.......	146.3	24.5	170.8	180
1862:				
January........	165.2	74.6	239.8	250
April..........	151.1	131.0	282.1	300
June..........	142.9	166.1	309.0	330
October.......	181.5	287.3	468.8	500
1863:				
January........	239.1	410.5	649.6	690
April..........	257.1	561.7	818.8	870
June..........	267.5	637.3	904.8	960
October.......	274.7	792.4	1,067.1	1130
1864:				
January........	268.1	826.8	1,094.9	1160

* These figures are not adjusted for interbank deposits and are therefore biased upward.

serves. They created the potential for banks to grant large amounts of loans and add sizably to the rise in prices. Actually, however, bank notes and deposits did not expand rapidly from January, 1861, to January, 1864. As shown in Table 1, they expanded less than three times during this period.[9]

The demand for money was high during the war. Profit margins were high because wages lagged behind prices. Producers knew the market demand for any war or import competing commodity was certain. Further-

9. Tables 1, 2, and 3 are reproduced from my article, "Money, Prices, and Wages in the Confederacy, 1861–65," *Journal of Political Economy*, LXIII (February, 1955), 21. In this article I describe in detail how the estimates for these series were made.

more, the continuous rise in commodity prices meant that all loans would be repaid in depreciated dollars. Why then did bankers use such remarkable restraint in creating deposits?

The most important reason was that commercial banks had no central bank to support them during a crisis. Southern bankers expected mass withdrawals whenever Union troops approached. They were therefore forced to protect themselves in the only way they could—by limiting the expansion of credit and by increasing their reserves. Georgia banks held 47 per cent reserves in June, 1862, and 69 per cent in June, 1863; the Bank of Fayetteville, North Carolina, held 21 per cent in May, 1861, and 46 per cent in November, 1863; the Bank of South Carolina held 5 per cent in January, 1861, and 30 per cent in October, 1863; the Bank of the Valley in Virginia held an average of 41.2 per cent in 1861, 56.5 per cent in 1862, 57.2 per cent in 1863, and 66.4 per cent in 1864.

In the North during the war years, $1.49 was created per dollar printed by the government.[10] In the South, as of January, 1864, only $1.20 was created per dollar printed by the government. Had southern bankers not increased their reserve ratios, the stock of money, and therefore prices, would have risen still more.

V. THE PRICE RISE

The general commodity price index of the Confederacy (Table 2) increased steadily from the outbreak of war in April, 1861, until May, 1864. In response to a currency reform enacted in February, 1864, prices stopped rising and, indeed, fell slightly until November. In December, 1864, the price index started to climb again and continued to rise sharply until the war's end.

The rapid rise in prices after the outbreak of war reduced the real value of Confederate notes. Lenders refused to extend credit unless they were repaid in gold, leather, or some other commodity, and creditors refused to accept payment for obligations incurred before the war. A client wrote J. D. Davidson, an attorney in Lexington, Virginia, that "some time about the 1st of the present month, Mr. Jack Jordan again came to me when I refused to take the money [for his debt] owing to the condition of the currency."[11] The creditor wanted Davidson to prevent the debtor from repaying his obligation. In the North, where the inflation was not

10. Milton Friedman, "Prices, Income and Monetary Changes in Three Wartime Periods," *American Economic Review*, XLII (May, 1952), 635.

11. University of Wisconsin Historical Society, McCormick Collection, Special Davidson Collection, Charles Aenentrout to James D. Davidson, March 13, 1864, Fol. Jan., 1863–65.

nearly so severe, William McCormick wrote his brother Cyrus, then in England, that events reminded him of Dr. Witherspoon's allusion to the time when "creditors were seen running away from their debtors and their debtors pursued them in triumph and paid them without mercy."[12]

As early as 1862 some southern firms stopped selling their products for currency alone, and customers were forced to offer commodities as well as notes to buy things. Manufacturers were compelled to pay part of their

TABLE 2

GENERAL PRICE INDEX OF THE EASTERN
SECTION OF THE CONFEDERACY
(First Four Months of 1861 = 100)

MONTH	YEAR				
	1861	1862	1863	1864	1865
January...........	101	193	762	2,801	5,824
February..........	99	211	900	2,947	6,427
March............	101	236	1,051	4,128	8,336
April.............	101	281	1,178	4,470	9,211
May..............	109	278	1,279	4,575	....
June.............	109	331	1,308	4,198	....
July.............	111	380	1,326	4,094	....
August...........	120	419	1,428	4,097	....
September.........	128	493	1,617	4,279	....
October..........	136	526	1,879	4,001	....
November.........	161	624	2,236	4,029	....
December.........	172	686	2,464	4,285	....

employees' salaries in commodities. One complained that "money will buy little or nothing here, and unless I can find some means of getting food for my workmen, I fear I shall lose them."[13]

In the North the McCormicks protected themselves from the continuous rise in prices by purchasing durable goods and real estate. William McCormick "felt that paper money kept on deposit was unwise . . . and bought nearly 3000 tons of pig iron,"[14] a supply large enough to last the firm two years. The McCormicks bought paints, nails, lead, and lumber in such quantities that storage space had to be enlarged. Land and property were bought with a minimum down payment and a maximum mortgage "to have a place to put our depreciated notes if [the inflation] gets worse."

12. McCormick Collection, letter from William S. McCormick to Cyrus H. McCormick, January 23, 1863.

13. Letter from J. Ralph Smith, general supervisor of the State Works of South Carolina, to William Gregg, September 4, 1863 (Thian [ed.], *op. cit.*, II, 140).

14. Letter from William S. McCormick to Cyrus H. McCormick, August 3, 1862.

Many southerners protected their wealth in the same manner, but were accused of speculation and burned in effigy. The Confederate Congress, trying to "get" the speculators, enacted a tax law allowing property bought before January 1, 1862, to be assessed at its 1860 value. Property bought after January 1, 1862, was to be assessed at its purchase price.

The continuous and rapid rise in prices caused Secretary Memminger to write in December, 1863, that "the continuance of the notes as a circulating medium to their present extent involves the ruin of public and private credit, and will deprive the government of the means of defending the lives and property of its citizens."[15] Some program to effectively reduce the stock of money was imperative.

On February 17, 1864, the Confederate Congress enacted a currency reform. All existing currency and call certificates, except one-, two-, and five-dollar bills could be converted, dollar for dollar, into 4 per cent bonds until April 1, 1864. The notes still outstanding on April 1 were to be exchanged for new issues at the rate of three for two. With this one law, one-third of the South's cash was erased.

In anticipation of the currency reform southerners tried to reduce their cash balances and drove up prices more sharply than at any time since the war began. In the single month between February 15 and March 15, 1864, the price index increased 23 per cent. In medieval times the crown debased coins in periods of falling prices and restored the specie content in periods of rising prices. Such policies "gave surprising stability to prices in the long run," but Professor Hamilton indicated that they may have "intensified short term instability."[16] The attempt of the Confederacy to stabilize prices through a well-publicized currency reform had just that effect.

In May, 1864, the currency reform took hold, and the stock of money was reduced. Dramatically, the general price index dropped. This price decline took place in spite of invading Union armies, the impending military defeat, the reduction in foreign trade, the disorganized government, and the low morale of the Confederate army. Reducing the stocks of money had a more significant effect on prices than these powerful forces.

Taxes, however, were still uncollectable, bonds unsalable, and the government expenditures continued large. The printing press was again resorted to, and by December, 1864, prices began to rise. They continued rising until the end of the war.

15. Memminger, "Report of December 7, 1863" (Thian [ed.], *op. cit.*, IV, 189).

16. Earl J. Hamilton, "Prices and Progress," *Journal of Economic History*, XII (fall, 1952), 329.

VI. THE REAL VALUE OF MONEY

The general commodity price index of the Confederacy increased twenty-eight fold from the first quarter of 1861 to January, 1864. During the same period the stock of money increased only eleven fold. The difference between these ratios is attributable to increases in the velocity of money and to decreases in the South's real output. Unfortunately, the statistical data are not adequate to determine with accuracy the amount

TABLE 3

THE REAL VALUE OF MONEY

Date (1)	Increase in Stock of Money (Jan., 1861 = 100) (2)	Index of Commodity Prices (Jan., 1861 = 100) (3)	Real Value of the Stock of Money (Col. [2]÷ Col. [3]) (4)
1861:			
January	100	100	100
April	129	100	129
June	127	108	117
October	180	135	134
1862:			
January	253	191	133
April	298	279	107
June	337	328	102
October	496	522	95
1863:			
January	687	756	90
April	666	1,168	57
June	959	1,296	74
October	1,129	1,858	61
1864:			
January	1,159	2,776	42

each of these forces changed. A measure of their combined strength is given by the real value of the stock of money. This statistic increases when velocity falls or real income rises and declines when velocity rises or real income falls.

Estimates of changes in the real value of Confederate cash balances are shown in Table 3. Until June, 1862, the index of real value was greater than 100, the level of January, 1861. Instead of reducing their cash holdings immediately, southerners held notes longer, suggesting that they were slow to realize that inflation was under way. In October, 1862, when it was clear that more inflation was in store, the value of cash balances fell below the January, 1861, level. After this date, prices rose more than the stock of money increased.

This pattern, in which the aggregate real value of cash balances first rises, then falls, has been found in every major inflation for which statistical data are available. Keynes, in describing the inflations of post–World War I in Europe, accounted for this repeated occurrence as follows:

At first there may be a change of habit in the wrong direction which actually facilitates the Government's operation [of collecting taxes by issuing notes]. The public is so much accustomed to thinking of money as the ultimate standard, that, when prices begin to rise, believing that the rise must be temporary, they tend to hoard their money and to postpone purchases, with the result that they hold in monetary form a larger aggregate of real value than before. . . . But sooner or later the second phase sets in. The public discovers that it is the holder of notes that suffer taxation and defray the expenses of government and they begin to change their habits and to economize in their holding of notes.[17]

On January 10, 1863, Secretary Memminger stated that velocity had fallen to two-thirds of its prewar rate. If this estimate were correct, the real income of the South declined 40 per cent by January, 1863. If he were correct only in that velocity fell, the decline in the real value of money by January, 1863, would still be attributable to the drop in the South's real output.

During the first two years of the war the real income of the South fell because the Confederate army drained large numbers of white men from the labor force. General Clement A. Evans estimated that approximately 40 per cent of the white men of military age were in the army.[18] Colonel Thomas L. Livermore put the number still higher. The jobs left vacant could not be filled immediately. Old men, women, slaves, or wounded veterans were the replacements for men called to service; these workers were not so productive as the men they replaced.

As war continued, the invading Union armies, the northern blockade, and the reallocation of southern labor tended to reduce output. These disturbing forces, however, were partly offset. Since prices rose much faster than wages, real wages fell. Southern laborers tried to maintain their prewar living standards by working longer hours and holding down more than one job. In many cases wives and children entered the labor force for the first time to supplement the family income. Patriotism also made workers become more efficient at their jobs, work longer hours, and discover "short cuts" in production. Large numbers of army privates re-

17. John M. Keynes, *A Tract on Monetary Reform* (New York: Harcourt, Brace & Co., 1924), pp. 50–51.

18. *Confederate Military History* (Atlanta: Confederate Publishing Co., 1899), VII, 500.

ceiving eleven dollars a month deserted to work on their farms back home. Like France during World War I, the Confederacy realized it was over-mobilized and sent soldiers home to work in factories. These increases in the labor force reduced the most important "bottleneck" in southern production and increased the South's real output. If the conflicting forces just described offset each other, the army's heavy drain on manpower caused a "once and for all" drop in real output—a drop felt most seriously during the first two years of the war.

The continuing decline in the real value of cash balances was caused by increases in velocity. Like all people who live through prolonged and rapid price rises, southerners came to realize that the only way to avoid the tax of inflation was to reduce their cash holdings. Some resorted to limited forms of barter and refused to accept cash alone for their products. Others adopted more stable currencies, such as northern greenbacks, or made their notes payable in commodities. Durable goods, land, precious metals, and jewelry were kept as ultimate reserves instead of notes or deposits. As velocity increased, prices rose still higher and the real value of cash balances declined.

Taxing through printing money was as appealing to the Confederate government as it was to the Continental Congress in earlier years of American history and to so many governments since that time. What is remarkable is that so large a fraction of the southern war effort could, in fact, be financed by currency issue. It betokens the enormous importance that people attach to having a currency, even a depreciating one, and the great amount of real resources they are willing to pay for it.

V

Monetary Velocity in the United States

RICHARD T. SELDEN

Monetary Velocity in the United States

I. THE PROBLEM

> An examination of the circumstances by which the circulation of money is liable to be affected, appears to me to be still a desideratum in the theory of commerce.[1]

> In the developed quantity theory of money . . . there has always been a weak spot, namely, the velocity of circulation. The Quantity of Money is an observable phenomenon, and the proximate causes, at least, which govern it, may be specified. . . . Velocity is also observable, but the causes which govern it are less easy to distinguish.[2]

Economists have been talking about the velocity of circulation of money and related concepts for nearly three hundred years.[3] Despite this fact, the subject remains a fertile field for study. The importance of the concept can scarcely be denied. A given change in the quantity of money will have widely varying effects on the level of prices and incomes, depending on the behavior of monetary velocity.

Prior to the Great Depression most economists "solved" this problem by assuming velocity to be essentially constant for short "normal" periods.[4] Since the early 1930's, however, there has been a growing conviction that the velocity of money is highly volatile and undependable and that better results can be attained through an entirely different ap-

1. Dugald Stewart, "Notes on the Bullion Report," Appendix II to Vol. I of his *Lectures on Political Economy*, ed. Sir William Hamilton (Edinburgh: T. & T. Clark, 1877), p. 433.

2. Roy F. Harrod, *The Trade Cycle* (Oxford: Clarendon Press, 1936), pp. 125–26.

3. M. W. Holtrop ("Theories of the Velocity of Circulation of Money in Earlier Economic Literature," *Economic History* [supplement to the *Economic Journal*], January, 1929, pp. 503–34) gives an excellent short history of early thought in this field. He states that Petty (*Verbum sapienti* [1664]) was the first to "touch upon the problem of the velocity of circulation."

4. I do not imply that earlier economists had no elements of a theory of velocity or that they were unaware of large variations in velocity during both (1) "transition" periods and (2) long time spans. Monetary literature abounds with discussions of the determinants of cash holdings relative to payments (see Arthur W. Marget, *The Theory of Prices*, Vol. I [New York: Prentice-Hall, Inc., 1938], for many references to such discussions). However, the elements of a theory of velocity have not been adequately integrated yet or tested empirically for the most part.

proach to monetary problems. An important corollary of this position has been the general rejection in recent years of monetary policy as a major instrument of stabilization.

The present study examines two questions: (1) How has the income velocity of money in the United States behaved? (2) What caused the changes that have occurred? Terminologies and definitions are discussed in Section II. Section III examines the observed behavior of income velocity. Sections IV–VI attempt to explain the facts revealed in Section III.

II. Alternative Terminologies and Definitions

A. VELOCITY

The velocity (V) of money is the ratio of a money flow during a time period to the average money stock during that period.

Much ambiguity has resulted from the practice of using "velocity," without modifiers, to denote particular money-flow–money-stock ratios. For instance, the money flow may be viewed broadly, as in *transactions velocity*, which is the ratio of the money volume of total monetary transactions for the period to the average total money stock $(V_t = PT/M$, where $P =$ general price level and $T =$ real value of all monetary transactions). Or the flow may include only some transactions, as in *income velocity*, which is the ratio of the money value of monetary income for the period to average total money stock $(V_y = Y/M)$. Furthermore, the velocity of particular components of the money stock may be examined, as in *deposit turnover*, the ratio of total debits against bank deposits to average total stock of bank deposits. Other velocities will not concern us in this study. I shall use the unmodified term "velocity" only in statements which apply equally to both income and transactions velocity.

B. VELOCITY, CASH BALANCES, AND THE DEMAND FOR MONEY

Discussions of monetary velocity are sometimes complicated by the fact that they make no mention of the term itself. In particular, the "Cambridge" or "cash-balances" monetary equation has no explicit term for V: it sets real balances (M/P) equal to real monetary income (y) or transactions (T) times a number, k. Algebraically, of course, $V = 1/k$, and any analysis in terms of the proportion that desired cash holdings bear to income or total transactions can easily be restated in terms of the velocity of money.[5]

5. The fact that the Cambridge equation has usually been of the "income" type (e.g., see Alfred Marshall, *Money, Credit, and Commerce* [London: Macmillan & Co., 1923], p. 44), whereas the velocity equation is most often associated with the "total transactions" approach (e.g., see Irving Fisher, *The Purchasing Power of Money* [2d ed.; New

Similarly, one frequently encounters the statement that "the demand for money rose" during a period of declining velocity. What is actually involved is the distinction between a function and a particular value of the function rather than alternative modes of expressing the same idea. And the fact that the demand function for money has been defined in various ways has added to the confusion.[6]

Throughout this study the phrase "demand for money" denotes the function relating desired money relative to total monetary transactions (M/PT) to the cost of holding money (r) and other variables (O) specified later. Symbolically,

$$D_m = \frac{M}{PT} = D\,(r;O)\ .$$

Of course, M/PT is the Cambridge k in its total transactions form. This definition has the merit that demand for money and transactions velocity are unambiguously related to each other.

C. THE CONCEPT OF INCOME VELOCITY

Since the income-velocity concept, on which this study focuses, has been strongly attacked by such diverse critics as Keynes[7] and Marget,[8] this choice requires explanation. There are two reasons for concentrating on V_y—one a matter of expediency, the other a question of principle. The governing reason is the absence of reliable estimates of V_t for the total money stock,[9] owing primarily to the paucity of data on the volume of currency transactions. However, even estimates of check transactions are

---

York: Macmillan Co., 1911]), presents no problem. See D. H. Robertson, *Money* (rev. ed.; New York: Harcourt, Brace & Co., 1948), p. 180, on the algebraic relation between the two equations. Note that k in the real balances equation of J. M. Keynes, *Tract on Monetary Reform* (London: Macmillan & Co., 1923), chap. iii, differs from that of Marshall and Robertson.

6. For instance, classical economists (e.g., Pigou, "The Value of Money," *Quarterly Journal of Economics*, Vol. XXXII) have sometimes treated the demand for money as a rectangular hyperbola, relating the value of money to its quantity. On the other hand, Keynes, in *The General Theory of Employment, Interest, and Money* (New York: Harcourt, Brace & Co., 1936), related desired money to the interest rate and other variables. He treated as synonyms the terms "demand for money," "liquidity preference," and "propensity to hoard" (*ibid.*, pp. 166 and 194).

7. J. M. Keynes, *A Treatise on Money*, Vol. II (London: Macmillan & Co., 1930), p. 24. V_y is viewed as "a hybrid conception having no particular significance." In *The General Theory* (p. 299) Keynes states that the use of V_y "has led to nothing but confusion."

8. Marget, *op. cit.*, pp. 368 ff.

9. Fisher's ingenious attempt notwithstanding (*op. cit.*, p. 285).

not entirely satisfactory. This is particularly true for the study of secular trends, since comprehensive bank-debit data exist only for the period since 1919.[10]

Suppose, however, that we possessed a reasonably good index of V_t over a long time period. In my judgment it would still be desirable to concentrate on V_y in a study such as this, because V_y explicitly relates the quantity of money to the level of money income, a variable of great interest to economists. The student of income determination who wishes to use some form of velocity analysis may take either of two basic approaches. He may follow the advice of Keynes and Marget: first analyze the determinants of the volume of monetary payments in current dollars (PT), with the aid of sector velocities, and then examine the factors influencing the size of non-income payments.[11] Alternatively, he may take the income-velocity approach. In that case the list of income determinants is precisely the same, but the concept of money income is kept in view at all times. The magnitude of non-income payments must be considered in a full analysis, no matter which velocity concept one adopts.[12]

But controversy does not end here. Many definitions of V_y have appeared in the literature, and we must decide which is most appropriate for this study. Should the denominator of V_y include time deposits and government cash holdings? Should the numerator consist of gross national product, net national product, national income, personal income, or disposable income? Should "income in kind" and government spending for goods and services be deducted from the numerator?

These questions are discussed at length in Appendix A (pp. 234 ff.), where the following conclusions are reached. The denominator of V_y is best defined as the sum of currency outside banks and all deposits, including United States Government holdings of "Treasury cash" and deposits in all banks. The most appropriate numerators are national income and personal income, minus non-monetary income.

10. Board of Governors of the Federal Reserve System, *Banking and Monetary Statistics* (Washington, D.C.: Board of Governors, 1943), p. 231. For a discussion of these data see George Garvy, *The Development of Bank Debits and Clearings and Their Use in Economic Analysis* (Washington, D.C.: Board of Governors, 1952). Quite apart from statistical complications, bank debits do not accurately indicate the volume of transactions effected by checks. Checks made payable to cash should be excluded from the total. On the other hand, many checks are negotiated more than once.

11. See Marget, *op. cit.*, pp. 389 and 395. Keynes and Marget argue that the V_y ratio relates variables that have no close relationship to each other—payments into or out of income and a total money stock which is held to meet other payments as well.

12. This argument is elaborated in Sec. V.

III. THE BEHAVIOR OF INCOME VELOCITY
IN THE UNITED STATES

I have never met with any attempt to determine in any country the average rapidity of circulation, nor have I been able to think of any means whatever of approaching the investigation of the problem, except in the inverse way. If we knew the amount of exchanges effected, and the quantity of currency used, we might get by division the average number of times the currency is turned over; but . . . the data are quite wanting.[13]

A. PREVIOUS ESTIMATES OF V_y FOR THE UNITED STATES

Twenty years after Jevons wrote the above words, the method he suggested was employed by Pierre des Essars[14] in the first extensive empirical investigation of the velocity of money. A decade later E. W. Kemmerer,[15] following the lead of Des Essars, made the first estimate of velocity for the United States. Kemmerer's estimate (for a single year, 1896) pertained solely to the velocity of *currency* in *all* currency transactions. Fisher's estimates, published in 1911, were also of the transactions type, although they were not restricted to currency.[16]

The first income-velocity series for the United States did not appear until 1933. At least thirty-eight V_y time series have been assembled since that time (Table 1). Hereafter I shall refer to these series by the numbers assigned them in Table 1. James W. Angell (V-1) and Lauchlin Currie (V-2) share the distinction of having first published V_y series; their initial estimates both appeared in the *Quarterly Journal of Economics* in November, 1933. The following year Currie made two slightly revised V_y series (V-3 and V-4), and in 1936 Angell published six new series (V-5 to V-10). In 1941 Angell constructed still another time series for V_y (V-11). During the subsequent decade the list was lengthened by Fellner, Warburton, Wernette, Hart, McKean, Hansen, Villard, Gordon, Chandler, and Goldenweiser. Nearly half of the series listed in Table 1 are the work of two men, Warburton and Angell.

Most of these are annual series, but there are six quarterly and one monthly series. The periods covered vary greatly, of course. They extend

13. W. Stanley Jevons, *Money and the Mechanism of Exchange* (1875), p. 336, quoted by E. W. Kemmerer, *Money and Credit Instruments in Their Relations to General Prices* (New York: Henry Holt & Co., 1909), p. 108.

14. "La Vitesse de la circulation," *Journal de la Société de Statistique de Paris*, April, 1895.

15. *Op. cit.*

16. *Op. cit.*

TABLE 1

INCOME VELOCITY ESTIMATES FOR THE UNITED STATES

Series	Estimator and Reference*	Time Unit of Numerator and Period Covered
V-1.......	James W. Angell, "Money, Prices and Production: Some Fundamental Concepts," *QJE*, November, 1933, p. 75, n. 4	Year, 1909–28
V-2.......	Lauchlin Currie, "Money, Gold, and Income in the United States, 1921–1932," *QJE*, November, 1933, Table V	Year, 1921–30
V-3.......	Lauchlin Currie, "A Note on Income-Velocities," *QJE*, May, 1934, p. 354	Year, 1921–30
V-4.......	Lauchlin Currie, *The Supply and Control of Money in the United States* (Cambridge, Mass.: Harvard University Press, 1934), p. 6	Year, 1921–29
V-5.......	James W. Angell, *The Behavior of Money* (New York: McGraw-Hill Book Co., 1936), Table VIII	Year, 1909–28
V-6.......	*Ibid.*	Year, 1909–28
V-7.......	*Ibid.*	Year, 1913–28
V-8.......	*Ibid.*	Year, 1913–28
V-9.......	*Ibid.*	Year, 1929–32
V-10.....	*Ibid.*	Year, 1929–32
V-11.....	James W. Angell, *Investment and Business Cycles* (New York: McGraw-Hill Book Co., 1941), Appendix II	Year, 1899–1941
V-12.....	William J. Fellner, *A Treatise on War Inflation* (Berkeley: University of California Press, 1942), Table 3	Year, 1939–41
V-13.....	*Ibid.*	Year, 1939–41
V-14.....	*Ibid.*	Year, 1939–41
V-15.....	Clark Warburton, "The Volume of Money and the Price Level between the World Wars," *JPE*, June, 1945, Table 1	Year, 1919–43
V-16.....	J. Philip Wernette, *Financing Full Employment* (Cambridge, Mass.: Harvard University Press, 1945), Table 8	Year, 1800–1910 (decennially), 1911–40
V-17.....	Clark Warburton, "Quantity and Frequency of Use of Money in the United States, 1919–1945," *JPE*, October, 1946, Table 1	Year and quarter, 1919–45
V-18.....	*Ibid.*	Year and quarter, 1919–45
V-19.....	*Ibid.*, Table 2	Year, 1938–45
V-20.....	*Ibid.*	Year, 1940–45
V-21.....	Albert G. Hart, *Money, Debt, and Economic Activity* (New York: Prentice-Hall, Inc., 1948), Fig. 3 and Appendix C	Year, 1909–47
V-22.....	*Ibid.*	Year, 1909–47

* The following abbreviations are used in this table: *QJE, Quarterly Journal of Economics; JPE, Journal of Political Economy;* and *AER, American Economic Review.*

184

TABLE 1—*Continued*

Series	Estimator and Reference*	Time Unit of Numerator and Period Covered
V-23......	Roland N. McKean, "Fluctuations in Our Private Claim-Debt Structure and Monetary Policy" (unpublished doctoral dissertation, University of Chicago, 1948), Table 4	Month, 1929–41 and 1945–47 (at annual rates)†
V-24......	Henry H. Villard, "Monetary Theory," chap. ix of H. S. Ellis (ed.), *A Survey of Contemporary Economics* (Philadelphia: Blakiston Co., 1948), p. 318	Year, 1929–47
V-25......	Clark Warburton, "Index Numbers of Elements of the Equation of Exchange," presented at a joint meeting of the Econometric Society and the American Statistical Association, December 28, 1948. (Mimeographed.)	Year and quarter, 1919–47
V-26......	*Ibid.*	Year and quarter, 1919–47
V-27......	Clark Warburton, "The Secular Trend in Monetary Velocity," *QJE*, February, 1949, Table 2	Year, 1799–1939 (decennially)
V-28......	*Ibid.*, Table 3	Year, 1909–47
V-29......	*Ibid.*	Year, 1909–47
V-30......	Alvin H. Hansen, *Monetary Theory and Fiscal Policy* (New York: McGraw-Hill Book Co., 1949), Table 1	Year, 1800–1900 (decennially), 1905–45 (quinquennially), 1947, and 1948 (first half)
V-31......	*Ibid.*, Table 5	Year, 1892, 1895–1945 (quinquennially), 1947 and 1948 (first half)
V-32......	R. A. Gordon, "The Treatment of Government Spending in Income-Velocity Estimates," *AER*, March, 1950, Table 1	Year, 1939–48
V-33......	*Ibid.*	Year, 1939–48
V-34......	*Ibid.*, Table 2	Year, 1939–48
V-35......	*Ibid.*, Table 3	Year, 1939–48
V-36......	Lester V. Chandler, *Inflation in the United States, 1940–48* (New York: Harper & Bros., 1951), Table 90	Quarter (at annual rates), 1945–48
V-37......	*Ibid.*, Table 91	Year, 1929–48
V-38......	E. A. Goldenweiser, *American Monetary Policy* (New York: McGraw-Hill Book Co., 1951), Appendix, Table 1	Year, 1919–38, half-year (at annual rates), 1939–42; and quarter (at annual rates), 1943–50

† The income figures used as V_y numerators in V-23, V-36, and the latter portion of V-38 are the annual figures that would have resulted had the normal seasonal pattern been maintained.

backward in time to 1799, though continuous annual estimates begin only in 1899. Quarterly estimates go back to 1919, while the monthly series begins in 1929.

For many years only one estimate of V_y has been made. On the other hand, twenty-three estimates have been made for 1940, most of them differing from one another. Differences among V_y measures reflect variations in definitions, in basic data, or in methods of handling data, definitional differences being the most important source of discrepancies. Angell's V-5 series most nearly meets the criteria advanced in Section II, although other series by Angell (V-7 and V-9), Wernette (V-16), and Warburton (V-17, V-25, and V-27) do not diverge greatly from these criteria. Among these seven series, Warburton's are least subject to criticism in terms of quality of basic data and computational methods.[17]

B. NEW ESTIMATES OF INCOME VELOCITY

For many purposes Warburton's V_y series (V-17, V-25, and V-27) may suffice. However, since close study of V_y requires the best possible estimates, I have constructed several new measures of V_y that avoid most of the difficulties found in existing series. The new series are numbered V-39 to V-45. They appear in Appendix C (p. 252), with detailed descriptions of the data used.

V-39 is a decennial series, 1839–1939, and may be compared with series by Wernette (V-16), Warburton (V-27), and Hansen (V-30) covering the entire nineteenth century. V-39 excludes the first four decades of the century, because money estimates are particularly poor for those years. The numerator of V-39 is the same as that of V-27. The denominator (for 1839–99) was derived from several sources (see Appendix C). Since it deviates from the denominator of V-27 by no more than ± 10 per cent, V-39 does not differ greatly from the most reliable previous series for the same period.

V-40, an annual series for the period 1899–1938, most closely resembles Angell's V-11 series. The main differences are that: (1) V-40 uses a single income series throughout; (2) Federal Reserve money figures are used in V-40; and (3) time deposits are included in V-40's denominator.

V-41, also an annual series, covers the period 1909–46. The numerator consists of an early Department of Commerce "national income" series— the only such series published by that agency for years prior to 1929. V-41 resembles Hart's V-21 series but uses national income instead of gross national product. Although neither V-40 nor V-41 is an entirely satisfac-

17. In Appendix B (p. 238) the thirty-eight series in Table 1 are analyzed from each of these standpoints.

tory velocity series, they are the best available for the pre-1929 period and permit study of long-run trends during the early decades of this century.

V-42 and V-43, for 1929–51, use national income and net national product, respectively, as numerators. The basic income data were taken from the 1951 "National Income Supplement" to the *Survey of Current Business*, as revised by the July, 1952, issue of that periodical. Data for both series were adjusted by deducting expenditures in kind wherever possible. The denominators conform to the criteria advanced in Section II and Appendix A. December–June–December averages were computed, with the December figures each weighted one-quarter and the June figure weighted one-half.[18] There is little choice between these series. Perhaps the estimates of national income are more precise than those of net national product; if so, V-42 is the preferable series.

V-44 and V-45, 1943–51, are quarterly counterparts of V-42 and V-43, respectively, except that expenditures in kind cannot be deducted from quarterly income series. No seasonal adjustments have been made for these series.

C. THE SECULAR TREND OF INCOME VELOCITY

The problem of the secular trend of V_y is one of the most interesting and controversial in the field of monetary economics. As one commentator has stated, "In the literature there is disagreement on the trend of money velocity: it is viewed as basically stable [Angell]; or rising in the long run [Fisher, Hart]; or decreasing [Warburton]."[19]

Actually this controversy is more imaginary than real. Some statements about the trend of velocity clearly refer to transactions velocity[20] or to virtual velocity,[21] and it is by no means certain that those who have made such statements would apply them to V_y as well. In addition, one must distinguish between untested hypotheses and opinions based on ex-

18. See Appendix B, p. 249, for the rationale of this procedure.

19. Ernest Doblin, "The Ratio of Income to Money Supply: An International Survey," *Review of Economics and Statistics*, August, 1951, p. 201.

20. Fisher, *op. cit.*, pp. 79 ff. and 110; Carl Snyder, "New Measures in the Equation of Exchange," *American Economic Review*, December, 1924, p. 699; and Arthur F. Burns, "The Quantity Theory and Price Stabilization," *American Economic Review*, December, 1929, p. 572.

21. Knut Wicksell, *Lectures on Political Economy* (London: Routledge & Kegan Paul, 1935), II, 66: "At every stage in commercial progress . . . we note a new, and generally higher, average velocity of circulation of the medium of exchange." Virtual velocity is defined as total transactions divided by total currency (see *ibid.*, pp. 67–70). It seems clear that Wicksell is referring to virtual velocity in this quotation.

tensive empirical work. The viewpoints of Chandler,[22] Halm, [23] Fisher,[24] and Wicksell[25] fall into the former category, and so does at least one of Hart's statements.[26] Virtually all remaining disagreements reflect differences in definitions or in the particular periods selected for study.

There are two schools among those who have done empirical work on V_y. Angell,[27] Hart,[28] and Villard[29] hold that V_y was essentially constant before 1929 but has declined sharply since then. They believe that a basic discontinuity occurred in 1929, so that it is meaningless to apply a single trend line to both periods. The other view is that of Warburton,[30] who concludes that "the downward trend in monetary velocity is not of recent origin, since it apparently extends back a century and a half." Hansen[31] and Wernette[32] also support this general position.

Two facts should be noted: first, Angell, Hart, and Villard base their conclusions on V_y measures that exclude time deposits from the denominator and, second, their V_y series begin with 1899 at the earliest. Warburton, Wernette, and Hansen, on the other hand, include time deposits in money, and their series cover the entire nineteenth century, as well as more recent years. These disagreements would vanish if the nineteenth century were included in all series and if common definitions were employed. Indeed, Hart has said: "If we take total cash as de-

22. Lester V. Chandler, *The Economics of Money and Banking* (New York: Harper & Bros., 1948), p. 565.

23. George N. Halm, *Monetary Theory* (2d ed.; Philadelphia: Blakiston Co., 1946), p. 76.

24. *Op. cit.*

25. *Op. cit.*

26. Albert G. Hart, *Money, Debt, and Economic Activity* (New York: Prentice-Hall, Inc., 1948), p. 167.

27. James W. Angell, *Investment and Business Cycles* (New York: McGraw-Hill Book Co., 1941), pp. 153 and 279–83.

28. *Op. cit.*, p. 167; also "Postwar Effects To Be Expected from Wartime Liquid Accumulations," *American Economic Review, Proceedings*, May, 1955, p. 343.

29. Henry H. Villard, "Monetary Theory," chap. ix in H. S. Ellis (ed.), *A Survey of Contemporary Economics* (Philadelphia: Blakiston Co., 1948), p. 317. Villard's position is based upon Angell's work.

30. Clark Warburton, "The Secular Trend in Monetary Velocity," *Quarterly Journal of Economics*, February, 1949, p. 81; "Volume of Money and the Price Level between the World Wars," *ibid.*, June, 1945, pp. 153–55; and "Quantity and Frequency of Use of Money in the United States, 1919–45," *ibid.*, October, 1946, pp. 447–48.

31. Alvin H. Hansen, *Monetary Theory and Fiscal Policy* (New York: McGraw-Hill Book Co., 1949), p. 1.

32. J. Philip Wernette, *Financing Full Employment* (Cambridge, Mass.: Harvard University Press, 1945), pp. 36–37.

nominator . . . a case can be made out for a downtrend in velocity."[33] It should be recalled that Angell's work was done prior to that of Warburton, Wernette, and Hansen, and he has not disputed their findings.[34]

Furthermore, simple linear regression lines of velocity on time for V-11 (Angell) and V-22 (Hart) both yield negative slopes, although, when the years after 1929 are omitted, small positive slopes result.[35] These calculations were repeated for V-21, the counterpart of V-22 for time deposits as well as currency and demand deposits; although the regression slope for the entire series was less steep than that of V-22, the slope of the 1909–29 segment was nearly the same as that of the entire series. This is a highly significant result, since it means that the 1929 "discontinuity" observed by Hart and Angell largely disappears when time deposits are included in money. The "discontinuity" reflects the shift from time to demand deposits after 1929.

It is worth noting that all but five of the thirty-eight series in Table 1 have negatively sloped regression lines, despite the wide variety of time periods and the numerous discrepancies noted earlier. The exceptions are V-2 to V-4 (Currie) and V-6 and V-8 (Angell), all of which exclude time deposits and cover only the period 1909–30.

The new V_y series (V-39 to V-43) tell a more complex story. There can be no doubt that V_y fell sharply from 1839 to 1939. The regression slope of V-39 (1839–1939) is -0.0628, which closely agrees with the slopes of -0.0586 and -0.0594 computed for the comparable years of V-16 (Wernette) and V-27 (Warburton).[36] Greater underreporting of money figures in the earlier years may have exaggerated the degree of downtrend, but a sizable decline in V_y persists even when very large allowances are made for this factor.

Cyclical variations may have distorted the trend of V_y even though the estimates themselves are accurate. For instance, each of the estimates for the early portion of V-39 might have hit cyclical peaks, while those for the latter portion coincided with troughs. The negatively sloped

33. *Money, Debt, and Economic Activity,* pp. 166–67.

34. In an earlier publication Angell argued that the trend of V_y is downward (see Angell, "Money, Prices, and Production: Some Fundamental Concepts," *Quarterly Journal of Economics,* November, 1933, p. 75).

35. Entire series: V-11, -0.0171, V-22, -0.0397; with years after 1929 omitted: V-11, 0.0059, V-22, 0.0072. It may be objected that linear regressions are inadequate trend indicators. The fitting of trend lines is a complicated subject on which there is little unanimity. I have used the linear regression because it is a simple descriptive technique with which nearly everyone is familiar.

36. This regression slope is considerably less steep than the slopes of V-16 and V-27 for the entire period 1799–1939 (-0.0978 and -0.1173, respectively).

trend line would thus be spurious in part. According to the business-cycle reference dates of Burns and Mitchell,[37] 1839, 1869, 1899, and 1929 are years of business-cycle peaks; a trough occurred in 1919, although the aftermath of war finance produced relatively high V_y figures for that year. Apparently 1849, 1859, 1879, 1889, 1909, and 1939 were years of mixed tendencies. This disperison of cyclical peaks and troughs is not likely to produce an important bias in the trend of V_y.

The regression slopes of V-40 (1899–1938) and V-41 (1909–46) are about the same: -0.0167 and -0.0235, respectively. Both are much less steep than that of V-39. The regression lines of V-42 and V-43 (1929–50) actually have small positive slopes: 0.0090 and 0.0062, respectively. These differences in regression-line slopes are not surprising. The differences between V-39, on the one hand, and V-40 and V-41, on the other, merely underline the fact that a single linear trend line does not give a satisfactory fit to V-39. The close approximation of the regression slopes of V-40 and V-41 to that of V-39 (-0.0211) for the period 1879–1939 illustrates this. To state the point differently, the graph of V-39, when plotted on an arithmetic scale, is concave upward; it corresponds closely to the graphs of V-40 and V-41 for comparable years.[38] The differences between (1) V-40 and V-41 and (2) V-42 and V-43 are largely a result of the relatively short time spans of the latter series, which make them unduly sensitive to cyclical and wartime changes.[39] Conceptual differences are also of some importance.

Thus the following conclusions are well established: (1) there was a marked decline in V_y from 1839 to 1939; (2) a decline also shows up in V_y series covering the period 1899–1938 and 1909–46; (3) there was little net change in V_y from 1929 to 1951, although regression lines for this period have slight positive slopes; and (4) a single linear trend line fits the entire data poorly.

Before we leave the topic of secular trends, Warburton's use of trend lines deserves comment. Warburton has experimented with exponential trend lines for V_y, and he has concluded that a line that declines 1.33 per

37. Arthur F. Burns and Wesley C. Mitchell, *Measuring Business Cycles* (New York: National Bureau of Economic Research, 1946), Table 16, p. 78.

38. The graph of V-39 is concave upward even when plotted on a logarithmic scale.

39. A comparison of regression slopes for the common years, 1929–38 and 1929–46, demonstrates the validity of this statement. The following values result: 1929–38, V-40, -0.0333, V-41, -0.0285, V-42, -0.0218, and V-43, -0.0206; 1929–46, V-41, -0.007, V-42, $+0.0088$, and V-43, $+0.0068$.

cent per year gives a highly satisfactory fit to his data.[40] He derived this figure initially by computing an exponential trend line for the so-called normal period 1923–28; when this line was extended forward and backward in time, he found it a good trend indicator for his entire series.

If one wishes to obtain a single line that represents *the* trend of V_y, Warburton's method is preferable to simple computation of regression lines. By basing his trend line on a "normal" period, he has avoided distortions arising from cyclical and wartime variations in V_y. But there are objections to his procedure. It may be questioned whether 1923–28 was a "normal" period, whatever that may be. More important is the sensitivity of Warburton's trend line to small changes in the V_y estimates for the base years.

The downward-sloping trend line plays a crucial role in Warburton's approach to monetary policy. For Warburton the trend line is a predictive tool: he predicts that, in the absence of disequilibrating changes in the money stock, V_y next year will be 1.33 per cent below this year's value. From this he concludes that price-level stabilization is feasible if the monetary authority increases the money stock each year by 1.33 per cent because of the anticipated decline in V_y and by 3.60 per cent because of real growth of the economy. Significant deviations of V_y from its trend line are solely a result of failure to follow this stabilization rule.[41]

Warburton's use of trend lines is questionable, quite apart from the objections noted above. Nowhere does he give a satisfactory account of the causal factors responsible for V_y's secular decline.[42] He assumes that the causes of past changes, whatever they may be will continue to produce annual declines in V_y of 1.33 per cent. Simple trend-line extrapolation can be treacherous, as developments since 1947 indicate.[43] Most of the remainder of this study will attempt to supply a more satisfactory basis for predicting changes in velocity.

40. "Index Numbers of the Elements of the Equation of Exchange," presented at a joint meeting of the Econometric Society and the American Statistical Association, December 28, 1948, p. 16, n. 2, "Charts and Tables." (Mimeographed.)

41. *Ibid.*, pp. 12 ff., and all his previously cited works.

42. For his fullest account of these factors see *Quarterly Journal of Economics*, February, 1949, pp. 84–89.

43. For instance, application of a 1.33 per cent annual rate of decline to Warburton's figure for 1925 results in the following approximate values after 1947: 1948, 1.30; 1949, 1.28; 1950, 1.26; 1951, 1.24. The values of V-43 for the same period (after multiplying by 1.044 to adjust it to Warburton's concept) were: 1948, 1.36; 1949, 1.35; 1950, 1.43; 1951, 1.60. By 1951 Warburton's figure must have been nearly 30 per cent above trend.

D. SHORT-RUN VARIATIONS IN V_y

Although V_y has been declining for more than a century, the decline has not been uninterrupted. All V_y series for the United States show characteristic short-run rises and declines, which may be summarized as follows: (1) V_y generally rises during business expansions and falls during contractions; (2) a seasonal low appears to occur in the first quarter and a high in the last quarter of each year; and (3) during both world wars V_y apparently rose initially, fell during years of full military effort, and rose again in the early postwar period.

Annual V_y series conform closely to the National Bureau's cyclical reference dates[44] for the period 1900–1938 (Table 2). Of the 272 reference phases covered by these V_y series, 235 (86.4 per cent) conformed to the cyclical pattern indicated above (i.e., rose during expansions and fell during contractions). Eight series (V-6, V-9, V-10, V-22, V-24, V-37, V-42, and V-43), covering 40 reference phases, conformed without exceptions. In 5 cases of non-conformity V_y neither rose nor fell. Most of the failures to conform (25 of the 37 instances) occurred during the contraction of 1919 (5 of 13 series), the expansion of 1920 (13 of 19), and the expansion of 1926 (7 of 15). All series conformed during the contractions of 1900, 1904, 1911, 1914, 1921, 1923, 1932, and 1938 and the expansions of 1910, 1923, and 1929.

These annual series, of course, are poor indicators of the timing of cyclical changes in V_y; the various quarterly series in Table 1 and Appendix C serve this purpose better. However, the problem of seasonal movements must be considered first. There are eight quarterly V_y series for the United States: V-17 and V-18 (1919–45), V-25 and V-26 (1919–47), V-36 (1945–48), V-38 (1944–50), and V-44 and V-45 (1943–51). Only V-44 and V-45 employ entirely unadjusted data. The other series are hybrid in nature: the numerators consist of seasonally adjusted income series, while the denominators consist of raw-money data. A glance at the completely raw series, V-44 and V-45, suggests a small seasonal movement in V_y since 1946, low values occurring during the first quarter with successive rises throughout the year. This pattern is not characteristic of all years, nor is it as evident in V-44 as in V-45.

Unadjusted quarterly income series are not available prior to 1939, and Warburton's quarterly money series are the only ones for years prior to 1943. These lacks hamper study of prewar seasonal variations in V_y. By using a seasonally adjusted numerator, does Warburton eliminate or mini-

44. Arthur F. Burns and Wesley C. Mitchell, *Measuring Business Cycles*, p. 78.

DIRECTIONS OF MOVEMENT OF ANNUAL V_y SERIES IN SUCCESSIVE NATIONAL BUREAU CYCLICAL REFERENCE PHASES,* 1900–1938

Series Number	C† 1900	E‡ 1903	C 1904	E 1907	C 1908	E 1910	C 1911	E 1913	C 1914	E 1918	C 1919	E 1920	C 1921	E 1923	C 1924	E 1926	C 1927	E 1929	C 1932	E 1937	C 1938
V-1							−	+	−	+	−	+	−	+	−	−	−	+			
V-2														+	+	+	−	+			
V-3														+	o	+	o	+			
V-4														+	o	+	o				
V-5														+	−	−	−		−	−	
V-6														+	−	+	−		−	+	
V-7														+	−	−	−		−	+	
V-8														+	−	+	−		−	+	
V-9									−	+	−	+	−								
V-10	−	−	−	+	+	+	−	+	−	+	−	+	−								
V-11							−	+	−	−	−	+	−								−
V-15												+	−	+	−	+	−	+	−	+	−
V-16							−	+	−	+	−	−	−	+	−	+	−	+	−	+	−
V-17							−	+	−	+	+	−	−	+	−	−	−	+	−	+	−
V-18											o	−	−	+	−	+	−	+	−	+	−
V-21												−	−	+	−	+	−	+	−	+	−
V-22												+	−	+	−	+	−	+	−	+	−
V-24							−	−	−	+	−	+	−	+	−	+	−	+	−	+	−
V-25							−	+	−	+	−	−	−	+	−	+	−	+	−	+	−
V-26												−	−	+	−	+	−	+	−	+	−
V-28							−	+	−	+	+	−	−	+	−	+	−	+	−	+	−
V-29							−	+	−	+	+	−	−	+	−	+	−	+	−	+	−
V-37									−	+	−		−	+	−	−	−	+	−	+	−
V-38	−	−	−	−	−	+								+	−	−	−	+	−	+	−
V-40							−	+	−	+	+	−	−	+	−	−	−	+	−	+	−
V-41							−	+	−	+			−	−					−		−
V-42												−	−						−		−
V-43												−	−								−
Total	2	2	2	2	2	2	11	11	13	13	13	19	19	22	22	22	22	17	20	18	18
Conform	2	0	2	1	1	2	11	10	13	12	8	6	19	22	19	15	20	17	20	17	18
Non-conform	0	2	0	1	1	0	0	1	0	1	5	13	0	0	3	7	2	0	0	0	0

* Arthur F. Burns and Wesley C. Mitchell, *Measuring Business Cycles* (New York: National Bureau of Economic Research, 1946), p. 78.
† Contraction ending in 1900.
‡ Expansion ending in 1903.

mize the seasonal pattern in V_y?[45] If there were no seasonal in the money stock, a seasonally adjusted income series would provide a fully deseasonalized V_y measure. On the other hand, if money varied seasonally in the same general pattern as income, though with less amplitude, the use of a seasonally adjusted numerator would convert the seasonal highs of the raw V_y index into seasonal lows. Casual inspection of Warburton's series suggests that this may have happened throughout the 1920's. However, it seems improbable that such a spurious seasonal pattern (if it exists) is of much importance in influencing the dating of turning points.

Comparison of the National Bureau's quarterly reference dates[46] with V-17, V-18, V-25, and V-26 shows complete cyclical conformity in all reference phases from the expansion of 1920 to the contraction of 1938. The turning points in V_y correspond precisely to the turning points in business activity in only four of the eleven cases covered, however. In four instances V_y lagged behind, and in three it led the cyclical turning points.[47]

The amplitudes of these cyclical movements of V_y are irregular—as are those for business activity in general (see Table 3). For the period 1919–38 the greatest declines appear in 1920–21 and 1929–33, which corresponds to the intensity of general business contractions. The greatest rise is that of 1933–37, representing recovery of V_y from the unusually low values of the preceding depression. This evidence indicates that a well-defined cyclical pattern in V_y exists.[48]

Wartime movements of V_y present a confused picture. During World War I twelve of the thirteen series recorded moderate rises from 1914 to 1915, but only five series rose during the following year. Two series registered peak values for the war period in 1915, four in 1917, five in 1918, and two in 1919. V-40 and V-41, which are probably more reliable than the other eleven series, reached peaks in 1918 and 1917, respectively. V-40 then fell continuously to 1922; V-41 fell in 1918 but returned to its peak value in 1919.

45. The question is obviously important from the standpoint of Warburton's theory of business fluctuations. He computed deviations of V_y and the money stock from their trend lines; he observed that V_y almost invariably has departed from its trend after money has; and he concluded that major downturns in business activity are caused by monetary deficiency (see Clark Warburton, "The Theory of Turning Points in Business Fluctuations," *Quarterly Journal of Economics*, November, 1950, pp. 525–49). It would be interesting to see whether his findings would hold up with a fully deseasonalized V_y series.

46. Burns and Mitchell, *op. cit.*, p. 78.

47. A full analysis, of course, would require adjustment for trend.

48. The National Bureau's study of cyclical behavior of Snyder's index of deposit activity supports these findings (see Burns and Mitchell, *op. cit.*, pp. 98–99).

During World War II all series tell much the same story. V_y rose sharply from 1940 to 1941 or 1942 but fell drastically during the years of full military effort. Most series reached a low in 1946 and then rose sharply, with a postwar peak moderately (15–20 per cent) above the 1939 figure but less than the early wartime peak.

Such, then, has been the behavior of V_y. This behavior presents a problem of interpretation, to which we now turn.

TABLE 3

CYCLICAL AMPLITUDES OF V-25 AND V-26, 1919–38

	V_y AS PERCENTAGE OF PRECEDING PEAK OR TROUGH	
EXPANSIONS AND CONTRACTIONS	V-25	V-26
1919 (ii) to 1919 (iv).........	106.0	108.4
1919 (iv) to 1922 (i)..........	82.3	80.6
1922 (i) to 1924 (i)...........	112.0	112.9
1924 (i) to 1924 (iii)..........	90.4	90.0
1924 (iii) to 1926 (i)..........	106.3	106.7
1926 (i) to 1928 (ii)..........	90.2	91.5
1928 (ii) to 1929 (i)..........	108.5	110.0
1929 (i) to 1933 (i)...........	62.3	57.9
1933 (i) to 1937 (iii)..........	135.4	140.7
1937 (iii) to 1938 (ii).........	89.4	89.8

IV. TOWARD A THEORY OF MONETARY VELOCITY:
THE COST OF HOLDING MONEY

The preceding section has described the behavior of V_y in the United States. When common definitions are used, there is no longer any serious dispute about the *facts* of velocity's behavior. This is not true of the theory of velocity. If "theory" is taken to mean "framework of analysis," there is substantial agreement regarding important parts of velocity theory; but in another sense of "theory"—as tested hypothesis or prediction—there is scarcely any agreement whatever. The existing analytic framework, incomplete though it is, has not been used to explain velocity's observed behavior. The remainder of this study attempts to develop the theory of V_y in both aspects. I shall begin by examining the relation between velocity and the cost of holding money in this section.

A. FIRST APPROXIMATION: UNADJUSTED INTEREST RATES

In Section II[49] demand for money, D_m, was defined as the function relating the Cambridge $k(M/PT)$ to the cost of holding money and other

49. P. 181.

variables. Since $k = 1/V$, it is obvious that changes in V_t may reflect changes either in the cost of holding money or in the other variables as yet unspecified.

It is conceivable that velocity's behavior is influenced mainly by the cost of holding money. Wald,[50] Behrman,[51] and Warburton[52] have tested this hypothesis, using unadjusted interest rates as indexes of the cost of holding money. Wald and Behrman found close positive relations between interest rates and various measures of velocity for 1909–46 and 1919–40, respectively—though Wald made a trend allowance in his computations. Warburton agreed that such a relation exists in some periods, particularly between short-term rates and deposit turnover,[53] but insisted that there is no significant relation between V_y and long-term interest rates over the period 1889–1939. Warburton concluded, in opposition to Tobin's view,[54] that the decline in V_y "cannot reasonably be interpreted as a result of a changing interest rate."[55]

These studies raise several problems. First, should D_m pertain to desired money relative to *all* payments or only to *income* payments? In other words, should V_t or V_y be related to the cost of holding money? Wald and Warburton have taken the latter point of view, whereas Behrman and Tobin favor broader definitions of payments (and hence of velocity).[56] This question is important, since there is not always a strict proportionality between V_t and V_y.

Factors causing lack of proportionality are discussed in Section V; they need not concern us here. The question we must answer may be framed as follows: Suppose that the cost of holding money is constant but that changes in other variables cause V_t and V_y to diverge. Will this divergence of velocities take the form of (1) a decline in V_y, with no change in V_t; (2) a rise in V_t, with no change in V_y; or (3) both a decline in V_y and a

50. Haskell Wald, "The Expanded Money Supply and Economic Activity," *Survey of Current Business*, May, 1946, pp. 8–15.

51. J. N. Behrman, "The Short-Term Interest Rate and the Velocity of Circulation," *Econometrica*, April, 1948, pp. 185–90; also "Addendum," *ibid.*, October, 1948, p. 370.

52. Clark Warburton, "Monetary Velocity and Monetary Policy," *Review of Economics and Statistics*, November, 1948, pp. 304–14; and "Monetary Velocity and the Rate of Interest," *ibid.*, August, 1940, pp. 256–57.

53. "Monetary Velocity and the Rate of Interest," *op. cit.*, p. 257.

54. James Tobin, "Rejoinder," *Review of Economics and Statistics*, November, 1948, pp. 314–17.

55. Warburton, "Monetary Velocity and the Rate of Interest," *op. cit.*, p. 257.

56. Wald, *op. cit.*, pp. 10–11; Warburton, "Monetary Velocity and Monetary Policy," *op. cit.*, p. 311; Behrman, *op. cit.*, p. 186; and Tobin, *op. cit.*, p. 316.

rise in V_t? If the first of these alternatives is correct, then Behrman and Tobin are right in favoring broad velocity concepts. On the other hand, Wald and Warburton are right if the second alternative is correct. This is one of the unsettled questions in the theory of velocity, and I shall defer its examination until Sections V and VI. For present purposes, however, relating cost of holding money to *both* V_t and V_y may illuminate the issue.

A second problem these studies raise is, Should time deposits be included in money? Wald, Behrman, and Tobin excluded time deposits; Warburton included them.[57] Warburton's procedure is preferable, for reasons discussed in Appendix A.

A third problem is, How should the cost of holding money be measured? Wald[58] used Durand's[59] series on basic yields of corporate bonds, thirty-year maturities. Warburton[60] used yields on long-term government bonds and Macauley's[61] adjusted index of railroad-bond yields. Behrman[62] and Tobin,[63] on the other hand, relied on short-term commercial paper rates. Since the pattern of rates has changed from time to time, it is likely that some rates will be more closely related to velocity than others.

But let us consider the problem more generally. The holder of cash sacrifices a number of alternatives. Wealth held in this form could be consumed; it could be converted to tangible earning assets or titles to such assets (equities); or it could be lent under a variety of circumstances for a fixed interest income. Each economic unit strives to allocate its wealth to equalize the marginal utilities of dollars devoted to the several alternatives. The cost of holding money may be measured in terms of any of these alternatives.

This is helpful as a general rule. It tells us that equity yields or interest rates on loans can and must (since the marginal utilities of other alternatives are essentially immeasurable) be used to measure the cost of holding

57. Wald, *op. cit.*, p. 10; Behrman, *op. cit.*, p. 186; Tobin, *op. cit.*, pp. 315–16; and Warburton, "Monetary Velocity and Monetary Policy," *op. cit.*, p. 310.

58. *Op. cit.*, p. 11.

59. David Durand, *Basic Yields of Corporate Bonds, 1900–1942* (Technical Paper No. 3 [New York: National Bureau of Economic Research, 1942]).

60. "Monetary Velocity and the Rate of Interest," *op. cit.*, p. 257.

61. F. R. Macauley, *Some Theoretical Problems Suggested by the Movements of Interest Rates, Bond Yields and Stock Prices in the United States since 1856* (New York: National Bureau of Economic Research, 1938).

62. *Op. cit.*, pp. 188–89.

63. *Op. cit.*, p. 316.

money.[64] However, it does not tell us how to distinguish among rates on loans of differing maturities, which is the problem under discussion.

If we apply ordinary price analysis to money, a case can be made for long rates as measures of the cost of holding money. We speak of the price of beef as so many units of generalized purchasing power (money). We also say that the demand for beef is a function of the prices of related commodities, such as pork and lamb. The demand for money can be treated in the same way. The "price" or cost of holding money is a rate of return earned by lenders and sacrificed by holders of cash balances. But *which* rate of return? The rates on loans that are least liquid[65] seem most appropriate, for these rates best reflect the value the community places on being liquid. Long-term loans experience greater price volatility and therefore are less liquid than short terms.

Short-term loans, on the other hand, are close substitutes for money (from the lender's standpoint); hence D_m undoubtedly is influenced by short-term rates. A rise (fall) in these rates will cause D_m to decrease (increase), since the "cost" of obtaining liquidity from money substitutes has fallen (risen).[66] Thus, while I agree with Wald and Warburton that long rates are better than short rates as indicators of the cost of holding money, it is clear that a study of velocity cannot ignore short rates. They will be considered subsequently, along with several other factors.

There are many long rates, however, including (1) yields on bonds, both private and public; (2) dividend yields on equities, both common and preferred; and (3) earnings-price ratios on equities. One would expect the cyclical (and perhaps secular) behavior of these yields to differ. Certainly price-level changes influence equities differently from bonds and money, and on this ground bond yields are superior to equity yields as indicators of the cost of holding money. Bonds, being fixed claims, will depreciate (appreciate) in real terms during inflation (deflation) in the same way as money. This depreciation presumably will affect bond prices and yields. Equity yields, on the other hand, require an explicit adjust-

64. This statement is true only under a stable price level. See pp. 202–3 for a discussion of problems introduced by price-level changes.

65. See J. Marschak and H. Makower, "Assets, Prices, and Monetary Theory," *Economica*, August, 1938, pp. 261–88, for the concept of liquidity used here.

66. "Cost" here is really the lost income resulting from holding wealth in the form of money substitutes rather than in highly illiquid forms. If long rates are constant, a rise in short rates implies a lower cost of holding money substitutes, and D_m will fall— just as a fall in the price of pork will cause the demand for beef to decrease. See p. 208 below for further discussion of money substitutes.

ment to account for the influence of price-level changes.[67] There appears to be little choice between dividend yields and earnings-price ratios.

Regardless of which yield series one uses to measure cost of holding money, allowance should be made for the fact that income from stocks and bonds is taxable, while non-monetary income from cash holdings is not. Since the rise in income-tax rates over time may have had an important bearing on the relative attractiveness of money and other assets, one ought to deduct from yields the average portion paid in taxes. However, the magnitude of this deduction cannot be calculated simply, largely because progressive rates and other statutory provisions differentiate among taxpayers. The following analysis ignores taxes, but their influence should be kept in mind.

To test the hypothesis that cost of holding money is the chief determinant of velocity's behavior, let us examine the relation between each of three long-term yield series and each of two annual velocity series, 1919–51 (Table 4). If other determinants of D_m played minor roles during this period, we would expect to find a strong positive relation between velocity and cost of holding money. The yield series selected are annual averages of corporate bond yields,[68] earnings-price ratios for common stocks, and dividend yields on common stocks. The velocity series are: (1) a spliced V_y series consisting of V-42, 1929–51, and 93.3 per cent of V-41, 1919–28; and (2) a deposit-turnover series obtained by splicing two debits-deposits ratios published by the Board of Governors. The period since 1919 was chosen because deposit-turnover measures begin in that year.

The strongest of the six correlations computed between yields and velocity (see Table 5, Items 1–3) is that between deposit turnover and bond yields ($+0.73$). The only other strong positive correlation is between V_y and earnings-price ratios ($+0.68$). There is actually a small negative correlation between deposit turnover and dividend yields.

B. SECOND APPROXIMATION: DEDUCTION OF THE YIELD ON MONEY

None of the studies mentioned above takes account of interest paid on deposits. Clearly the "yield on money" should be deducted from yields on loans and equities in computing the cost of holding money.[69]

The yield on money is the ratio of total interest paid on all bank de-

---

67. See p. 203 below. This point was brought to my attention first by Phillip Cagan.

68. See footnotes to Table 4 for citations to these time series.

69. Keynes, *The General Theory*, p. 196, recognizes this point explicitly.

TABLE 4

DATA USED IN STUDYING THE RELATION BETWEEN COST OF HOLDING MONEY AND VELOCITY

Year	Income Velocity*	Deposit Turnover†	Bond Yields‡	Dividend Yields§	Earnings Yields‖	Yield on Money#	Rate of Change, Wholesale Prices**
1919	1.76	24.5	6.3	5.8	10.6	1.9	5.6
1920	1.61	23.8	7.1	6.1	10.1	1.9	11.4
1921	1.27	20.8	7.0	6.5	4.2	2.0	−36.8
1922	1.41	21.6	6.0	5.8	8.2	2.0	− 0.9
1923	1.51	20.8	6.0	5.9	11.4	2.1	4.0
1924	1.44	20.7	5.8	5.9	10.3	2.1	− 2.5
1925	1.42	21.7	5.5	5.2	11.2	2.1	5.5
1926	1.41	22.2	5.2	5.3	10.0	2.1	− 3.4
1927	1.35	23.4	5.0	4.8	7.6	2.2	− 4.6
1928	1.33	26.2	4.9	4.0	7.3	2.3	1.4
1929	1.40	29.9	5.2	3.5	6.2	2.2	− 1.4
1930	1.21	22.4	5.1	4.3	4.7	2.2	− 9.3
1931	0.97	18.1	5.8	5.6	3.0	1.9	−15.5
1932	0.75	14.8	6.9	6.7	0.7	1.7	−11.2
1933	0.77	15.3	5.9	4.1	3.4	1.4	1.7
1934	0.88	16.0	5.0	3.9	3.9	1.1	13.6
1935	0.95	15.8	4.5	3.9	5.2	0.9	6.8
1936	1.00	16.2	3.9	4.4	5.9	0.7	1.0
1937	1.10	16.1	3.9	4.9	6.2	0.6	6.8
1938	0.99	14.0	4.2	4.3	3.9	0.6	− 8.9
1939	1.01	13.6	3.8	4.1	5.7	0.5	− 1.9
1940	1.06	12.9	3.6	5.4	7.2	0.4	1.9
1941	1.23	14.0	3.3	6.4	9.5	0.3	11.1
1942	1.44	13.3	3.3	6.9	10.7	0.3	13.2
1943	1.39	12.4	3.2	5.2	8.0	0.2	4.4
1944	1.22	12.0	3.0	5.1	7.6	0.2	0.9
1945	1.01	11.4	2.9	4.4	5.9	0.2	1.7
1946	0.95	11.7	2.7	4.1	6.2	0.2	14.5
1947	1.08	13.4	2.9	5.3	9.7	0.2	25.6
1948	1.20	14.6	3.1	5.9	12.6	0.2	8.5
1949	1.15	14.3	3.0	6.9	11.5	0.2	− 5.0
1950	1.24	15.6	2.9	6.0	13.7	0.2	3.9
1951	1.39	16.4	3.1	5.8	12.2	0.2	11.3

* For 1929–51, V-42, Appendix C; for 1919–28, 93.3 per cent of V-41, Appendix C.

† 1919–41, "Annual Turnover Rate," demand and time deposits at all commercial banks, Table 55, *Banking and Monetary Statistics;* 1942–51, 95 per cent of ratio of: (1) "debits to total deposit accounts, except interbank accounts, all reporting centers," *Federal Reserve Bulletins,* to (2) total deposits, all reporting centers, derived from *Federal Reserve Bulletins* by dividing debits figures for New York City and 333 other centers by their respective turnover rates.

‡ 1919–47, "Moody's corporate bond yields, averages of daily figures," from Irwin Friend, "Business Financing in the Postwar Period," *Survey of Current Business,* March, 1948, pp. 10–16, Table 5; 1948–49, from Loughlin F. McHugh, "Current Financial Position of Corporations," *Survey of Current Business,* January, 1951, Table 6; 1950–51, extrapolated on basis of "Moody's corporate bond yields," *Federal Reserve Bulletins.*

§ 1919–51, "Dividend Yields" and "Earnings-price ratios," from McHugh, *op. cit.,* Table 6; figures for 1919–38 attributed to Cowles Commission Monograph No. 3, *Common Stock Indexes;* subsequent figures extrapolated on basis of movements of Moody's earnings, stock prices, and dividends series. 1951, extrapolated on same basis as 1939–50.

‖ *Ibid.*

See n. 70 below.

** Percentage changes in the BLS wholesale price index (1926 = 100); 1949–51 computed from revised index, 1947–49 = 100.

posits to average total money stock in each year.[70] Although this yield was 2 per cent or more throughout the 1920's, it has fallen steadily since 1928 and is now about two-tenths of 1 per cent. Deducting this series from the various long-term yield series reveals that the much-discussed decline in interest rates is largely fictitious from the standpoint of holders of money. Bond rates minus the yield on money show a modest fall, but dividend and earnings rates adjusted for this factor both have upward trends, 1919–51. The six correlations of yields and velocity (Table 5) were

TABLE 5

SIMPLE CORRELATION COEFFICIENTS BETWEEN EACH OF EIGHT MEASURES OF
COST OF HOLDING MONEY AND EACH OF TWO MEASURES OF
MONETARY VELOCITY, 1919–51*

Cost of Holding Money	Deposit Turnover	Income Velocity
1. Bond yields.	+0.73	+0.22
2. Earnings-price ratios.	+0.10	+0.68
3. Dividend yields.	−0.08	+0.35
4. Bond yields minus yield on money.	+0.26	−0.01
5. Earnings-price ratios minus yield on money.	−0.12	+0.54
6. Dividend yields minus yield on money.	−0.60	−0.03
7. Rate of change of price level minus yield on money.	−0.31	+0.06
8. Total yields on common stocks minus yield on money.	+0.11	+0.22

* All variables defined in footnotes to Tables 4 and 6.

repeated with adjusted yields, and the results are striking. Small negative correlations exist in four cases. The correlation coefficient between deposit turnover and bond yields minus the yield on money is only +0.26. The strongest positive relation is between adjusted earnings ratios and V_y, +0.54.

70. See Table 4. The yield on money was obtained from Federal Reserve data in the following manner. For 1927–51 member-bank figures for interest on time deposits and interest on demand deposits (less service charges) were divided by June 30 net time and demand deposits, respectively, of member banks. The resultant interest rates were then applied to time deposits and demand deposits adjusted at all banks (June 30) to obtain estimated interest paid on all deposits. Postal savings were computed separately at a rate of 2 per cent. Total interest on deposits was then divided by total deposits adjusted plus currency outside banks (June 30) to obtain the yield on money. For 1919–26 separate figures for demand and time deposit interest payments are unavailable. Hence I have applied the rates as computed for 1927 to total demand and time deposits as of June 30, 1919–26, to obtain an estimate of total interest paid; the yield on money is the ratio of total interest paid to total deposits and currency outside banks.

C. THIRD APPROXIMATION: ADJUSTMENT FOR PRICE-LEVEL CHANGES

The above-mentioned studies did not take account of the influence of price-level changes on the cost of holding money.[71] The real value of money and other fixed claims falls as prices rise. Holding wealth in goods rather than in money avoids this capital loss. Thus, where holding tangible assets is an alternative to holding cash, the cost of holding money increases. For these reasons the rate of change of the price level is probably not inferior to equity yields (adjusted only for the yield on money) as an index of the cost of holding money.

But one must choose among available price indexes and take account of the time unit to which the price index applies. Undoubtedly there are lags between (1) alterations in the rate of change, (2) recognition of these alterations, and (3) consequent adjustment of cash balances relative to payments.[72] Brown selected the annual change in the monthly wholesale price index during the year preceding that to which the velocity measure pertains.[73] There seems to be no a priori justification of these choices. However, comparison of wholesale and consumer price indexes for 1919–51 indicates that the choice of a particular index does not greatly affect results.

For 1919–51 I correlated year-to-year percentage changes in wholesale prices,[74] minus the yield on money, with deposit turnover and income velocity, obtaining coefficients of −0.31 and +0.06. Again there is little relation between velocity and cost of holding money.

In addition to measuring the cost of holding money directly, price-level

71. Avram Kisselgoff ("Liquidity Preference of Large Manufacturing Corporations [1921–39]," *Econometrica*, October, 1945, p. 337) suggests that the "rate of change in the price level . . . may affect to some extent the propensity to hoard." A. J. Brown, ("Inflation and the Flight from Cash," *Yorkshire Bulletin of Economic and Social Research*, September, 1949, pp. 33–42) gives a thorough discussion of the relation between rate of change of prices and velocity. I am particularly indebted to Milton Friedman for many helpful suggestions on this topic.

A relation between demand for money and changing prices has long been recognized· Alfred Marshall (*Official Papers* [London: Macmillan & Co., 1926], p. 6) stated the point concisely in 1886: "The demand for a metal for the purposes of hoarding is increased by a continued rise in its value and diminished by a continued fall, because those people who hoard believe that what has been rising in value for some time is likely to go on rising and *vice versa*."

72. Such lags may apply to interest rates and the yield on money as well.

73. *Op. cit.*, pp. 35–36.

74. These figures are shown in Table 4. They were computed from the BLS wholesale price index, all commodities (1926 = 100). The years 1949–51 were computed from the revised index, 1947–49 = 100.

changes are likely to influence another indicator of the cost of holding money—equity yields.[75] Since equity prices usually rise during inflationary periods, the holder of money sacrifices a capital gain as well as dividend income. One can compute this measure of the cost of holding money from price and yield data for common stocks, 1919–51 (Table 6). The coefficients of correlation between this measure of cost of holding money (minus the yield on money) and two velocity series for 1919–51 are +0.11 (deposit turnover) and +0.22 (income velocity).[76] The degree of positive relationship between adjusted dividend yields and velocity increases considerably when one takes account of changes in capital values but still is not impressive.

D. A FINAL TEST: MULTIVARIATE ANALYSIS

Up to now I have treated the various measures of cost of holding money as *alternatives*, any one of which ought to be adequate for studying cash-balance behavior or velocity. This is appropriate for a world characterized by perfect markets and where good data exist for all variables. In the real world, however, the measures of cost of holding money may be *joint* determinants of velocity. I have therefore included several of the variables discussed above in a multiple regression analysis for the period 1919–51. First I treated V_y as the dependent variable, taking bond yields, rate of change of wholesale prices, and total yields on common stocks (each minus the yield on money) as independent variables.[77] Then I repeated the operation, substituting deposit turnover for V_y. These analyses yielded the following regression equations:

$$V_y = 0.780 + 0.109 r_b + 0.003 r_p + 0.006 r_e , \qquad (1)$$

$$V_t = 11.290 + 1.640 r_b - 0.146 r_p + 0.084 r_e , \qquad (2)$$

where r_b denotes bond yields, r_p the rate of change of wholesale prices, and r_e total yields on common stocks. The multiple correlation coefficients turned out to be low, 0.19 and 0.36, respectively. Fisher's z-test was applied to both equations, and both were significant at the 10 per cent level.

It is evident that multivariate analysis does not alter the general view derived from a study of simple correlations between cost of holding money and velocity. Both multiple correlation coefficients are within the range of values recorded in Table 5; indeed, they are noticeably lower than several.

75. Bond yields are free from this influence (see p. 198 above).

76. See Table 5.

77. See Tables 4 and 6.

TABLE 6

STOCK PRICES, TOTAL YIELDS, AND THE COST OF HOLDING MONEY, 1919–51

Year	Common-Stock Price Index*	Total Yields, Common Stocks†	Cost of Holding Money‡
1918.........	60.7	....	....
1919.........	70.7	23.2	21.3
1920.........	64.2	− 3.7	− 5.6
1921.........	52.2	−13.4	−15.4
1922.........	67.7	18.0	16.0
1923.........	69.0	8.0	5.9
1924.........	72.8	11.7	9.6
1925.........	89.7	29.7	27.6
1926.........	100.0	17.4	15.3
1927.........	118.3	23.9	21.7
1928.........	149.9	31.8	29.5
1929.........	190.3	31.4	29.2
1930.........	149.8	−17.9	−20.1
1931.........	94.7	−33.2	−35.1
1932.........	48.6	−45.3	−47.0
1933.........	63.0	35.0	33.6
1934.........	72.4	19.4	18.3
1935.........	78.3	12.3	11.4
1936.........	111.0	47.9	47.2
1937.........	111.8	5.6	5.0
1937.........	117.5	....	....
1938.........	88.2	−22.7	−23.2
1939.........	94.2	11.2	10.7
1940.........	88.1	− 1.5	− 1.9
1941.........	80.0	− 3.5	− 3.8
1942.........	69.4	− 7.5	− 7.8
1943.........	91.9	38.9	38.7
1944.........	99.8	13.8	13.6
1945.........	121.5	26.8	26.6
1946.........	139.9	19.8	19.6
1947.........	123.0	− 7.6	− 7.8
1948.........	124.4	7.0	6.8
1949.........	121.4	4.0	3.8
1950.........	146.4	28.2	28.0
1951.........	176.5	27.9	27.7

* Common-stock price index derived from Cowles Commission Monograph No. 3, *Common Stock Indexes*, pp. 66–67, for 1918–37, and from U.S. Department of Commerce, *Business Statistics* (supplement to *Survey of Current Business*), 1951 ed., pp. 98–99, for 1937–50. The former includes all stocks listed on the New York Exchange, while the more recent figures, taken from Moody's Investment Service, include a sample of 200 common stocks.

† Total yields on common stocks take account of capital gains and losses (whether realized or not) as well as dividend payments. The following computational method was used. The dividend yield (see Table 4) was multiplied by the stock-price index for each year, and this product was added to the first difference of the stock-price index column. This sum was then divided by the stock-price index of the preceding year to obtain the total yield on common stocks.

‡ Total yields on common stocks less the yield on money (Table 4).

The above findings offer little support to the hypothesis that velocity movements are mainly a result of changes in the cost of holding money. Whatever role the cost of holding money may have had during some periods of our history, it cannot account for the major velocity changes between 1919 and 1951. A likely explanation of these weak relationships will become apparent in the next section.

Thus a more complex hypothesis is needed. Section V takes up this task.

V. ELABORATION OF THE HYPOTHESIS

A. INTRODUCTION

Rejection of the proposition that the cost of holding money is the primary determinant of monetary velocity obliges one to seek and test alternative hypotheses. Both the large number of hypotheses in monetary literature and the paucity of information regarding most of them make this task difficult. Here the method of attack will be, first, to specify the "other variables" in the demand for money (D_m) referred to in Section II; next, to examine briefly some alleged determinants of D_m and V_t that seem inappropriate; then, to select some of the "other variables" for further empiricial testing; and finally, to broaden the analysis by considering the relation between V_t and V_y.

B. BASIC DETERMINANTS OF D_m

In discussing the demand function for any commodity, economists long have used a fivefold classification of variables: the price of the commodity, prices of related commodities, incomes, tastes, and expectations. There is no reason why D_m should be treated differently. As indicated in the previous section, the "price of the commodity" is the cost of holding money. A detailed analysis of the problem of related commodities and their "prices"—the problem of money substitutes—appears in the following subsection. In this subsection I shall confine my remarks to "incomes," "tastes," and "expectations."

1. Incomes. An individual's income and consumption include a number of non-cash items, and among them is the value of services received from his money holdings. In general, the proportion of income he consumes by providing for anticipated or contingent cash needs probably will vary with the level of his income.[78] For our purposes it is important to

---

78. A large number of economists have said that D_m is a function of real income (or wealth). A partial list follows: Fisher, *op. cit.*, p. 167; Hansen, *op. cit.*, pp. 1, 8; Keynes, *Monetary Reform*, p. 83; Marshall, *Money, Credit, and Commerce*, p. 44; Warburton, "The Secular Trend in Monetary Velocity," *op. cit.*, p. 89; and Wernette, *op. cit.*, p. 44.

emphasize that, as long as income elasticity of D_m for the economy as a whole is greater than zero (i.e., as long as money—relative to total transactions—is a superior "commodity"), a rise in real income will lead to an increase in D_m and a decline in V_t.[79]

Aside from the contradictory observations that real income has risen secularly while velocity has declined and that both variables have risen during prosperous times and fallen during recessions, little evidence is available on the income elasticity of D_m. Most budget studies fail to include data on cash holdings. Klein,[80] however, has found in an analysis of the 1949 Survey of Consumer Finances that the lowest and highest income deciles of sample households held the highest volume of liquid assets, excluding currency, relative to income. These data do not relate directly to D_m; nevertheless they suggest that D_m has low, perhaps even negative, income elasticity, since upper-income groups probably rely less on currency and more on money substitutes as sources of liquidity than do lower-income groups. But the relevance of this finding to the influence of income changes on D_m is doubtful for several reasons;[81] common observation and introspection are probably better guides.

Since negative income elasticity of D_m would mean that money (relative to total transactions) is an inferior "good," let us consider the nature of inferior goods. They usually are thought to consist of the "poorer qualities of goods offered for sale," potatoes and margarine being classic examples.[82] Frequently they are regarded generally as badges of low social status. Money (relative to total transactions)

79. It may seem that the text should read "greater than unity" rather than "greater than zero." This would be correct if D_m were defined in terms of real balances (M/P) rather than the Cambridge $k(M/PT)$. With the latter definition of D_m, unitary income elasticity means that a 1 per cent increase in real income will be associated with a 1 per cent increase in D_m and therefore a 1 per cent decrease in V_t. Obviously, an elasticity less than unity—but greater than zero—will also lead to a falling V_t as income rises.

80. Lawrence R. Klein, "Assets, Debt, and Economic Behavior," Conference on Research in Income and Wealth, *Studies in Income and Wealth* (New York: National Bureau of Economic Research, 1951), XIV, 210.

81. For example, the cost of holding money undoubtedly is higher for upper-income families, even after taxes, because of greater knowledge of the mechanics of investment, lower unit brokerage costs, and greater proficiency in analyzing investment opportunities. Although these factors are pertinent in explaining differences derived from budget-study data, for the most part they would be irrelevant in explaining changes over time. The same may be true of the availability of money substitutes, including lines of credit, which obviously cannot be tabulated in a survey. In addition, one should stress the great reluctance of many individuals to answer frankly when questioned about bank balances.

82. J. R. Hicks, *Value and Capital* (2d ed.; Oxford: Oxford University Press, 1946), p. 28.

certainly does not qualify as an inferior "good" in either of these senses. Money is the norm against which the liquidity of other assets is measured; it furnishes liquidity of the highest grade, and its possession is not considered bad taste or a symbol of low status. These arguments I find more convincing than the findings based on the Survey of Consumer Finances. On the other hand, the income elasticity of D_m, though probably positive, is limited by the fact that a sizable portion of all cash in recent decades has been held outside the household sector of the economy.[83] Long-run income changes would hardly influence D_m for governments and business firms. Obviously, our knowledge is far from adequate on this important topic.

2. *Tastes.* Let us turn to the counterpart of "tastes" in monetary analysis. Cash is desired as a medium of exchange and a store of value.[84] Changes in D_m may reflect changed attitudes toward the usefulness of money in either respect. As a medium of exchange money is held for contingent as well as normal transactions to satisfy what are usually termed the "precautionary" and "transaction" motives for holding cash. These motives are well-known and require little comment here.[85] The transaction motive reflects two objective factors, the frequency of payments and the degree of overlapping of payments and receipts.[86] D_m will increase if payments are less frequent or if the average interval between receipts and payments lengthens. As for the precautionary motive, D_m will increase if expectations become more subject to doubt (i.e., less certain).

There is a further source of variations in D_m and V_t related to tastes.

---

83. See Table 10, p. 224.

84. The other "functions of money" do not require that it actually be held.

85. Good general discussions of these and other determinants of D_m appear in the following: Fisher, *op. cit.*, pp. 79–88; Hart, *Money, Debt, and Economic Activity*, pp. 165–67 and 191–215; J. R. Hicks, "A Suggestion for Simplifying the Theory of Money," *Economica*, February, 1935, pp. 1–19; and Keynes, *The General Theory*, pp. 194–209. I do not imply that these determinants are free from all ambiguities; however, a full discussion of each of them would unduly lengthen the present study. Although the concept of the degree of overlapping of payments is particularly in need of clarification, its general meaning is clear enough, and this study will not undertake the task. For basic discussions of this concept see James W. Angell, "The Components of the Circular Velocity of Money," *Quarterly Journal of Economics*, LI (1937), 224–73, and H. S. Ellis, "Some Fundamentals in the Theory of Velocity," *Quarterly Journal of Economics*, LII (1938), 431–72. The latter and the Hicks article have been reprinted in *Readings in Monetary Theory*, ed. Friedrich Lutz and Lloyd W. Mints (Philadelphia: Blakiston Co., 1951).

86. A third and more important factor, the volume of transactions itself, has been incorporated into the analysis directly by the definition of D_m in terms of the Cambridge k.

Suppose that the demand for real balances as exchange media is constant, relative to total transactions, and that there is no change in the proportion of *wealth* that people wish to store in the form of cash. If the volume of transactions rises, the price level will decline, and therefore real balances will increase. However, if real balances are desired as a store of value as well as a medium of exchange, the price level will not decline by the same percentage as transactions have risen. This means that D_m will decrease and V_t will increase.[87] As we shall see, this may be one of the more important determinants of D_m.

3. Expectations. It is virtually impossible to generalize about the influence of "expectations" on D_m in view of the large number of variables cash holders must consider, including expected income and time of its receipt, size and timing of payments, availability of money substitutes, and cost of holding money. To complicate matters further, changes in expectations regarding the cost of holding money may induce either decreases or increases in D_m, depending on which measure of cost of holding money is expected to change. For instance, an expected fall in the rate of change of the price level will cause D_m to increase. Expectations of falling dividend yields, on the other hand, may induce purchases of securities in anticipation of capital gains, and D_m is likely to decrease.[88]

C. SUBSTITUTE SOURCES OF LIQUIDITY

Like other demand functions, D_m is influenced by the existence of substitutes and complements. As the following discussion indicates, the nature of this influence is complex.

There are three general sorts of money substitutes: liquid assets, negotiated options to borrow, and access to credit markets. The liquidity of an asset refers to the terms on which it can be converted to cash. A highly liquid asset possesses two primary characteristics: the demand schedule faced by potential sellers is infinitely elastic and price is stable or at least

87. These effects will vary with the nature of the transactions involved. If they consist entirely of non-income payments, the result will be that indicated in the text. However, if the increased transactions include additional income payments, the decrease in D_m will be limited; indeed, D_m may even *increase*, depending on the relative strengths of the transactions and income effects.

88. These conclusions are consistent with those reached by Keynes, *The General Theory*, pp. 170–71 and 196–99, in his discussion of the speculative motive for holding money. However, Keynes goes a step further and states that expectations of increased (bond) yields will occur when existing yields fall below "normal" yields to which investors have become accustomed. The present discussion says nothing about the conditions under which increased yields will be expected; I merely describe the probable influence of such expectations if they exist.

predictable over time.[89] Although equities and tangible assets in some instances possess a considerable measure of liquidity, they are generally inferior to claims (i.e., evidences of indebtedness *owned*) in this respect, particularly marketable claims with short maturities.

Options to borrow include such arrangements as lines of credit, trade accounts, credit cards, and overdraft facilities. Their importance in reducing desired cash holdings is probably far greater than the number of consummated transactions would indicate. The same comment applies to credit markets and their influence on desired money holdings.

The concept of money complements is less easy to formulate. McKean speaks of "the capacity of maturing debts to require the holding of cash balances."[90] Clearly, debts—particularly those with short maturities—are money complements. In addition, the concept apparently includes commitments to lend, which necessarily accompany negotiated options to borrow.[91]

Let us turn to the problem of how to measure the effect of money substitutes and complements on D_m. According to conventional price analysis, the demand for any commodity increases (decreases) if prices of close substitutes rise (fall), and decreases (increases) if prices of close complements rise (fall). In monetary analysis the counterpart of "prices of close substitutes" is, in the case of liquid assets, the differential between rates on long- and short-term loans. This differential, which I shall call the "cost of money substitutes," measures the income a lender sacrifices by lending on short rather than long term. From the borrower's point of view this differential indicates the cost of money complements. For him, of course, the "cost" is usually negative, reflecting the interest he saves by borrowing on short rather than long term. A rise in the differential between long- and short-term rates implies an increase in the cost of money substitutes and an equal decrease in the cost of money complements; on both counts D_m will increase. The opposite is true for a fall in this differential.

The preceding paragraph relates solely to liquid assets and debts. With respect to equities and other assets there seem to be no clear-cut counterparts to "prices of substitutes." Access to credit, however, is less

89. For discussion of these points see Marschak and Makower, *op. cit.*

90. Roland N. McKean, "Fluctuations in Our Private Claim-Debt Structure and Monetary Policy" (unpublished doctoral dissertation, University of Chicago, 1948), pp. 69–70.

91. However, commitments to lend, like ownership of durable goods subject to unpredictable maintenance costs, might be treated in terms of the precautionary motive for holding cash.

troublesome: the cost of this important money substitute is simply the effective interest paid by borrowers. D_m will decrease if borrowers' rates fall.[92] This statement may seem paradoxical after the argument of Section IV that D_m will *increase* if the cost of holding money falls. The "paradox" vanishes when one considers that *lenders' rates* were used in measuring cost of holding money, while *borrowers' rates* are used here. The two rates differ by the amount of brokers' fees. In the short run they will probably move together, with the result that the effect of a decline in cost of holding money will usually be offset by a simultaneous decline in cost of money substitutes. If this is correct, it explains the poor correlations between cost of holding money and velocity presented in Section IV.

During the past century or more the gap between borrowers' and lenders' rates probably has diminished steadily as credit markets have improved. Regardless of whether the cost of holding money has risen or the cost of money substitutes has fallen, this development has tended to reduce D_m and therefore to raise V_t.

These conclusions concerning the effects of credit on D_m must be modified when fractional reserve banking becomes an integral part of the financial system. In general, credit institutions obtain money in exchange for claims and then lend it in exchange for their customers' debts. The distinctive feature of modern banks is that the claims they create (i.e., "deposits") are virtually perfect substitutes for money and appear in statistical estimates of the money stock. Clearly, inclusion of deposits in money results in much larger cash holdings relative to transactions than otherwise would be the case, but this does not tell us the net effect of fractional banking on D_m. Actually three separate effects are discernible. First, cost of holding money falls as service charges decline. Second, cost of money complements probably falls as short-term rates decline. Third, cost of money substitutes falls as borrowers' rates fall. The first two effects tend to increase D_m, while the latter tends to lower it. Thus the net effect of fractional banking on D_m is uncertain.

D. OTHER ALLEGED DETERMINANTS OF D_m

The preceding subsections contain a comprehensive framework for analyzing D_m and V_t, modeled after orthodox demand analysis. Each of the usual determinants of demand has been shown to have its counterpart in D_m. However, it may be asked whether the foregoing list is truly comprehensive. The vast literature on velocity and demand for money contains many discussions of so-called determinants of D_m not mentioned above. This study does not deal primarily with the history of

92. Throughout this discussion it is important to remember that the existence of credit rationing reduces the significance of borrowers' rates of interest.

monetary thought, but it may be worthwhile to consider two of these alleged causal agents.

Conceivably, D_m may increase because of basic shifts in the structure of the economy such that "high hoarders" become relatively more important. Fisher[93] states that "an increased trade in the southern states, where velocity of circulation of money is presumably slow, would tend to lower the average velocity in the United States." Changes in income distribution, ethnic composition of the population, and so forth, are further possible examples. Of course, knowledge of which groups are typically high hoarders, coupled with information regarding the relative importance of these groups, would increase our understanding of shifts in D_m. However, these structural shifts are really changes in tastes, from an aggregate point of view, and therefore are not independent determinants of D_m.

Several economists have asserted that the rapidity of transportation of money influences D_m.[94] There appear to be two somewhat different problems here, one of which involves "mail float," the other "bank float." Mail float means that the effective quantity of money is overstated during the interval between the mailing of a check by the drawer and its receipt by the payee. The drawer presumably deducts the check from his balance at once, but there is no immediate increase in the payee's balance. Thus the total money stock, as measured by bank records, exceeds the effective money stock, as viewed by depositors. More rapid transportation, by lessening the difference between these two views of the money stock, will cause D_m to decrease—if D_m is defined in terms of bank-record money.

Bank float, which occurs when a check is deposited in a bank other than the drawer's, leads to a further discrepancy between bank records and depositors' records: the check is carried in two different accounts until settlement between the banks themselves. Deduction of bank clearings from the total money stock easily corrects this discrepancy. Does the relative size of these clearings influence D_m? Or, stated alternatively, does the speed of the clearing process influence D_m? If D_m refers to total money minus clearings, the answer appears to be "No." The effective money stock and the price level will be affected, not D_m.[95]

93. Fisher, *op. cit.*, p. 166.

94. Cf. Knut Wicksell, *Interest and Prices* (New York: Macmillan Co., 1936), pp. 54–55; Fisher, *op. cit.*, p. 88; Chandler, *The Economics of Money and Banking*, p. 548; and Keynes, *Treatise*, II, 38.

95. However, some depositors use the clearing system as a source of interest-free credit by writing checks against balances that do not exist until shortly before the checks are cleared to drawee banks for payment. An increase in the speed with which checks are cleared reduces opportunities for interest-free borrowing of this sort. To the extent that such borrowing declines, D_m will increase.

E. FURTHER EMPIRICAL TESTS

The demand function for money, as outlined in the preceding discussion, takes the following form:

$$D_m = M/PT = D(r_m, r_{ms}, y/N, E, U),$$

where r_m is cost of holding money; r_{ms}, cost of money substitutes; y/N, real income per capita; E, expectations; and U, tastes. The first three variables (r_m, r_{ms}, and y/N) are identified collectively below as *objective* determinants of D_m. This terminology reflects the fact that these variables, in contrast to expectations and tastes, can be described satisfactorily as numerical quantities.

TABLE 7

SIMPLE CORRELATION COEFFICIENTS BETWEEN REAL INCOME PER CAPITA
AND COST OF MONEY SUBSTITUTES AND EACH OF TWO MEASURES
OF MONETARY VELOCITY, 1919–51*

Independent Variables	Deposit Turnover	Income Velocity
1. Real income per capita......................	−0.51	+0.12
2. Cost of money substitutes (bond yields minus rates on 4–6-month commercial paper)...............	−0.69	−0.77

* All variables defined in footnotes to Tables 4 and 8.

Section IV examined empirical tests of the hypothesis that changes in D_m and velocity result primarily from changes in cost of holding money. I rejected this hypothesis for the period 1919–51. Let us now subject the other two objective variables, r_{ms} and y/N, to the same test (see Tables 7 and 8).

The correlations between velocity and real income per capita are not notably strong. A weak positive relation of $+0.12$ exists between V_y and this variable rather than the negative relation one would expect to find. Deposit turnover conforms much better to expectation, with a correlation coefficient of -0.51.

As a measure of cost of money substitutes I have taken bond yields minus rates on four- to six-month prime commercial paper in New York City. This measure is more appropriate for present purposes than an index of interest rates paid by borrowers, for two reasons: First, it would be difficult to put together a meaningful time series of borrowers' rates because of credit rationing and borrowing costs other than "interest." Second, borrowers' rates correspond closely to the cost of holding money,

TABLE 8

REAL INCOME PER CAPITA AND THE COST OF MONEY SUBSTITUTES, 1919–51

Year	Real Income per Capita*	Cost of Money Substitutes†
1919.	$ 553	0.9
1920.	477	−0.4
1921.	392	0.4
1922.	474	1.5
1923.	534	0.9
1924.	520	1.8
1925.	533	1.5
1926.	542	0.9
1927.	540	0.9
1928.	551	0.1
1929.	586	−0.6
1930.	510	1.5
1931.	437	3.2
1932.	342	4.2
1933.	341	4.2
1934.	401	4.0
1935.	456	3.7
1936.	510	3.7
1937.	556	3.0
1938.	515	3.4
1939.	634	3.2
1940.	614	3.0
1941.	740	2.8
1942.	871	2.6
1943.	1,003	2.5
1944.	1,056	2.3
1945.	1,016	2.1
1946.	914	1.9
1947.	864	1.9
1948.	887	1.7
1949.	852	1.5
1950.	926	1.5
1951.	970	0.9

* Real income per capita derived from two series for national income, divided by annual population estimates (U.S. Department of Commerce, Bureau of the Census, *Historical Statistics*, Series B-31) and a consumer price index (*ibid.*, Series L-41). The national income estimates for 1929–51 were taken from U.S. Department of Commerce, *Survey of Current Business, National Income Supplement* (July, 1951), Table 1, as revised by the July, 1952, issue. The figures for 1919–28 were derived by multiplying the national income series in U.S. Congress, Senate, Committee on Banking and Currency, Print No. 4 (79th Cong., 1st sess. [1945]), *Basic Facts on Employment and Production*, Table E-2, by 1.0492.

† Cost of money substitutes is bond yields (see Table 4) minus rates on prime commercial paper (four to six months) (Board of Governors of the Federal Reserve System, *Banking and Monetary Statistics* and *Federal Reserve Bulletins*).

and it is likely that these variables largely neutralize one another.[96] As Table 7 indicates, fairly strong negative relations exist between this measure of cost of money substitutes and both velocity concepts. Thus a decline (increase) in cost of money substitutes is associated with a rise (fall) in velocity, as one would expect.

The evidence presented so far in this study suggests that cost of money substitutes has been a more important determinant of D_m in the United States during the period 1919–51 than either cost of holding money or real income per capita. Whatever the value of this finding, it is probably true that each objective variable, as well as expectations and tastes, has influenced D_m to some extent. These variables should be regarded as supplementing one another rather than as competing explanations of changes in D_m. Clearly this is a problem calling for multivariate analysis.

Taking deposit turnover as dependent variable and the three objective determinants of D_m as independent variables,[97] I obtained the following regression equation:

$$\text{Deposit turnover} = 42.82 - 2.1478\,r_m \tag{3}$$
$$- 0.0190 y / N - 2.8562\,r_{ms} \,.$$

The correlation coefficient has the unusually high value of 0.937, and the standard error of the estimate is 1.58.

Although these results are striking, they should not be accepted hastily, especially since equation (3) has the peculiar property of a negative coefficient for cost of holding money. This is not altogether surprising, since a decline in bond yields has at least two aspects: money is less expensive to hold in terms of sacrificed income, but less cash need be held, since credit is available on better terms. There is no reason to expect these opposing tendencies to offset each other precisely.

Actually, adjusted bond yields add little to the multiple regression analysis of deposit turnover and the objective determinants of D_m. In fact, dropping bond yields from the analysis scarcely affects the correlation: computation on this basis yielded a coefficient of 0.915, with standard error of 1.87. The following equation describes this relationship:

$$\text{Deposit turnover} = 32.09 - 0.0137\ y / N - 2.8727\,r_{ms} \,. \tag{4}$$

In twenty-one of the thirty-three years equation (4) gives estimates of deposit turnover as good as or better than those obtained from (3).

96. See p. 210.

97. I have taken bond yields minus the yield on money as cost of holding money. See Tables 4 and 8 for sources of data.

Partial correlation analysis provides further clues regarding the influence of adjusted bond yields on D_m. When y/N and r_{ms} are held constant, the partial correlation coefficient between deposit turnover and adjusted bond yields is -0.43. The partial coefficients are -0.83 for deposit turnover and y/N and -0.90 for deposit turnover and r_{ms}. It is clear that bond yields, adjusted for the yield on money, are not related to velocity in the positive manner usually assumed. Thus the conclusions of Section IV are reinforced by multivariate analysis involving other determinants of D_m as well as cost of holding money.

Quite apart from such questions, however, it would be premature to conclude from equations (3) and (4) that the cost of money substitutes and real income per capita alone determine V_t. These equations "prove" too much, as the historical analysis of the following section indicates. There are periods during which tastes and expectations must have greatly influenced V_t. As I argued earlier in discussing tastes, changes in the volume of transactions will almost certainly lead to variations in V_t. Further, as the following subsection suggests, non-proportionality of velocities probably affects V_t as well as V_y; there have been important instances of this since 1919, if deposit turnover is accepted as a rough index of V_t.

It is obvious that the high correlations associated with equations (3) and (4) reflect mainly the trends of deposit turnover, cost of money substitutes, and real income per capita since 1919. The pitfalls of attaching significance to correlation analysis of time series are well known and need not be elaborated here.

F. THE TRANSITION TO V_y

Up to this point little has been said about the central concept of this study, V_y. Ordinarily one would expect proportionate movements in V_t and V_y,[98] but divergent or convergent movements may occur for several reasons. Since V_t and V_y have identical denominators, divergence or convergence implies variation in the ratio of their numerators, PT/Y. Variations in this ratio must reflect either relative price movements or changes in T/y, where y is the real value of monetary income. I shall discuss each of these cases in terms of *divergence* of velocities; obviously changes the opposite of those to be discussed will lead to convergence.

1. *Relative price movements.*—Let us assume a decline in prices of cur-

---

98. If money and volume of transactions are constant, V_t can rise only if the price level rises proportionately. But prices of currently produced goods will rise along with other prices, and, if real income is constant, it follows that money income and V_y must also rise.

rently produced ("income") goods and services and a compensatory rise in prices of other goods and services, P remaining constant. If M and T are constant, then $V_t(=PT/M)$ is unchanged; but Y and hence $V_y(=Y/M)$ will fall if y is constant. Alternatively, the relative decline in prices of income goods may occur through a rise in P, in which case the divergence between V_t and V_y will take the form of a rise in V_t, V_y being unchanged. Or, the divergence may involve a rise in V_t *and* a fall in V_y, the rise and fall in this case being of lesser magnitudes.

2. *Changes in* T/y.—There are at least three ways in which the ratio T/y may change, with resultant divergence of velocities.[99] The first pertains to the volume of financial transactions. Monetary payments are either financial (T_f) or non-financial (T_{nf}). Financial transactions are those "outside" the flow of currently produced goods and services (e.g., sales of securities and real estate). If T_{nf}, M, and y are unchanged, an increase in T_f will bring about divergence. Since T has increased, either V_t must rise, thus diverging from a constant V_y, or P, Y, and V_y must fall, divergence again taking place. Such an increase in T_f might be associated with periods of intense speculative activity, or it might occur secularly as brokerage costs decline or wealth accumulates relative to income.

A second type of variation in T/y may result from vertical disintegration.[100] Disintegration may take either of two forms: (1) with a constant composition of output firms may become more specialized or (2) products involving greater specialization may become relatively more important in the economy. In either case there will be an increase in T_{nf} because of greater interfirm transactions, and divergence of velocities will result.[101] A third conceivable source of divergence is that T/y may increase because of a shift of barter transactions to the monetary economy. The same effect will result from a shift of income payments *away from* the monetary economy: y will fall relatively more than T, and hence T/y will increase.

The particular reasons for non-proportionality of velocities are less important than the *form* it takes. Divergence may mean a rise in V_t, with V_y stable; a fall in V_y, with V_t stable; or a rise in V_t and a fall in V_y.

99. The changes discussed may induce relative price movements in addition to variations in T/y. The present discussion ignores such movements.

100. Many economists have vigorously debated the relation of integration to velocity. For references to this controversy see A. W. Marget, "The Relation between the Velocity of Circulation of Money and the 'Velocity of Circulation of Goods,' " *Journal of Political Economy*, August, 1932, pp. 490–96, and H. S. Ellis, *German Monetary Theory, 1905–1933* (Cambridge, Mass.: Harvard University Press, 1937), pp. 134–37 and 148–53.

101. If small firms hold larger cash balances in relation to payments than large firms, vertical disintegration will cause further declines in V_t, P, and V_y.

Obviously, the student of money income must determine which of these possibilities corresponds to the facts.

The answer depends largely on the relative importance of cash as a medium of exchange and as a store of value.[102] If the former function is paramount, divergence implies a decline in V_y, with V_t stable. Assume, for instance, that T_f increases while T_{nf}, y, M, and relative prices are unchanged. The increased volume of transactions will lead to a desire for more money in real terms. Since M is fixed, real balances can rise only if prices fall. If the rise in desired real balances is proportional to the rise in T, these changes will not affect V_t. V_y, however, will fall to the same relative extent as T has increased.

The crucial assumption here is that the demand for real balances is proportional to T. If some real balances are held as a store of value independently of T, the results will differ.[103] The price level will not decline as much as T rises. Hence V_t will rise somewhat, and V_y will not fall as much as under the first set of assumptions.

If one pushes this line of reasoning to an extreme, one can imagine a situation in which money has no value as a medium of exchange. A rise in T_{nf} would then have no effect on desired real balances. P and V_y would therefore be unchanged, while V_t would rise to the same relative extent as the increase in T.

Clearly, the last set of assumptions is a caricature of reality: divergence and convergence certainly do not affect V_t alone. In my judgment it is also unlikely that only V_y changes when divergence occurs. The issue is whether V_t or V_y is the stabler magnitude, in the absence of changes in the determinants of D_m. There is little evidence bearing on this question, although it is interesting to note that when one substitutes V_y for deposit turnover in equation (3), the correlation coefficient is substantially lower: 0.763 for V_y as against 0.937 for deposit turnover. The following regression equation describes this relationship:

$$V_y = 0.800 + 0.0831 r_m + 0.0002 y/N - 0.1445 r_{ms} . \quad (5)$$

The standard error of the estimate is 0.153. A possible explanation of the difference between equations (3) and (5) is that divergence and convergence, which neither equation takes account of, have a greater influence on V_y than on V_t. This interpretation is supported somewhat when equation (5) is reformulated by replacing r_m with the ratio, deposit turn-

102. See my earlier discussion of tastes, pp. 207–8.

103. It is conceivable that proportionality between desired real balances and T would not exist even though money were valued solely as a medium of exchange.

over $/V_y$. The resultant correlation coefficient is 0.843, the standard error 0.127. This regression is described by equation (6):

$$V_y = 2.614 - 0.0492 \text{ deposit turnover}/V_y$$
$$- 0.0006y/N - 0.1596r_{ms} \ . \tag{6}$$

Even if one concludes that non-proportionality of velocities affects V_y more than V_t, it seems clear nevertheless that this factor is an important determinant of D_m and V_t. As we shall see in Section VI, this hypothesis agrees well with observed velocity behavior since 1919.

VI. An Interpretation of Changes in Income Velocity

A. INTRODUCTION

The preceding section dealt with two main problems: the elaboration of a framework for analyzing changes in velocity and the formulation of particular hypotheses concerning these changes. I examined these hypotheses with the aid of several time series for the thirty-three-year period 1919–51. It is desirable to supplement this discussion by investigating the great secular fall in V_y before 1919.[104] Further, a study of relatively short subperiods since 1919 may help overcome the trend problem noted in Section V;[105] in addition, it may provide clues about the specific causes of non-proportionality between deposit turnover and V_y.

B. THE SECULAR DECLINE IN V_y: 1839–1919

Explanations of the secular decline in V_y fall into two groups. Those that imply diverging trends for V_t and V_y include (1) a decrease in prices of currently produced goods and services relative to the general price level; (2) an increase in financial transactions relative to income; (3) an increase in non-financial transactions relative to income (i.e., vertical disintegration); and (4) a shift of non-income barter transactions to the monetary economy, or a shift of monetary income to the non-monetary economy. The other explanations, which imply proportionality between V_t and V_y, are the determinants of D_m defined in Section V: (5) a decreased cost of holding money; (6) an increased cost of money substitutes; (7) a rise in real income per capita; (8) a change in tastes, including under this heading an increased volume of transactions; and (9) a change in expectations. For periods during which V_t and V_y were more or less proportional the first four hypotheses become irrelevant, and the problem is then one of selecting among hypotheses (5) through (9).

The only clue to the trend of V_t before 1919 is the ratio of bank clear-

---

104. See pp. 187–90.   105. See p. 215.

ings to deposits, a crude indicator of V_t at best. It completely ignores the velocity of currency—a shortcoming of deposit turnover as well. Nor are clearings necessarily a constant percentage of bank debits. The scope of clearings series has increased over time, and clearings-deposits ratios therefore have an upward bias.[106] Hart's ratio of clearings to total deposits has a slight downward trend for 1875–1914.[107] In view of the upward bias of this series, it is likely that V_t fell during this period. The tenuous evidence does not indicate whether the rate of decline was the same as that of V_y, but the trends of the two velocities probably did not differ greatly during this period. Prior to 1875 we have no indication whatever of the relation between V_y and V_t.

If V_t and V_y fell at about the same rate during 1875–1919,[108] causal factors associated with divergences between V_t and V_y were not responsible for these changes. The determinants of D_m must have played the major role. Speculation about changes in tastes and expectations during this early period is pointless, except for the indisputable fact that total transactions must have risen steadily. This change tended to decrease D_m and increase V_t and V_y, provided the accompanying rise in real income did not completely (or more than) offset this effect. It is possible, of course, that wealth rose even more rapidly than transactions, in which case the reverse effects took place.

One can speak more definitely about the objective determinants of D_m —cost of holding money, cost of money substitutes, and real income per capita. The cost of holding money, although not closely related to V_y during 1919–51 (see Sec. IV), may have been more important in earlier years. Annual data for measures of cost of holding money begin in 1857 (railroad bond yields) and 1871 (dividend yields on common stocks), but there are no continuous annual V_y series before 1899. However, V-39 provides annual estimates once a decade after 1839. Table 9 presents the relevant portions of V-39, V-40, and three measures of cost of holding money. Data for 1859–99 suggest a fairly close relation between V_y and cost of holding money: both V-39 and railroad-bond yields fell sharply during this period.

For 1899–1919 the following correlation coefficients were obtained for V-40 and cost of holding money: $+0.24$ (bond yields), $+0.16$ ("total" yields), and $+0.15$ (rate of change of wholesale prices).[109] Deduction of

106. For a detailed description of clearings and debits data see Garvy, *op. cit.* In the text I have assumed that deposits data are less subject to this bias.

107. *Money, Debt, and Economic Activity,* Fig. 3, p. 164.

108. Both probably *rose* during 1914–19.

109. See footnotes to Table 9 for descriptions of these series.

the yield on money from cost of holding money might strengthen these weak relationships, but this cannot be done because deposit-interest data are lacking.[110] It seems clear that this correction would have negligible effects on the correlations computed above. Cost of holding money may

TABLE 9*

ESTIMATES OF INCOME VELOCITY AND THE COST OF
HOLDING MONEY, SELECTED YEARS, 1839–1919

Year	V-39	V-40	Total Yields, Common Stocks	Railroad-Bond Yields	Rate of Change, Wholesale Prices
1839........	6.35				
1849........	7.91				
1859........	6.09			6.368	
1869........	3.23			6.717	
1879........	2.50			4.922	
1889........	2.20			3.599	
1899........	1.87	1.87	28.5	3.226	7.63
1900........		1.77	1.8	3.202	7.47
1901........		1.66	32.4	3.219	− 1.43
1902........		1.65	10.7	3.364	6.51
1903........		1.66	− 9.9	3.586	1.19
1904........		1.64	1.8	3.565	.17
1905........		1.58	32.2	3.491	.67
1906........		1.60	11.4	3.600	2.83
1907........		1.58	−14.2	4.062	5.50
1908........		1.56	4.1	3.841	− 3.53
1909........	1.64	1.64	30.2	3.727	7.47
1910........		1.63	1.0	3.866	4.14
1911........		1.55	3.6	3.873	− 7.81
1912........		1.53	1.8	3.931	6.47
1913........		1.59	− 6.1	4.138	1.01
1914........		1.53	− 0.4	4.225	− 2.44
1915........		1.55	8.9	4.285	2.06
1916........		1.58	21.6	4.086	23.02
1917........		1.63	− 3.3	4.695	37.43
1918........		1.79	− 4.7	4.824	11.74
1919........	1.75	1.75	23.2	4.927	5.56

* Sources: (1) "Total Yields, Common Stocks," computed in same manner and from same sources as "Total Yields, Common Stocks" column of Table 6; (2) "Railroad-Bond Yields" (adjusted index), F. R. Macaulay, *Some Theoretical Problems Suggested by the Movements of Interest Rates, Bond Yields and Stock Prices in the United States since 1856* (New York: National Bureau of Economic Research, 1938), pp. A 142– A 161 ("highs"); and (3) year-to-year percentage changes in the Bureau of Labor Statistics' Wholesale Price Index (1926 = 100). See Appendix C for descriptions of V-39 and V-40.

110. The deposits-money ratio is a rough indicator of the yield on money. Beginning in 1899 at 0.824, this ratio rose steadily to 0.912 in 1917, then fell to 0.887 in 1918 and 0.890 in 1919. Thus the yield on money probably rose steadily from 1899 to 1917 and fell from 1917 to 1919. If this is true, cost of holding money would have shown a slightly stronger downward trend during 1899–1917, when V-40 was falling, and the reverse would have been true for 1917–19, when V-40 was rising.

have played an important part in the decline of V_y before 1899, but we may conclude that it was a minor factor from 1899 to 1919.

Let us consider the cost of money substitutes, as measured by the difference between long- and short-term interest rates. A rise (fall) in this variable implies a rise (fall) in D_m and hence a fall (rise) in V_t. Except for the period 1873–78, rates on prime commercial paper (four to six months) were generally substantially above rates on long-term railroad bonds until 1915.[111] From about 1890 to 1915 the trends of the two interest series converged, which means that the cost of money substitutes was rising, as one would expect while velocity was falling. A weak negative correlation coefficient (-0.18) exists between V-40 and railroad-bond yields minus prime commercial paper rates for 1899–1919.

On the other hand, presumably credit markets were improving throughout the period before 1919. The reduced spread between effective rates borrowers paid and those lenders received should have exerted an upward influence on V_t, and therefore on V_y. In view of the fact that V_y (and apparently V_t) *fell* during these years, this factor complicates the problem of explaining observed changes in V_y.

Real income per capita rose steadily from 1869 to 1919 except for cyclical downturns.[112] If the income elasticity of D_m was greater than zero for the American economy during those years, this rise caused V_t and V_y to fall. I have already reviewed the meager evidence we have about this elasticity.[113] In my judgment it is undoubtedly positive. Along with the decline in cost of holding money and perhaps a moderate divergence of velocities associated with increased transactions relative to income, the rise in real income per capita during 1839–1919 probably is responsible for most of the observed decline in V_y.

C. DIVERGENCE OF VELOCITIES, 1919–29

During the 1920's, and particularly from 1924 to 1929, the two velocities diverged, if deposit turnover is used as an index of V_t: V_y fell, and deposit turnover rose.[114] As previously indicated, this divergence springs from one or more of the following causes: (1) a fall in prices of currently

111. The relation between long and short rates can be studied conveniently from charts prepared by the Board of Governors of the Federal Reserve System, *Federal Reserve Charts on Bank Credit, Money Rates, and Business, Historical Supplement* (Washington, D.C., September, 1952), p. 39.

112. See Robert F. Martin, *National Income in the United States, 1799–1938* (New York: National Industrial Conference Board, 1939), Table 1, pp. 6–7.

113. See pp. 205–7.

114. For a description of the deposit-turnover series used throughout this chapter see footnotes to Table 4.

produced (i.e., "income") goods relative to prices in general; (2) an increase in financial transactions relative to income; (3) an increase in non-financial transactions relative to income (i.e., vertical disintegration); and (4) a shift of non-income barter transactions to the monetary economy or of income payments to the non-monetary economy.

It does not seem possible to explain the divergence of velocities in terms of the fourth of these causes. Agriculture has been declining in relative importance for many decades, and cash crops have become more important within agriculture. Both trends imply that income payments in kind have been shrinking faster than other payments in kind. Moreover, financial transactions (bank clearances, brokers' accounts, etc.) increasingly take place on a barter basis. These developments tend to make V_t and V_y converge.

Prices of income goods showed little net change from 1919 to 1929, while a more comprehensive price index rose moderately.[115] All indexes reached postwar troughs in 1922. From 1922 to 1929 the consumer price index rose from 119.7 to 122.5, the wholesale index fell from 96.7 to 95.3, and the general index rose from 158 to 179.[116] Rising stock prices account for most of the disparity between the general price index and the others. These relative price movements account for a minor part of the divergence between V_t and V_y. In 1929 V_t was 49.4 per cent higher than it would have been had the 1919 ratio to V_y continued; on the other hand, general prices in 1929 were only 4.4 per cent higher than they would have been on the basis of the 1919 ratio to consumer prices.

Thus divergence of velocities in the 1920's was probably due either to an increase in financial payments relative to income or to vertical disintegration. The former undoubtedly had a potent influence in this direction: from 1919 to 1929 the number of shares traded on the New York Stock Exchange increased nearly fourfold.[117] Angell's finding that the rise in V_t during the late 1920's was more pronounced in New York City than in 140 other cities supports this.[118]

There is less agreement about the trend of vertical integration during the 1920's. Most economists regard that decade as a period of increasing

115. Consumer and wholesale indexes are the best indicators of prices of final output (see U.S. Department of Commerce, Bureau of the Census, *Historical Statistics of the United States* [Washington, D.C.: Government Printing Office, 1949], Series L-15, L-40, and L-41). A "general" price index, computed by Carl Snyder and Rufus S. Tucker, is reproduced *ibid.*, Series L-1.

116. See *ibid.* for sources. The base years are not identical, of course.

117. U.S. Department of Commerce, Bureau of the Census, *Historical Statistics*, Series N-228.

118. *The Behavior of Money*, Chart XIV.

business concentration through mergers.[119] However, many of these mergers involved firms that had not formerly made payments to one another, and they probably did not reduce the volume of non-financial payments appreciably. Furthermore, the pronounced movement of the economy away from agriculture, and particularly away from subsistence farming during the 1920's, meant that a larger part of total output originated in sectors where the division of labor had proceeded far and where interfirm payments were consequently great. Even aside from such shifts in the composition of output, it is likely that growth of market areas resulted in the shedding of functions by established firms to newly formed and more specialized firms.[120]

If interfirm payments increase relative to total payments, and if firms maintain their customary payments-money ratios, firms will hold a larger fraction of total money. Thus a study of the changing distribution of cash among sectors of the economy may provide important clues to the causes of divergence and convergence. Here again the needed data are crude or totally lacking, 1929 being the earliest year for which we have information. The best available estimates of the 1929–50 distribution of cash (Table 10) indicate that in 1929 corporate businesses (excluding insurance companies) held only 18.6 per cent of the total money stock.[121] If businesses held as little as 5 per cent of all money in 1839, and if every dollar held by businesses supported five times the volume of expenditures supported by dollars held elsewhere in both years, then rising interfirm payments would have caused at most a 40 per cent decline in V_y relative to V_t.[122] Actually V_y had fallen by more than 75 per cent of its 1839 value in 1929. Even on the basis of these generous assumptions, vertical disintegration leaves unexplained a major portion of the secular decline in V_y since 1839 and particularly of the more than 30 per cent decline in V_y relative to V_t from 1919 to 1929. It appears that the increase in financial

119. George W. Stocking and Myron W. Watkins, *Monopoly and Free Enterprise* (New York: Twentieth Century Fund, 1951), pp. 39–41.

120. George J. Stigler, "The Division of Labor Is Limited by the Extent of the Market," *Journal of Political Economy*, June, 1951, pp. 185–93.

121. Of course, this figure would be slightly higher if cash holdings of unincorporated businesses had been included.

122. This result is derived from the following relationship:

$$V_t / V_y = a\, n / (1 - a) + 1 ,$$

where a is the percentage of all cash held by businesses and n is the ratio of sector velocities, $V_{t(\text{business})}/V_{t(\text{non-business})}$. The ratio V_t/V_y was computed for 1839 and 1929; then, on the assumption that V_t was the same in 1839 and 1929, the ratio $V_{y(1929)}/V_{y(1839)}$ was obtained.

payments, in which the general public actively participated, was the principal cause of divergence of velocities during the 1920's.

The above analysis related only to the causes of *divergence*. When one turns to the broader problem of why V_y declined, three interpretations are possible. First, divergence may have affected only V_y, causing it to fall in spite of other forces that pushed V_t upward. Second, divergence may have affected only V_t, causing it to rise in spite of forces that pushed V_y downward. Third, divergence may have been partly responsible for *both* the fall in V_y and the rise in V_t.

The first interpretation agrees poorly with the facts during this period. Between 1919 and 1929 the objective determinants of D_m all implied *declines* in V_t and V_y: cost of holding money fell slightly, cost of money

TABLE 10

PERCENTAGE OF TOTAL MONEY HELD BY MAJOR
SECTORS OF THE ECONOMY, 1929–50

YEAR	TOTAL MONEY (BILLIONS)	PERCENTAGE OF TOTAL HELD BY				
		U.S. Government	Rest of World	Corporate Businesses	State and Local Governments	All Others
1929......	55.5	0.4	2.2	18.6	4.1	74.8
1930......	54.2	0.6	2.0	18.3	4.0	75.1
1931......	49.0	1.0	1.8	16.3	3.9	76.9
1932......	45.7	1.1	1.5	16.6	3.7	77.0
1933......	42.8	2.3	0.9	16.6	4.2	75.9
1934......	48.4	3.7	1.0	16.1	5.4	73.8
1935......	53.3	2.8	1.9	16.1	5.8	73.4
1936......	58.3	2.0	2.2	15.6	5.7	74.4
1937......	57.6	1.7	2.4	14.8	5.7	75.3
1938*.....	60.7	3.0	3.0	15.8	5.9	72.3
1938†.....	63.2	7.1	3.0	15.3	5.8	68.7
1939*.....	65.9	2.3	4.2	16.2	5.3	71.9
1939†.....	68.4	5.7	4.4	15.8	5.3	68.8
1940......	75.2	4.4	4.9	17.4	5.3	68.0
1941......	82.2	6.0	4.1	16.8	5.1	68.0
1942......	104.3	10.9	3.4	16.9	4.4	64.3
1943......	127.9	10.4	3.4	16.9	3.9	65.4
1944......	156.0	15.1	2.9	13.8	3.3	64.8
1945......	180.8	15.4	2.8	12.0	3.2	66.5
1946......	171.7	3.4	3.0	13.3	4.0	76.4
1947......	175.3	2.1	2.9	14.3	4.4	76.3
1948......	176.1	2.8	3.2	14.1	4.8	75.1
1949......	177.3	3.0	3.3	14.6	5.0	74.0
1950......	184.4	2.7	3.4	14.6	5.1	74.2

* Data for these and all preceding years are from Solomon Shapiro, "The Distribution of Deposits and Currency in the United States, 1929–39," *Journal of the American Statistical Association*, December, 1943.

† Data for these and all succeeding years are from Daniel H. Brill, "Progress Report on the Money-flows Study" (Washington, D.C.: Board of Governors of the Federal Reserve System, 1951). (Mimeographed.) There may be substantial revisions in these data.

substitutes rose somewhat, and real income per capita continued to rise. If the rise in financial payments relative to income is counted as a factor tending to decrease V_y, we have several explanations of the behavior of V_y but only tastes and expectations remain to account for a large increase in deposit turnover. Almost certainly divergence was responsible in part for the changes in both velocities. Therefore, the determinants of the moderate decline in V_y during 1919–29 appear to be the rises in financial payments relative to income, cost of money substitutes, and real income per capita, and the fall in cost of holding money. Deposit turnover probably rose during this period because of the growth in transactions, both absolutely and relative to income, and changed expectations.

D. PROPORTIONATE CHANGES: 1929–33

This period of crisis and depression was marked by sharp and roughly proportionate drops in V_y and deposit turnover with partial recoveries in 1933. The problem of interpretation here is particularly difficult, for it is probably true that an explanation of changes of velocity during such circumstances would amount to an explanation of the business cycle itself·

Nevertheless, certain general inferences may be made about the forces responsible for the sharp decline in velocity during this period. The cost of holding money may well have been one of these; the rate of change in wholesale prices and total yields on common stocks both fell drastically from 1929 to 1932 and recovered strongly in 1933.[123] However, a third measure of cost of holding money, bond yields minus the yield on money, actually increased from 3.0 in 1929 to 4.2 in 1932. Perhaps a more important factor was the dramatic rise in cost of money substitutes, as short rates fell far below long rates for the first time since 1866.[124] In addition, credit rationing was much more stringent than a few years earlier.

On the other hand, real income per capita fell sharply, a change that should have been associated with rising velocity, according to the hypothesis presented in Section V. Apparently the uncertainty and adverse expectations created by rapid declines in income overwhelmed the income effect itself. Throughout the period 1929–33 the threat of reduced incomes and unemployment undoubtedly induced people to build up contingency reserves. This factor, together with the changes in cost of holding money and cost of money substitutes noted above, appears to account adequately for changes in velocity in this period.

123. See Tables 4 and 6 for these series.

124. Short rates were slightly below long rates in 1878, 1905, 1906, 1924, 1925, and 1926.

V_y rose steadily during the next decade except for declines in 1938 and 1943. Deposit turnover had the same general pattern of movements during 1933–38 but rose less rapidly than V_y. It fell in 1939, 1940, and 1942, while V_y was rising, and rose in 1943, while V_y fell. By the end of the period, V_y was 80 per cent above its 1933 value, while deposit turnover had fallen by 19 per cent. Thus there was a strong convergence of the two series—more than enough to reverse the trend of the 1920's.

A fall in the general price level relative to prices of current output could have caused this convergence, but examination of various price indexes indicates that relative price movements alone would have produced *divergence* of velocities. From 1933 to 1938 an index of general prices rose at almost the same rate as a wholesale index. A consumer price index, on the other hand, rose less rapidly.[125] The general price index terminates in 1938, but for the entire period 1933–43 wholesale prices increased by about 56 per cent, as compared with a 34 per cent rise in consumer prices. Since stock prices showed little net change from 1939 to 1943, prices in general may have risen somewhat less than the wholesale index. Even so, it seems likely that they at least kept pace with prices of current output during 1933–43.

The analysis of changes in non-monetary transactions during the 1920's applies here as well.[126] The percentage of national income originating in agriculture continued to decline slowly.[127] This and other developments probably caused income payments in kind to fall relative to other payments in kind and thereby tended to bring about convergence of velocities.

Vertical integration could have been a further cause of convergence. However, an examination of cash holdings by major sectors of the economy (Table 10) does not support this hypothesis: corporate businesses held a slightly greater portion of all money in 1943 than in 1933.[128] Unless business D_m increased relative to D_m in other parts of the economy, convergence of velocities did not result from a reduction in non-financial payments relative to income.

125. See U.S. Department of Commerce, Bureau of the Census, *Historical Statistics* Series L-1, L-15, and L-41.

126. See p. 222.

127. U.S. Department of Commerce, *Survey of Current Business, National Income Supplement, 1951*, Table 13.

128. Of course, vertical integration does not necessarily imply a reduction in interfirm payments. Integrated firms may continue to hold their own cash balances and to make money payments to other units of the combine.

Probably the major reason for convergence of velocities during 1933–43 was the decline in financial payments relative to income. In 1933 the ratio of debits at weekly reporting banks in New York City to debits at all reporting centers was 0.489. This ratio declined steadily to a low of 0.354 in 1942.[129] A large portion of debits at New York banks consists of financial payments. The volume of trading on the New York Stock Exchange declined substantially—further evidence that financial payments fell relative to all payments.[130] Also, in 1933, 14.4 per cent of national income originated in the financial, insurance, and real estate sectors; in 1943 only 7.2 per cent of the national income came from those sources, indicating a decline in the importance of brokerage and other financial services.[131]

As in the case of the 1920's, three interpretations of velocity movements from 1933 to 1943 are possible: that convergence caused V_y to rise in spite of other forces that decreased deposit turnover, that it caused deposit turnover to fall in spite of other forces that increased V_y, or that it was responsible in part for both the fall in deposit turnover and the rise in V_y. Empirically there is little basis for choice among these alternatives. The behavior of some determinants of D_m implied falling velocity; others implied the reverse. Changes in the cost of holding money and real income per capita were velocity-reducing in nature. Bond yields minus the yield on money fell somewhat, while two other measures of cost had no discernible trend. Real income per capita rose sharply during this period and may have depressed velocity. On the other hand, cost of money substitutes fell, a change that must have induced greater reliance on non-cash sources of liquidity. In addition, the adverse expectations and increased demand for contingency balances that had characterized the preceding period gradually reversed. On balance, it is likely that convergence contributed to both the rise in V_y and the fall in deposit turnover.

F. WARTIME DIVERGENCE: 1943–46

In 1943 V_y was at its highest level since 1925, and in the following year it was only slightly lower. By 1946, however, it had fallen by about 32 per cent, reaching its lowest value since 1935. Deposit turnover behaved somewhat differently. It had been at an early wartime peak in 1941 still far below its 1929 value. Deposit turnover declined by about 14 per cent

129. Computed from U.S. Department of Commerce, Bureau of the Census, *Historical Statistics*, Series N-76 and N-77.

130. *Ibid.*, Series N-228 and N-229.

131. Computed from U.S. Department of Commerce, *Survey of Current Business, National Income Supplement, 1951*, Table 13.

during 1943–46 to an all-time low in 1945. On net V_y fell moderately in relation to deposit turnover: in 1943 the ratio was 0.108; in 1946 it was only 0.085.

Relative price movements probably caused much of the wartime divergence of velocities. The wholesale index rose by 17.5 per cent during 1943–46, as compared to a 12.7 per cent rise in the consumer price index. Since stock prices rose by more than 35 per cent in this period, it is clear that prices in general rose more than prices of current output.[132]

A minor factor causing divergence was the growth of payments in kind.[133] However, the basic pattern of divergence remains even when consumption expenditures in kind are included in the numerator of V_y.

Apparently there was no increase in interfirm payments relative to income. On the contrary, cash holdings of corporate businesses fell sharply relative to total money during 1943–46 (see Table 10), suggesting that interfirm payments fell rather than rose in relation to national income.

Financial transactions probably increased somewhat during the war and thereby contributed to divergence between V_y and deposit turnover. The ratio of debits at New York City reporting banks to debits at all reporting centers rose from 0.374 in 1943 to 0.415 in 1945 and 0.398 in 1946.[134] The volume of trading on registered securities exchanges rose sharply,[135] and the percentage of national income originating in the financial, insurance, and real estate sectors rose slightly.

During this period the cost of holding money fell moderately if measured by either bond yields or total yields on common stocks (both less the yield on money). The rate of change of wholesale prices fell from 1942 to 1944 but increased markedly from 1945 to 1946.[136] These changes in cost of holding money have doubtful significance as determinants of velocity. Nor do changes in cost of money substitutes and real income per capita satisfactorily explain wartime velocity behavior: short rates drifted upward as long rates declined; real income per capita rose from 1943 to 1944 but declined in the next two years as velocity continued to fall.

132. U.S. Department of Commerce, Bureau of the Census, *Statistical Abstract of the United States, 1949*, Tables 339, 345, and 515. Price, income, and velocity figures are undoubtedly understated (although not uniformly) during the period of wartime price control.

133. U.S. Department of Commerce, *Survey of Current Business, National Income Supplement, 1951*, Table 39.

134. Computed from U.S. Department of Commerce, Bureau of the Census, *Statistical Abstract, 1949*, Table 472.

135. *Ibid.*, Table 512.

136. See Tables 4 and 6.

If the wartime declines in V_t and V_y were not in fact spurious, they probably resulted from various sorts of changes in tastes. One important change was the great increase in the federal government's economic activity, which meant that its cash behavior had a greater impact on aggregate D_m. Increased government spending might be expected to produce a *decrease* in D_m and *rising* velocity, but such was not the case. The ratio of government expenditures to government-held cash declined much more sharply than either V_y or deposit turnover during this period.[137] And, although government probably holds less cash relative to expenditures than do households as a rule, it holds much more than do businesses.

A second change in tastes was the increased precautionary demand for cash. During the war this reflected the extensive movement of people about the country. As demobilization got under way, uncertainty about jobs provided an additional source of demand for contingency balances.

Tastes changed in a different sense as a result of direct governmental controls. Because many commodities were rationed explicitly and others (e.g., automobiles) were totally unavailable for the civilian population, the range of alternatives to the holding of cash decreased. Income that in the absence of controls would have been spent on certain commodities was allocated to other uses. Among the latter, of course, was the increased consumption of the services of money through holding larger cash balances.

The arguments of the three preceding paragraphs explain most of the wartime velocity changes, but they do not tell the whole story. In part the changes themselves are spurious in that they have been computed from income figures that reflect fictitious prices. The velocity of money did not fall as much as official statistics indicate.

G. PROPORTIONATE CHANGES: 1946–51

V_y and deposit turnover both rose from 1946 to 1948, fell in 1949, and rose again in 1950 and 1951. A rough proportionality was maintained between the two series over this period: V_y rose by 46 per cent; deposit turnover, by 40 per cent.

Two measures of cost of holding money, bond yields and total yields on common stocks (both minus the yield on money), had rising trends, as

---

137. The following rough estimates of government spending in relation to cash holdings were made by dividing the government money figures implicit in Table 10 into federal government expenditures, as presented in U.S. Department of Commerce, *Survey of Current Business, National Income Supplement, 1951,* Table 8: 1943, 6.5; 1944, 4.1; 1945, 3.1; and 1946, 6.39.

one would expect during a period of rising velocity. The rate of change of wholesale prices, on the other hand, was high in 1946, very high in 1947, low in 1948, negative in 1949, low in 1950, and fairly high in 1951—a net fall but no clearly defined trend either way. Once again no strong relationship between cost of holding money and velocity appeared. A change of some importance may have been the fall in real income per capita in 1947. However, this variable rose between 1949 and 1951 as velocity *increased*.

A more significant change during this period was the sharp rise in short-term interest rates, both absolutely and in relation to long-term rates. As a result the cost of money substitutes was halved, and D_m must have fallen somewhat. Still more important reasons for the velocity increases of 1946–48, however, are reversals of the wartime changes in tastes discussed above: the diminished economic role of government, the reduction in job uncertainty, the cessation of direct controls, and the return to authentic prices. By 1949 these forces had spent themselves, and the velocity rise in 1951 undoubtedly was largely expectational in nature.

H. IMPLICATIONS OF HISTORICAL ANALYSIS

The preceding historical analysis has important implications for the theory of monetary velocity. One of the conclusions of Sections IV and V—that cost of holding money, as measured by yields on various long-term securities, has played a minor role in velocity movements in the United States—has been confirmed by extension of the study to the years before 1919 and by the analysis of subperiods since then. The rise in per capita real income emerges as the major determinant of the secular decline in V_y.

On the other hand, analysis of subperiods since 1919 indicates that short-term movements are more closely related to tastes, the factors responsible for non-proportionality of velocities, and the cost of money substitutes. This brings us back to the question raised at the close of Section V concerning the validity of equations (3) and (4). The high correlation coefficients associated with these equations lose much of their significance when one examines the period 1919–51 in greater detail. Taken collectively, the objective determinants of D_m included in equations (3) and (4)—cost of holding money, cost of money substitutes, and real income per capita—fail to explain developments within most of these shorter segments of time.

One of the most interesting implications of the historical analysis is that the "store of value" function is an important motive for holding cash. As I indicated in Section V, if this motive is strong, a rise in transactions may decrease D_m and increase V_t and V_y. Moreover, if the ratio T/y increases as transactions rise, V_y will diverge from V_t. Velocity movements of the 1920's are difficult to explain if one denies importance to the "store of value" function of money. Apparently, the rise in transactions of that period—particularly in relation to income—was partly responsible for the sharp increase in deposit turnover and at the same time contributed to the decline in V_y.

VII. Concluding Remarks

The foregoing study of monetary velocity is an exploratory work. Much of it has dealt with definitional matters, examination of previous studies, and the creation of a suitable analytic framework. The difficult but important task of testing velocity hypotheses was barely begun.

On the analytic side, my basic approach has been to view velocity in terms of an orthodox demand function rather than as an arbitrary or mechanically determined number. This immediately suggests that velocity's determinants should be classified under the headings employed in traditional demand analysis: the price of the commodity, prices of related commodities, incomes, tastes, and expectations. Formulation of monetary counterparts has been troublesome for the first two headings, which I have termed "the cost of holding money" and "the cost of money substitutes," but I believe I have demonstrated beyond reasonable doubt the feasibility of analyzing velocity in this manner.

Empirically the study has not adequately explained all velocity changes in the United States, but it has narrowed the range of uncertainty. One of the study's main findings was that the cost of holding money, however measured, has been insignificant as a velocity determinant in the twentieth century. Probably this is because interest rates represent the cost of money substitutes to those who rely on credit to satisfy contingency needs. A rise in the rate of interest therefore means both that the holding of cash is more costly in terms of sacrificed alternatives and that the attractiveness of credit as a source of liquidity has diminished. The former tends to decrease the demand for money, while the latter tends to increase it, and the net effect may be negligible.

A further finding of some interest was the strong correlation for the period 1919–51 between deposit turnover and two independent variables, the cost of money substitutes and real income per capita. However, detailed study of this period dispelled the notion that velocity movements can be explained by only two key determinants. On analytic grounds it is apparent that non-proportionality between V_t and V_y probably affects both velocities in some measure. The experience of the 1920's supports this view: changes in cost of money substitutes and real income per capita both implied falling velocity, but deposit turnover rose sharply. The explanation probably lies in the marked divergence of velocities resulting from increased transactions relative to income. As long as a significant portion of cash is held as a store of wealth rather than as a medium of exchange, a rise in transactions relative to income will cause V_t to rise. Thus it is evident that the factors responsible for non-proportionality, and probably also tastes, must be added to the list of important determinants of velocity.

The main reason for non-proportionality has been the varying volume of financial payments relative to income rather than relative price movements, changes in non-monetary transactions, or variations in the degree of business integration. This implies that financial activities are more important determinants of income velocity and money income than they are usually thought to be.

Finally, the study has reached conclusions regarding the secular trend of V_y. Warburton's contention that V_y has fallen drastically during the past century or more is well founded. However, nearly all of the decline took place before 1919, and this hampers study of the trend's determinants. For several reasons it is unlikely that divergence caused a major portion of the decline in V_y. Probably the rise in real income per capita was much more important, aided perhaps by the decline in cost of holding money.

Perhaps it is worth asking why the theory of velocity has developed so slowly. One is tempted to blame Keynes and his followers, who have not been content with the development of a new analytic framework but have often ridiculed the few practitioners of monetary orthodoxy. However, the problem goes deeper than the rise of Keynesianism. For decades, as Keynes emphasized,[138] monetary theory was divorced from the main body of economic thought, and few economists understood the basic similarity between the demand for money and the demand for anything else. The Cambridge economists were on the right track, but unfortunately they presented the demand for money in the sterile form of a rectangular hyperbola, relating quantity of money to its *value* rather than to its *cost*.[139] In the United States Fisher did not analyze velocity in the traditional demand-and-supply framework, although he recognized several factors that influence the amount of money people wish to hold. The succeeding generation of economists, working with defective analytic tools, was unable to advance matters substantially. They tended to become pre-

138. *General Theory*, p. 292.   139. E.g., see Pigou, *op. cit.*

occupied with arithmetic examples designed to illuminate more or less mechanical aspects of money flows and did not develop the idea of a velocity function—a demand function for money.[140]

Hicks, in his famous 1935 article,[141] and Keynes, in the *General Theory*, deserve much credit for getting velocity theory back on the main track— although, paradoxically, both go out of their way to denounce the concept. The great merit of these works is that they view the demand for money in terms of the alternatives sacrificed by holders of cash. Once the dust settled after the "Keynesian Revolution," it became increasingly apparent that there was no conflict between this way of looking at money and the traditional velocity approach.

Ultimately, of course, the fate of the velocity concept will depend on its usefulness in economic forecasting, as compared with the Keynesian or other approaches. Nothing in the preceding pages bears directly on this issue: no income predictions were attempted, let alone comparison of such predictions with those yielded by other analytic frameworks. In my judgment, in any such comparison we should use not simple extrapolations of velocity but rather expressions derived from regression equations such as those presented in Section V. This is a neglected area of monetary research.

Undoubtedly the reliability of velocity-estimating relationships can be improved by studying velocity data from other countries, extending annual V_y series for the United States to the period before 1899, and studying quarterly velocity series more closely. Another promising line of attack is the development of sector velocities. This can be done at least crudely for corporate businesses as a whole as well as for subgroups within that sector.[142] It can also be done for the government sector. Sector velocities may throw new light on the reasons for variations in aggregate velocity. The Federal Reserve "flow-of-funds system of national accounts,"[143] while not set up ideally for velocity analysis, will nevertheless be useful in studies of differential cash-balances behavior by the major sectors of the economy.

In these and other ways, therefore, the concept of monetary velocity may soon be developed into a more useful tool of economic analysis than it has been up to now.

140. As a prime example see Ellis, *op. cit.*

141. J. R. Hicks, "A Suggestion for Simplifying the Theory of Money," *Economica*, II (new ser., 1935), 1–19.

142. See Robert Dean, "Corporate Cash Balances, Relation to Asset Size and Industrial Activity" (unpublished Master's thesis, Vanderbilt University, 1955).

143. This system is described in the *Federal Reserve Bulletin*, October, 1955.

APPENDIX A
THE DEFINITION OF INCOME VELOCITY
GENERAL CONSIDERATIONS

Anyone who works with income-velocity estimates will be impressed with the great variety of definitions employed. Appendix B describes definitional differences among the thirty-eight V_y series listed in Table 1. The main disagreements relate to three general issues: (1) Which of the many possible income concepts should be used? (2) What assets should be counted as money? (3) How should the governmental sector of the economy be treated? In this appendix I shall examine each of these issues. However, some problems of a broader nature must first be discussed.

The term "velocity of money" is a misnomer if taken literally. Economists are interested not in the speed and direction of money as it moves through space but in a quite different idea—the frequency with which money is spent. Monetary velocity is simply the average volume of transactions per unit of money, irrespective of the fact that some units are not spent at all. If all monetary transactions are included, the frequency indicator is called "transactions velocity."

Obviously a large number of other velocity concepts may be formed by restricting transactions to particular types. The "income velocity of money" (V_y) measures the frequency with which money is received as or paid out of income. It would be equally appropriate to measure the "consumption velocity of money" and so forth. These less-than-global velocities are just as legitimate frequency indicators as transactions velocity, for it is no more meaningful to object that some money is spent in other types of transactions than to complain that some money is never spent.

But frequency indicators per se are scarcely more interesting than the velocity of money in its literal sense. As economists we seek concepts that are useful for analysis of real problems, and some frequency indicators have little analytic relevance. The problem is to select among many frequency indicators those that deserve primary emphasis as tools of analysis. The selection will vary, of course, with the particular problem being analyzed.

For purposes of this study we are seeking a velocity concept that will be helpful in analyzing the determinants of aggregate money income. There are three major variants of the "velocity" approach to income analysis. (1) One may center attention on V_t, in which case the income determinants are classified on a threefold basis: the quantity of money, the demand for money in relation to the volume of transactions, and the ratio of total transactions to income (however defined). (2) Alternatively, if one emphasizes V_y, a different classification results: the quantity of money, the demand for money in relation to monetary income, and the ratio of monetary income to total income. (3) Finally, one may abandon true frequency indicators and directly study the ratio of total income to the quantity of money. In each case the analysis may be supplemented by study of sector velocities, as urged by Keynes and Marget.[144]

Let us begin by comparing the first two approaches. The demand for money in relation to monetary income is influenced by all the factors affecting V_t (viz., the cost of holding money and money substitutes, real income per capita, tastes, and expectations) plus other factors that cause variations in the ratio of income to total monetary transactions. If the latter ratio were essentially stable, it would make little difference which approach one selected. This would be true even though a particular determinant of D_m (e.g., real income) had a much more important influence on desired cash holdings than the others.

Almost certainly, however, the ratio of income to total transactions varies substantially over time. If the basic desire for money reflects its services as a store of value more than as a medium of exchange, an increase in non-income transactions (income remaining unchanged) will not greatly increase the demand for real balances. The result will be a more or less stable V_y and a rising V_t. Under such conditions the second approach listed above would be somewhat simpler for analysis of income determinants than the first. But if money is valued mainly as a medium of exchange, such a rise in non-income transactions implies a falling V_y and a more or less stable V_t. The choice of approaches in this case is largely a matter of individual taste, for one must take into account the same list of income determinants either way. Since the first approach is not superior to the second under any circumstances, while the second is preferable if money is valued highly as a store of wealth, there seems to be a slight advantage in the second approach.

Let us now compare the second and third approaches. The only argument for direct study of total income-money ratios appears to be based on the assumption that real income per capita is the main determinant of desired cash holdings. In this case, it is argued, "velocity" will be represented as a stabler magnitude than if the second approach is used, since *total* income in money terms more closely approximates real income than does *monetary* income in money terms. Although this is correct, provided

144. See Marget, *The Theory of Prices*, pp. 389–90.

that the ratio of monetary to total income does not remain constant, it is not clear that the third approach is superior to the second. The findings of Section V of this study indicate that real income per capita is not the only important determinant of D_m. Furthermore, since the ratio of monetary to total income appears to change only gradually, there is little difference between the approaches in practice. A more important consideration, in my judgment, is that the third approach lumps together two essentially dissimilar problems: the demand for money and the relative importance of non-monetary income. A given increase in real income will affect income-money ratios differently depending on whether it is monetary or non-monetary income. It seems wiser to adopt the second of the above approaches to "velocity" analysis, which explicitly separates these two factors.

ALTERNATIVE CONCEPTS OF INCOME

The way is now clear for us to deal with the problem of which income concept to use in V_y measures. Specifically, we must decide whether or not to include non-monetary items (e.g., rental value of durable consumers' goods), whether to use a "factor-cost" or "final sales" concept, and which particular variant to select. The treatment of government is discussed below.

The preceding subsection dealt with the first of these three problems. The conclusion reached there was that the velocity numerator probably should exclude non-monetary income, since the factors responsible for changes in its relative importance have little to do with decisions about how much money to hold. The issue is important primarily in the analysis of secular trends. A relative decline in non-monetary income would probably produce a falling trend in the *total* income-money ratio, whereas the *monetary* income-money ratio would rise.

With respect to the second and third problems, it seems wisest to select the income concept (minus non-monetary elements) most relevant to decisions about desired cash holdings. This eliminates changes in velocity that otherwise might occur because of non-proportionality between the concept actually selected and whatever concept serves as a guide in determining the amount of cash to be held. Good cases can be made for national income, net national product, and personal income. Perhaps capital gains should be included as well. Since the choice among these three alternatives is not clear cut, I have selected the income concepts I am particularly interested in studying—national income and net national product.

THE DEFINITION OF MONEY

By all odds the main issue in the definition of money for V_y ratios is whether or not it should include time deposits as well as currency and demand deposits. Analytically it makes little difference how one treats time deposits. If excluded, they must be brought into the analysis as close money substitutes. One cannot ignore time deposits in any case.

Empirically, however, there is a strong case for inclusion of these deposits. (1) Prior to 1892 data for demand deposits alone do not exist; estimates of V_y before this date necessarily include time deposits in money. (2) The present system of differential reserve requirements for demand and time deposits at member banks did not begin until 1917. Classifications of deposits are particularly suspect for the period 1892–1917, since precise classification did not have the significance to bankers and depositors then that it has had more recently. (3) Since 1917 there have been shifts between demand and time deposits because of changes in the conditions attached to each type of deposit. These reasons for including time deposits in money are particularly compelling for study of long-run trends. Hence the analysis in the text deals exclusively with V_y measures so defined.

A further definitional issue concerns cash held by the United States government. The following subsection discusses this problem as part of the larger question of the treatment of government in V_y estimates.

THE TREATMENT OF GOVERNMENT

There are four basic methods of treating government in V_y estimates: (1) include government in both terms of the V_y ratio; (2) include government in the numerator only; (3) include government in the denominator only; and (4) exclude government from both terms of the V_y ratio.

The second approach has been adopted most frequently. It is inappropriate in my judgment, since it includes payments in the numerator against which none of the cash in the denominator is being held. The argument presented above concerning the propriety of including non-monetary transactions in the V_y numerator applies equally here. A shift of economic activity from the private to the public sector of the economy would influence the ratio of *total* monetary income to *privately* held cash, even though real income and the volume of transactions were unchanged.

Nor is there any obvious merit in the third approach, unless one assumes that income originating in the government sector has no influence on desired cash holdings. There is no reason to think that one type of income affects behavior differently than does another.

Gordon has favored a V_y measure of the fourth type.[145] This represents a compromise between V_y proper and the sector velocities advocated by Keynes in the *Treatise on Money*.[146] However, as an approximation to V_y it is subject to the same criticism as that made of the third approach; and as a sector velocity it fails to exclude cash held by businesses as well as government-held cash from the denominator. This is truly a "hybrid conception."

Only the first approach listed above avoids these objections. Accordingly, the present study follows this approach throughout.

SUMMARY

The preceding discussion indicates that V_y is best defined in the following way, for purposes of analyzing income changes:

1. The numerator should consist of national income, net national product, or personal income, minus all non-monetary elements but including income originating in the government sector.

2. The denominator should consist of all currency outside banks and total deposits adjusted, including government deposits at Federal Reserve banks.

The particular definition employed, however, is less important than an awareness of the consequences of using one definition rather than another.

APPENDIX B

COMPARISON OF INCOME-VELOCITY ESTIMATES
FOR THE UNITED STATES

V_y estimates for any year typically disagree. Such differences arise because of variations in definitions, in basic data, and in methods of handling data. This appendix analyzes each of these sources of discrepancies among V_y estimates in greater detail than was feasible in Section III.

DEFINITIONAL DIFFERENCES

1. *The definition of money.*—Seventeen V_y series define money broadly to include time deposits as well as currency outside banks and demand deposits: V-1, V-5, V-7, V-9, V-15 to V-21, V-25 to V-28, V-30, and V-38. Inclusion of time deposits in money obviously means that the denominator of V_y is much larger than it otherwise would be and that V_y itself is smaller. Also, since the relative importance of time deposits has shifted

---

145. R. A. Gordon, "The Treatment of Government Spending in Income-Velocity Estimates," *American Economic Review*, March, 1950, pp. 152–59.

146. II, 22 ff.

from year to year, the two types of estimates often fail to change proportionately to one another. Consider V-5 and V-6, which are identical except for the exclusion of time deposits from V-6. In 1909, the initial year of these series, V-5 was 1.81, V-6, 3.25; the former was 55.7 per cent of the latter. Seventeen years later V-5 had fallen to 1.56, whereas V-6 had risen to 3.29; V-5 was only 47.4 per cent of V-6. One can readily understand why Angell[147] was able to find a steady *fall* in V_y (during 1909–28) at the same time that Currie[148] was calling attention to the *rise* in V_y (1921–30). Angell's measure of V_y included time deposits in money, while Currie's did not.

Only two V_y series, V-17 and V-25, include all government balances in money. However, several others exclude only "Treasury cash." These series are V-5 to V-14. A further group of series, V-2 to V-4, V-16 (1895–1940), V-24, and V-27 (1899–1939), excludes government deposits at Federal Reserve banks as well. The denominators of the remaining twenty series exclude government cash holdings entirely.[149]

Will a V_y series that includes all government-held cash in its denominator differ greatly from one that excludes one or more of these components? Let us first compare the extreme positions, using Federal Reserve data.[150] For the period 1892–1950, privately held cash was between 83.5 and 99.2 per cent of all money (these extreme values occurring in 1945 and 1925, respectively). As one would expect, the percentage of total money held privately fell during both world wars, although the fall was greater during World War II (from 98.3 per cent in 1915 to 94.0 per cent in 1918, compared with a drop from 94.8 per cent in 1941 to 83.5 per cent in 1945). There was also a sharp fall in this percentage during the early 1930's, with a low of 90.4 per cent in 1934. Privately held cash, as a percentage of all money, remained at relatively low levels during the 1930's and 1940's but increased again during the postwar period to the level that was customary fifty years earlier (about 97 per cent). Thus sizable discrepancies among V_y estimates may result from this source, particularly

147. "Money, Prices, and Production: Some Fundamental Concepts," *op. cit.*, p. 75. His conclusions were based on the behavior of V-1, which closely approximates V-5.

148. Lauchlin Currie, "Money, Gold, and Income in the United States, 1921–31," *Quarterly Journal of Economics*, November, 1933, p. 6, n. 1.

149. V-18 excludes deposits of state and local governments also.

150. Board of Governors of the Federal Reserve System, *Banking and Monetary Statistics* (1943), Tables 9 and 104, for 1892–1941, and *Federal Reserve Bulletin* (1942–50). Data for "Treasury cash" for 1892–1913 are from *Annual Report of the Secretary of the Treasury, 1947*, p. 479.

during wartime. This is true for the interwar years, also: in 1934 V_y computed with total money was 9.6 per cent below V_y computed with privately held money; in 1928 this statistic was 0.9 per cent. Obviously, the trend lines differ, since V_y computed with privately held money was only slightly higher during the 1920's, but considerably higher during subsequent years, than the alternative measure.

Furthermore, a V_y series that excludes only Treasury cash may differ considerably at times from one using total money. During 1920–33 Treasury cash was an insignificant part of all money, varying between 0.4 and 0.6 per cent. However, Treasury cash increased eleven fold during the fiscal year 1934. This component was 6.0 per cent of total money for 1934, but the percentage has declined steadily since that time and has once more become a negligible magnitude (0.7 per cent in 1950).

Government deposits at Federal Reserve banks have never exceeded 1.5 per cent of all money, this figure being reached in 1939. The effect of excluding these deposits is therefore trivial for most years, although this results in a slightly higher slope for the trend line of V_y. I shall not discuss the effect of excluding only government deposits at commercial banks, since none of the thirty-eight series follows this practice.

The outcome of the above discussion is that exclusion of *all* components of government-held cash leads to large discrepancies among V_y estimates; that exclusion of Treasury cash alone may also produce significant (though lesser) discrepancies; and that inclusion or exclusion of Federal Reserve Bank deposits of the government is not a matter of great consequence.

2. *The definition of income.*—More than half the V_y series in Table 1 exclude all or part of non-monetary income from their numerators. These series are V-1, V-3 to V-11, V-15 to V-20, V-25 to V-29, and V-30 (1800–1905). It is difficult to determine precisely the importance of non-monetary elements, since most income estimates fail to indicate the extent to which they have been included. One may gain some notion of the size of non-monetary income during recent years from several sources. For 1929–50 the Department of Commerce gives data for major items of personal consumption expenditures in kind.[151] Deducting the sum of these

151. *Survey of Current Business, National Income Supplement, 1951,* Table 30, pp. 192–99, and Table 39, p. 203. For purposes of the computations in the text the following items were summed: Table 30, items I. 3, I. 4, II. 4, IV. 1, V. 19b, and VII. 12; Table 39, "meals furnished domestic servants and nurses," "employees' lodging," and "institutional depreciation." Derivation of most of these items is described *ibid.,* Part III, esp. pp. 83, 96, and 106–7. One sizable imputed item, "space-rental value of owner-occupied farm dwellings," is included in the Commerce estimates for personal consumption expenditures but cannot be ascertained, since it is merged with "space-rental value of rented farm dwellings" in Table 30.

items from net national product gives a reasonable approximation to "money expenditures for current output." On net this series has grown more rapidly than net national product in recent years: in 1929 it was equal to 89.5 per cent of net national product; by 1950 it was 92.7 per cent. For recent years a V_y series that excludes non-monetary income from the numerator may on that account be expected to be between 7 and 10 per cent lower than one that includes all these elements. Furthermore, the trend line of the former series will have a greater slope (algebraically) than that of the latter.

This conclusion is supported by a comparison of Currie's series, V-2 and V-3, which differ only because he attempted to eliminate the major items of non-monetary income from the latter. For 1921 V-3 was 91.5 per cent of V-2; by 1929 it was 93.7 per cent of V-2. The same general result is seen also when one compares Copeland's "money income" series[152] (used by Angell in V-7 and V-8) with his series on "total realized income." In 1913 the former series was 88.2 per cent of the latter, and by 1927 the figure had risen to 91.1 per cent.

The thirty-eight V_y series in Table 1 also differ in the income concepts they have adopted. Eight series (V-1, V-5, V-6, V-9, V-10, V-13, V-24, and V-33) used national income[153] as numerator; ten series (V-2 to V-4, V-7, V-8, V-11, V-12, V-16, V-23, and V-27) used variants of personal income; and eighteen series (V-14, V-15, V-17 to V-22, V-25, V-26, V-28, V-29, V-32, V-34 to V-38) used gross national product or similar concepts. Two series, V-30 and V-31, employed a personal-income type of concept for early years but subsequently switched to national income.

These differences are sometimes important.[154] During 1929–50 national income varied between 71.0 and 87.3 per cent of gross national product, these extremes occurring in 1933 and 1943, respectively. However, the two series showed similar net increases over the entire period. National income fell further during the 1930's and rose further during the 1940's than gross national product; hence for this period the trend line for national income has a greater slope than the trend line for gross national product. This means that when V_y is computed with national income rather than gross national product it will (for 1929–50) (1) be as much as

152. Morris A. Copeland, "The National Income and Its Distribution," *Recent Economic Changes*, II (1929), 763. Note that the numerators of V-2, V-3, V-7, and V-8 are factor-cost concepts; the sum of non-monetary payments to factors is not necessarily equal to the sum of non-monetary expenditures for currently produced goods and services.

153. Department of Commerce definitions of income are used throughout this discussion (see the *National Income Supplement, 1951*, Part III).

154. *Ibid.*, p. 150.

29 per cent lower and (2) have a trend line of somewhat greater slope. In addition, V_y will show wider cyclical swings if computed with national income rather than gross national product.

Comparison of national income with personal income also reveals differences that are not always negligible. The former exceeded the latter in 1929 and during 1940–50, whereas the reverse was true during the 1930's. National income was equal to 102.6 per cent of personal income in 1929, 84.6 per cent in 1932, 112.9 per cent in 1943, and 106.3 per cent in 1950. Thus national income fell further during the depression of the thirties and rose further during the wartime expansion than personal income. Consequently, the trend line of V_y will have a greater slope (for 1929–50) if national income is used as numerator rather than personal income. The greater cyclical variability of national income as compared with personal income means that the national income type of V_y will be as much as 15 per cent less than or 12 per cent greater than the personal income type.

The only other important definitional difference concerns the treatment of government in the numerator of V_y. Twenty-eight series included government expenditures for goods and services (or payments to factors) in the figure for "income." An additional eight series (V-15, V-18 to V-20, V-26, V-28, V-29, and V-35) compromised by including that portion of government's contribution which is tax-financed, and two series (V-23 and V-34) excluded government entirely.

Inasmuch as government's contribution to total expenditures for current output has been very large during recent years, measures of V_y for these years will be greatly influenced by the treatment accorded to government. For the period 1929–50 private spending[155] varied between 98.6 per cent (in 1929) and 55.8 per cent (in 1943) of net national product. Consequently, a V_y measure that uses net national product will (1) be higher and (2) have a greater trend-line slope than one that uses private spending alone.

The compromise definition, which puts tax payments on the same footing as private expenditures for goods and services, leads to a different conclusion during periods when tax payments exceed government expenditures for goods and services. In such circumstances V_y computed with net national product will actually be lower than the compromise concept. If by "taxes" we mean only personal taxes, this situation arose only once during 1929–50: in 1947 the compromise numerator was 101.2 per cent of net national product. During the 1930's this income measure

155. Net national product minus federal government expenditures for goods and services (computed from *ibid.*).

was about 95 per cent of net national product; like private spending, it fell sharply during World War II relative to net national product. Thus even this compromise concept of V_y will lead to large discrepancies when compared with a series that makes no adjustment for government spending.

DIFFERENCES IN UNDERLYING DATA

1. *Money data.*—The main sources of money data for the period since 1892 are *Banking and Monetary Statistics* (Washington, D.C., 1943) and the *Federal Reserve Bulletin* (Washington, D.C., monthly), both published by the Board of Governors of the Federal Reserve System. These publications contain time series for "currency outside banks," "demand deposits adjusted," "time deposits," "United States Government deposits" at all banks, and "Treasury cash," as well as numerous other pertinent monetary data. The deposit figures are given for *all* banks (including mutual savings banks and the Postal Savings System) and for less inclusive categories of banks. Interbank balances and "float" (items in process of collection) have been deducted.

For 1892–1922 the "all bank" data pertain to a single midyear call date (usually June 30). Beginning December 31, 1923, end-of-year figures are given also. Since 1943 estimates for the end of each month (the last Wednesday, since 1947) can be found in the *Federal Reserve Bulletin.*

Nineteen V_y series[156] use Federal Reserve money data exclusively (V-15 to V-18, V-23, and V-25 to V-38), and several others rely primarily on these data. Thus the denominator of V-19 (Warburton) was obtained essentially by subtracting corporate cash balances (as reported by the Treasury Department, *Statistics of Income*) from Federal Reserve data for cash balances of businesses and individuals. V-20 (also Warburton's) employed data presented in the *Federal Reserve Bulletin*'s yearly articles on "Estimated Liquid Asset Holdings of Individuals and Businesses." Hart (V-21 and V-22) has used the monthly currency estimates of the National Bureau of Economic Research[157] to adjust Federal Reserve June and December figures for the period 1918–1941. The main feature of these National Bureau data is that they are monthly. Comparison of the National Bureau's "currency in public circulation" and "U.S. Treasury currency assets"[158] with the Federal Reserve series "currency outside

---

156. V-16, V-27, and V-30 necessarily use data from other sources (described below) for years prior to 1892.

157. Anna J. Schwartz and Elma Oliver, *Currency Held by the Public, the Banks, and the Treasury* (New York: National Bureau of Economic Research, 1946). Hart's adjustment is discussed in the following section.

158. *Ibid.*, pp. 11–16.

SUMMARY OF MAJOR DEFINITIONAL DISAGREEMENTS AMONG
INCOME-VELOCITY ESTIMATES

Series	Time Deposits Included?	Government Balances Included?	Non-monetary Income Excluded?	National Income?	Government Real Expenditures Included?
V-1.......	Yes	No	Yes	Yes	Yes
V-2.......	No	Part*	No	Yes	Yes
V-3.......	No	Part*	Yes	Yes	Yes
V-4.......	No	Part*	Yes	Yes	Yes
V-5.......	Yes	Part†	Yes	Yes	Yes
V-6.......	No	Part†	Yes	Yes	Yes
V-7.......	Yes	Part†	Yes	Yes	Yes
V-8.......	No	Part†	Yes	Yes	Yes
V-9.......	Yes	Part†	Yes	No	Yes
V-10......	No	Part†	Yes	No	Yes
V-11......	No	Part†	Yes	Yes	Yes
V-12......	No	Part†	No	No	Yes
V-13......	No	Part†	No	Yes	Yes
V-14......	No	Part†	No	No	Yes
V-15......	Yes	No	Yes	No	Part‡
V-16......	Yes	Part*§	Yes	Yes	Yes
V-17......	Yes	Yes	Yes	No	Yes
V-18......	Yes	No	Yes	No	Part‡
V-19......	Yes	No	Yes	No	Part‡
V-20.	Yes	No	Yes	No	Part‡
V-21......	Yes	No	No	No	Yes
V-22......	No	No	No	No	Yes
V-23......	No	No	No	Yes	No
V-24......	No	Part*	No	Yes	Yes
V-25......	Yes	Yes	Yes	No	Yes
V-26......	Yes	No	Yes	No	Part‡
V-27......	Yes	Part*	Yes	Yes	Yes
V-28......	Yes	No	Yes	No	Part‡
V-29.	No	No	Yes	No	Part‡
V-30......	Yes	No	Part‖	Yes	Yes
V-31......	No	No	No	Yes	Yes
V-32......	No	No	No	No	Yes
V-33......	No	No	No	Yes	Yes
V-34......	No	No	No	No	No
V-35......	No	No	No	No	Part‡
V-36......	No	No	No	No	Yes
V-37......	No	No	No	No	Yes
V-38......	Yes	No	No	No	Yes

* Only United States government deposits at commercial banks are included.
† Only Treasury cash is excluded.
‡ Tax-financed expenditures are included. See Table B5, Appendix B, for details.
§ All government balances are included for the period 1895–1940.
‖ Non-monetary elements are excluded for the period 1800–1905.

banks" and "Treasury cash,"[159] for June, 1918–1941, shows no large differences. In the case of the outside currency series, the Federal Reserve data varied within the range of 98.6 per cent (in 1930) and 101.7 per cent (in 1923) of the National Bureau figures. Villard (V-24) used Federal Reserve data for 1940–47; however, he substituted Angell's money series for the period 1929–39.

Seven V_y series (V-1 to V-5, V-7, and V-9), all of which were assembled before publication of *Banking and Monetary Statistics* in 1943, relied exclusively on the "all bank" money data contained in the annual reports of the Comptroller of the Currency. These are June call-date figures, unadjusted for float.[160] The denominators of V-6 and V-8, for the period 1909–18, were also derived from the Comptroller; for 1919–39 Angell (in V-10 and V-11 as well as in V-6 and V-8) used the Comptroller's figures with adjustments based on Federal Reserve weekly data from reporting member banks. The remaining three series are V-12 to V-14 (Fellner). They, too, rely chiefly on the Comptroller's data, supplemented by Federal Reserve figures for member-bank "float" and currency outside the Treasury.

When the denominator of a series such as V-5, which uses Comptroller's data adjusted for float, is compared with a similarly defined Federal Reserve money series,[161] the differences are seen to be small: the denominator of V-5 is higher than the Federal Reserve series throughout the period 1914–32, with the latter varying between 96 and 99 per cent of the former; during the period 1909–13 the Federal Reserve series was slightly higher than the other. Obviously, only a small part of the differences between V_y series such as V-1 to V-14 and all other series can be attributed to differences in money figures.

The above remarks apply solely to the period since 1892. However, three V_y series, V-16, V-27, and V-30, cover the entire nineteenth century. A thorough study of monetary statistics for this period would be out of place here, but a brief description and evaluation may be in order. Wernette[162] and Warburton used the same basic sources in part, both relying heavily on deposit and currency data presented in the *Annual Report of the Comptroller of the Currency, 1876*, and in A. Piatt Andrew,

159. *Banking and Monetary Statistics*, pp. 34–35 and 395–96.

160. However, the compilers of these series have made their own adjustments for float.

161. "Total Deposits Adjusted and Currency outside Banks" plus "Treasury Deposits with Federal Reserve Banks."

162. Hansen (in V-30) merely reproduced Wernette's money series.

Statistics for the United States, 1876–1909.[163] Warburton's estimates are for the year preceding Wernette's in each case.

Money data for the period 1799–1830 are much less satisfactory than for later years. Wernette's deposit figures for 1800–1830 were obtained by extrapolation on the basis of the ratio of deposits to bank-note circulation in 1840 and 1850, even though it is likely that bank notes were relatively more important in the earlier years. His currency figures are from the Comptroller's report for 1876; no allowance was made for bank-held specie and notes. Both of these considerations support the conclusion that Wernette has overstated the money stock for these years. On the other hand, his exclusion of savings-bank deposits prior to 1875, coupled with the probable underreporting of deposits in 1840 and 1850 (as well as later years), would lead to an *under*statement of the quantity of money for 1800–1830. It is uncertain which of these counterbalancing errors has exerted the greater influence.

Warburton's estimates for 1799–1829 are free from the above flaws, yet one hesitates to select his as the more accurate series. His figures for bank-held specie, derived from Gallatin,[164] fail to deduct bank holdings of bank notes. This in itself would mean that Warburton's figures are too high. But his specie figures are undoubtedly too low, and the net effect is uncertain. The bank-specie figure for 1799 is assumed to be one-half of all specie in the country for 1800, and the figures for 1809, 1819, and 1829 are those of Gallatin for 1811, 1820, and 1828. Warburton's deposit figures are probably too small, particularly since it is doubtful whether mutual savings banks were included in Gallatin's totals. Consequently, it appears that Warburton's V_y estimates for this early period may be somewhat excessive. However, they certainly are not grossly excessive, as the general agreement with Wernette's independent estimates testifies.

After 1839 money data improve distinctly, except for the Civil War period. Wernette continued to exclude deposits of savings banks and to include bank-held specie. His deposit figure for 1870 is seriously understated because of the inadequate estimate for deposits of state banks. Warburton avoided this pitfall in his 1869 figure by using the estimate of the Federal Deposit Insurance Corporation,[165] based on collections from the federal tax on bank deposits. For 1879 Warburton used the Federal

163. National Monetary Commission, Senate Doc. 570 (61st Cong., 2d sess.).

164. Albert Gallatin, *Considerations on the Currency and Banking Systems of the United States* (Philadelphia, 1831), pp. 45, 49, and 53; republished in *Annual Report of the Comptroller, 1876*, p. xli.

165. *Annual Report of the Federal Deposit Insurance Corporation, 1934* (Washington, D.C., 1935), pp. 103–8.

Deposit Insurance Corporation's figure; he relied on the Comptroller's data for 1889 and 1899.[166]

2. *Income data.*—Three organizations have taken the lead in publication of national income statistics: the National Bureau of Economic Research, the National Industrial Conference Board, and the Department of Commerce. Although income estimates from each of these sources have been utilized in measures of V_y, Department of Commerce data have predominated. All but the first series in Table 1 employ Commerce data at least in part. Several use only these data: V-12 to V-14, V-19 to V-24, and V-32 to V-38. Various income series from the National Bureau were used in V-1 to V-10; in addition, several of Warburton's series (V-15, V-17, V-18, V-25, V-26, V-28, and V-29) contain National Bureau data together with data from the Department of Commerce and the Conference Board. Five series (V-11 for 1899–1929, V-16 for 1800–1908, V-27 for 1799–1929, V-30 for 1800–1905, and V-31 for 1895–1905) rely principally on the Conference Board estimates.

The main differences among these income series are conceptual. It would go beyond the scope of the present study to attempt to determine how much the series would differ *if* they were defined identically. However, the Department of Commerce has revised its estimates nearly every year as additional data have become available, and minor differences in V_y measures have resulted. Thus V-21, V-32, and V-37 used Commerce estimates for gross national product; V-21 and V-32 used the 1948 version for the period 1945–47, whereas V-37 used the 1949 figures, which were about 1 per cent higher. Similarly, the 1947 figures for national income were used in V-24 for 1944–46; the slightly different 1948 version was used in V-33 for the same years.

The above discussion pertains only to annual income estimates. Two different sorts of quarterly series have been used in V_y measures: (1) those of the Department of Commerce, since 1939 (V-36 and V-38) and (2) those of Warburton for 1919–47. The 1949 Commerce estimates for gross national product were used in V-36 for 1945–48, whereas the generally lower 1950 figures were used in V-38. Both of these income series are expressed as seasonally adjusted annual rates, in contrast to Warburton's series. The latter are essentially annual estimates of gross national product, allocated to quarters on the basis of data from various sources. These quarterly allocations are less adequate for 1919 and 1920 than for later years, since they are based solely on the Federal Reserve index of retail trade. The allocations for 1939–47 are the same as those of the De-

166. See Appendix C, below, for my own money series: 1839, 1849, . . . , 1899.

partment of Commerce. The small differences between V-17 and V-25 and between V-18 and V-26 appear to be due to minor conceptual variations.

The only monthly income series is the Department of Commerce personal income series, 1929 to date, at seasonally adjusted annual rates.

COMPUTATIONAL DIFFERENCES

The velocity denominator was defined in Appendix A as the *average* money stock during some time period. Unfortunately, existing money data permit only a poor approximation to the average money stock. Prior to 1923 the data consist of a single observation as of June 30 or some other late June date. Since 1923 the Federal Reserve series for all banks includes December call-date figures as well as those for June. There are monthly estimates since 1943.

Inferences may be made about the behavior of the total money stock between the June and December call dates by studying the member-bank call-date series since 1919; for most years two additional observations are thus made available.[167] Of the eighteen V_y series[168] that base their money estimates on more than a single observation, V-15, V-19, V-20, V-28, V-29, and V-37 (1929–42) use averages of June and December figures. Averages of the Federal Reserve monthly estimates were used in V-21 and V-22 (1942–47), V-36, and V-37 (1943–48). The denominators of another group of series consist of averages of monthly or quarterly money estimates prepared by the authors with the aid of member-bank data: V-6 (1919–28), V-8 (1919–28), V-10, V-11 (1919–39), V-17, V-18, V-24 (1929–39), V-25 and V-26.

Hart, in V-21 and V-22, apparently used the following complicated process to derive his deposit figures: (1) Federal Reserve all-bank data for December of the preceding year and June and December of the current year were averaged; (2) the same procedure was applied to member banks alone; (3) member-bank data for December of the preceding year and all call dates of the current year were averaged; (4) the latter averages were computed as percentages of the former (item 2); and (5) this percentage was used to adjust the original all-bank average. The Federal

167. *Banking and Monetary Statistics*, Table 18. This procedure could be extended by studying the weekly reporting member-bank series, Table 48.

168. V-6, V-8, V-10, V-11, V-15, V-17 to V-22, V-24 to V-26, V-28, V-29, V-36, and V-37.

Reserve outside currency series was adjusted similarly, the National Bureau's monthly series[169] being used for this purpose.

McKean's series (V-23), which is the only one not accounted for, consists of Federal Reserve monthly estimates of net demand deposits in all banks, 1929–41, and the familiar "demand deposits adjusted" for subsequent years.

Reflection on these computational methods suggests several comments. First, addition of the December call-date figures is preferable to sole reliance on June 30 data. Second, in computing averages from these data, the preceding and the current December figures should each be given weights of one-quarter and the June figure should be weighted one-half. This procedure avoids the overstatement which would otherwise result from the seasonal expansion of money in December. Most V_y series that have used the December money figures have included the preceding as well as the current December, but they have all applied equal weights to the three observations for each year. Similar remarks are applicable to averages of monthly estimates. Third, Hart's method seems inferior to that just described inasmuch as the additional call dates which he uses occur at irregular intervals, thus introducing a complicated weighting problem if seasonal disturbances are to be taken into account. Fourth, averages of monthly and quarterly money series that have been constructed on the basis of the weekly reporting member-bank data may or may not be an improvement over averages derived in other ways, depending upon the stability within seasons of the relative importance of these reporting banks in the economy. It is doubtful whether the increased accuracy that may result under this method is worth the additional computational cost.

The empirical importance of these refinements can be tested by making alternative computations where possible. A comparison of June 30 data with December–June–December averages, 1924–50, reveals that there have been sizable differences occasionally, as in 1924 and 1942; in both of these years the latter measure was more than 104 per cent of the former. Six times during this twenty-seven-year period the June figure exceeded the average figure.[170] Apparently the question of weighting procedures (second point, preceding paragraph) is of little empirical importance: in only one of four years for which sample computations were made did the

169. Schwartz and Oliver, *op. cit.*, pp. 11–16.
170. No influence on trend-line slopes from this source can be discerned.

two methods yield figures differing as much as 0.8 per cent. The effect of using monthly rather than December–June–December averages appears to be of the same order of magnitude. For three years Hart's technique was compared with the December–June–December method: Hart's figure was 99.7 per cent of the latter in 1929, 97.8 per cent in 1930, and 98.5 per cent in 1940. The 1930 figure suggests that deviations between series computed by these two methods may be sizable at times. By and large, however, differences in computational procedures can be expected to be of minor importance.

CONSISTENCY OF THE V_y ESTIMATES

There is a final point of comparison of the thirty-eight V_y series: Are they all consistent over time in the sense that the same definitions, sources of data, and computational methods have been followed throughout the series? The question is obviously important from the standpoint of secular trends.

V-6, V-8, and V-11 (Angell) contain a computational inconsistency which probably tilts the trend line downward slightly: June 30 money data were used prior to 1919, while averages of monthly estimates were used for subsequent years. The numerator of V-11 also lacks consistency: Angell's income figure for 1939 is from the Department of Commerce, whereas the figures for 1899–1939 are from the Conference Board. He linked these estimates by raising the entire Conference Board series enough so that the sum of the figures for the overlapping years (1929–39) was the same in the two series. The secular trend seems to be unaffected by this operation.

Nearly all of Warburton's series use data from different sources before and after 1929. In the case of V-27 there is a break in the denominator at 1899 and in the numerator at 1939. There seems to be no way of detecting secular bias in his series, however. His definitions and methods of computation are invariably consistent throughout each series (with the possible exception of his money figures for the nineteenth century, as noted above).

Wernette's series (V-16) contains several definitional inconsistencies: (1) deposits in savings banks are excluded for 1800–1870 and included for 1880–1940; (2) government balances are excluded for 1800–1890 and included for 1900–1940; and (3) bank-held currency is included for 1800–1890 and excluded for 1900–1940. The first two inconsistencies imply that the secular decline in V_y has been exaggerated by Wernette's series, while the third inconsistency works the other way. In addition, Wernette's numerator consists of two distinct segments which cannot be compared because of insufficient citation.

Hart's series contain at least three inconsistencies. His income figures for 1945–47 appear to be the revised Commerce estimates, which are as much as 7 per cent higher (1945) than the old series; Hart used a close approximation to this old series for 1909–44. Hence the trend-line slopes of V-21 and V-22 are slightly too high. Hart also changed his computational methods twice, in 1919 and in 1942. The probable effect is a slight downward tilt to his trend lines.

The monthly series (V-23), as McKean emphasized, [171] is inappropriate for the study of secular trends, since it contains definitional breaks at 1934 and 1942. Villard's money series (V-24) for 1929–39 is as much as 3.6 per cent higher than the alternative Federal Reserve figures which he used for 1940–47. As a result the trend-line slope for his V_y series is slightly too high.

Hansen (V-30 and V-31) switched from the Conference Board's income series to the old Department of Commerce in 1910, and in 1930 the latter was replaced by the revised Commerce estimates. The first of these changes had the effect of lowering the slope of the trend line of V-30 and V-31. The 1930 shift resulted in higher V_y estimates (by as much as 11 per cent) than would have been the case had the old series been retained; obviously the trend line was rotated in an upward direction.

Gordon's series are consistent in all respects, while Chandler's V-37 has a trivial computational inconsistency in the denominator as a result of his shift to monthly averages in 1943; Chandler used December–June–December averages for earlier years. V-38 (Goldenweiser) used different income series before and after 1929, and the trend-line slope was thereby raised.

171. *Op. cit.*

APPENDIX C
NEW ESTIMATES OF INCOME VELOCITY

TABLE C1
NEW ANNUAL ESTIMATES OF INCOME VELOCITY FOR THE UNITED STATES

Year	V-39	V-40	V-41	V-42	V-43
1839.......	6.35	....	....	....	....
1849.......	7.91	....	....	....	....
1859.......	6.09	....	....	....	....
1869.......	3.23	....	....	....	....
1879.......	2.50	....	....	....	....
1889.......	2.20	....	....	....	....
1899.......	1.87	1.87	....	....	....
1900......	....	1.77	....	....	....
1901......	....	1.66	....	....	....
1902......	....	1.65	....	....	....
1903......	....	1.66	....	....	....
1904......	....	1.64	....	....	....
1905......	....	1.58	....	....	....
1906......	....	1.60	....	....	....
1907	....	1.58	....	....	....
1908......	....	1.56	....	....	....
1909......	1.64	1.64	1.78	....	....
1910......	....	1.63	1.76	....	....
1911......	....	1.55	1.69	....	....
1912......	....	1.53	1.71	....	....
1913......	....	1.59	1.76	....	....
1914......	....	1.53	1.66	....	....
1915......	....	1.55	1.76	....	....
1916......	....	1.58	1.82	....	....
1917......	....	1.63	1.89	....	....
1918......	....	1.79	1.83	....	....
1919......	1.75	1.75	1.89	....	....
1920......	....	1.71	1.73	....	....
1921......	....	1.49	1.36	....	....
1922......	....	1.46	1.51	....	....
1923......	....	1.53	1.62	....	....
1924......	....	1.50	1.54	....	....
1925......	....	1.44	1.52	....	....
1926......	....	1.45	1.51	....	....
1927......	....	1.41	1.45	....	....
1928......	....	1.38	1.43	....	....
1929......	1.43	1.43	1.50	1.40	1.53
1930......	....	1.33	1.25	1.21	1.34
1931......	....	1.13	1.01	.97	1.14
1932......	....	1.02	.86	.75	.94
1933......	....	1.06	.99	.77	.98
1934......	....	1.05	1.00	.88	1.07
1935......	....	1.06	1.05	.95	1.10
1936......	....	1.12	1.11	1.00	1.17
1937......	....	1.14	1.17	1.10	1.24
1938......	....	1.04	1.08	.99	1.15
1939......	1.08	....	1.10	1.01	1.18
1940......	....	....	1.12	1.06	1.23
1941......	....	....	1.26	1.23	1.41
1942......	....	....	1.46	1.44	1.60

TABLE C1—*Continued*

Year	V-39	V-40	V-41	V-42	V-43
1943			1.34	1.39	1.51
1944			1.16	1.22	1.35
1945			.99	1.01	1.13
1946			.99	.95	1.06
1947				1.08	1.20
1948				1.20	1.30
1949				1.15	1.29
1950				1.24	1.37
1951				1.39	1.53

TABLE C2

NEW QUARTERLY ESTIMATES OF INCOME VELOCITY
FOR THE UNITED STATES

Quarter	V-44	V-45	Quarter	V-44	V-45	Quarter	V-44	V-45
1943—1	.390	.412	1946—1	.234	.254	1949—1	.314	.339
2	.383	.406	2	.251	.269	2	.317	.341
3	.368	.397	3	.265	.295	3	.318	.350
4	.350	.394	4	.279	.319	4	.310	.362
1944—1	.349	.375	1947—1	.299	.299	1950—1	.308	.338
2	.350	.375	2	.292	.314	2	.332	.353
3	.326	.360	3	.296	.320	3	.353	.384
4	.321	.365	4	.304	.355	4	.367	.416
1945—1	.309	.336	1948—1	.306	.324	1951—1	.366	.406
2	.307	.334	2	.326	.340	2	.379	.408
3	.207	.299	3	.333	.356	3	.386	.413
4	.250	.290	4	.334	.383	4	.384	.435

TABLE C3
MONEY FIGURES USED IN COMPUTING V-39 TO V-43

YEAR	MONEY (IN MILLIONS OF DOLLARS)				
	V-39	V-40	V-41	V-42	V-43
1839......	257	....	....	....	....
1849......	306	....	....	....	....
1859......	708	....	....	....	....
1869......	2,115	....	....	....	....
1879......	2,889	....	....	....	....
1889......	4,871	....	....	....	....
1899......	8,222	8,222	....	....	....
1900......	....	9,150	....	....	....
1901......	....	10,321	....	....	....
1902......	....	11,153	....	....	....
1903......	....	11,769	....	....	....
1904......	....	12,257	....	....	....
1905......	....	13,532	....	....	....
1906......	....	14,452	....	....	....
1907......	....	15,444	....	....	....
1908......	....	15,059	....	....	....
1909......	16,094	16,094	16,094	....	....
1910......	....	17,294	17,294	....	....
1911......	....	18,104	18,104	....	....
1912......	....	19,229	19,229	....	....
1913......	....	19,759	19,759	....	....
1914......	....	20,367	20,367	....	....
1915......	....	21,027	21,027	....	....
1916......	....	24,591	24,591	....	....
1917......	....	28,480	28,480	....	....
1918......	....	31,771	31,771	....	....
1919......	36,036	36,026	36,036	....	....
1920......	....	40,118	40,118	....	....
1921......	....	38,032	38,032	....	....
1922......	....	39,251	39,251	....	....
1923......	....	42,989	42,989	....	....
1924......	....	44,772	44,772	....	....
1925......	....	48,552	48,552	....	....
1926......	....	50,782	50,782	....	....
1927......	....	52,471	52,471	....	....
1928......	....	54,902	54,902	....	....
1929......	55,411	55,411	55,411	55,411	55,411
1930......	....	54,626	54,626	54,498	54,498
1931......	....	53,145	53,145	52,173	52,173
1932......	....	45,637	45,637	46,379	46,379
1933......	....	41,992	41,992	43,109	43,109
1934......	....	48,976	48,976	47,980	47,980
1935......	....	52,849	52,849	53,031	53,031
1936......	....	58,239	58,239	57,935	57,935
1937......	....	60,796	60,796	60,491	60,491
1938......	....	59,728	59,728	60,610	60,610
1939......	69,815	....	64,450	64,656	64,656
1940......	....	....	69,372	69,807	69,807
1941......	....	....	77,408	77,368	77,368
1942......	....	....	84,440	88,100	88,100

254

TABLE C3—*Continued*

YEAR	MONEY (IN MILLIONS OF DOLLARS)				
	V-39	V-40	V-41	V-42	V-43
1943			112,884	113,417	113,417
1944			139,118	139,433	139,433
1945			165,662	165,948	165,948
1946			174,321	174,270	174,270
1947				169,622	169,622
1948				172,486	172,486
1949				172,133	172,133
1950				177,264	177,264
1951				184,555	184,555

TABLE C4

MONEY FIGURES USED IN COMPUTING V-44 AND V-45

Quarter	Money (in Billions of Dollars), V-44 and V-45	Quarter	Money (in Billions of Dollars), V-44 and V-45	Quarter	Money (in Billions of Dollars), V-44 and V-45
1943—1	103.6	1946—1	179.2	1949—1	172.4
2	110.7	2	176.5	2	169.9
3	116.8	3	173.7	3	170.8
4	125.6	4	172.3	4	173.3
1944—1	129.1	1947—1	169.4	1950—1	174.4
2	131.9	2	167.3	2	174.3
3	141.9	3	168.8	3	176.4
4	145.3	4	172.5	4	178.7
1945—1	153.8	1948—1	172.4	1951—1	180.6
2	156.2	2	170.4	2	181.2
3	166.1	3	171.9	3	183.0
4	169.8	4	173.3	4	187.8

TABLE C5

SOURCES OF DATA USED IN NEW ESTIMATES
OF INCOME VELOCITY

Series	Sources of Data
V-39......	*Income:* Same as V-27. *Money:* See Table C6, below.
V-40......	*Income:* "Total Realized National Income," from National Industrial Conference Board, *National Income of the United States,* Table 1. *Money:* "Total Deposits Adjusted and Currency outside Banks," Board of Governors of the Federal Reserve System, *Banking and Monetary Statistics,* Table 9, plus "Treasury Cash" and "Treasury Deposits with Federal Reserve Banks," *ibid.*, Table 104, for 1914–38, and *Annual Report of the Secretary of the Treasury, 1947,* p. 479, "Money Held in Treasury" minus amounts held in trust against gold and silver certificates and against United States notes. Figures are for June call dates wherever possible.
V-41......	*Income:* "National Income," U.S. Department of Commerce estimates. For 1909–28, published in U.S. Congress, Senate, Committee on Banking and Currency, Print No. 4 (79th Cong., 1st sess. [1945]), *Basic Facts on Employment and Production,* Table E-2. For 1929–46, "National Income," U.S. Department of Commerce, *Survey of Current Business, National Income Supplement,* July, 1947, Table VII ("former concept, statistically revised"). *Money:* For 1909–38, same as V-40; for 1939–46, *Federal Reserve Bulletin.*
V-42......	*Income:* "National Income," U.S. Department of Commerce, *Survey of Current Business, National Income Supplement, 1951,* Table 1; minus the items listed in n. 152. Figures for 1951 obtained from the 1952 Commerce revisions, *Survey of Current Business,* July, 1952. *Money:* For 1929–41, sum of "Total Deposits Adjusted and Currency outside Banks," *Banking and Monetary Statistics,* Table 9, "Treasury Cash," *ibid.*, Table 104, and "Treasury Deposits with Federal Reserve Banks," *ibid.*, Table 104. Computed by summing June 30 figures and dividing by two. For 1942–51 the same procedure is applied to similarly defined money components derived from *Federal Reserve Bulletin.*
V-43......	*Income:* "Net National Product," same source as V-42, with identical adjustments. *Money:* Same as V-42.
V-44......	*Income:* "National Income, by Distributive Shares, Quarterly," U.S. Department of Commerce estimates. For 1943–48, *Survey of Current Business, National Income Supplement, 1951,* Table 40. For 1949–51, *Survey of Current Business,* July, 1952. *Money:* Same components as V-42. Quarterly averages of monthly figures from *Federal Reserve Bulletin,* computed in the following way: sum of one-half of figure for last month in preceding quarter, figures for first two months of current quarter, and one-half of figure for last month in current quarter; this sum is divided by three. All figures are for end of month or last Wednesday in each month.
V-45......	*Income:* "Net National Product, Quarterly." For 1943–48, obtained from U.S. Department of Commerce estimates for "Gross National Product, Quarterly," by deducting "capital consumption allowances," *Survey of Current Business, National Income Supplement, 1951,* Table 46. For 1949–51, same source as V-44. *Money:* Same as V-44.

TABLE C6*

DERIVATION OF DENOMINATOR OF V-39, 1839–89

(In Thousands of Dollars)

Component	1839	1849	1859	1869	1879	1889
1. Currency outside the Treasury	219,704	232,558	438,968	740,641	818,632	1,380,362
2. Less: Bank specie	45,133	43,619	104,538	149,200	190,200	488,400
Bank-held bank notes	27,373	12,708	18,858	11,524		
3. Currency outside banks (item 1 less item 2)	147,198	176,231	315,572	579,917	628,432	891,962
4. Individual deposits, state banks	90,240	91,179	259,568	361,140	410,276	507,100
5. Individual deposits, savings banks	13,344	36,074	128,658	457,675	802,490	1,425,230
6. Individual deposits, national banks				574,300	648,900	1,442,100
7. Individual deposits, trust companies					75,900	299,600
8. Individual deposits, private banks						83,200
9. Total individual deposits (sum of items 4 to 8)	103,584	127,584	388,226	1,393,115	1,937,566	3,757,230
10. Total privately held money (sum of items 3 and 9)	250,782	303,484	703,798	1,973,032	2,565,998	4,649,192
11. U.S. Government deposits	3,992	2,185	4,339	8,598	208,034	43,091
12. U.S. Government currency holdings	2,467			133,118	115,009	178,311
13. Total money (denominator of V-39) (sum of items 10, 11, and 12)	257,241	305,669	708,137	2,114,748	2,889,041	4,870,594

* Sources: *Item 1:* 1839–1959, *Annual Report of the Comptroller of the Currency, 1920,* Vol. II, Table 24; 1869–89, *Annual Report of the Secretary of the Treasury, 1947,* Table 88.

   Item 2: 1839–59, *Annual Report of the Comptroller of the Currency, 1876,* p. xcv; 1869–89, A. Piatt Andrew, *Statistics for the United States, 1867–1909,* Table 11. "Bank-held Bank Notes" for 1869 are from the Comptroller's report for 1876, p. 6 (national banks only).

   Item 4: 1839–59, *Annual Report of the Comptroller of the Currency, 1876,* p. xcv; 1869, *Annual Report of the Federal Deposit Insurance Corporation, 1934,* Table 45; 1879–89, Andrew, *op. cit.,* Tables 9 and 11.

   Item 5: 1839, estimated by distributing increase between 1830 and 1840 evenly over the decade; figures for 1830, 1840, and 1849–89 are from *Annual Report of the Comptroller of the Currency, 1920,* I, 241.

   Item 6: 1869–89, Andrew, *op. cit.,* Table 9.

   Item 7: 1879–89, *ibid.*

   Item 8: 1889, *ibid.*

   Item 11: 1839, David Kinley, *The Independent Treasury of the United States and Its Relations to the Banks of the Country* (U.S. Congress, Senate Doc. 587 [61st Cong., 2d sess. (1910)]), pp. 81–82; 1869–89, Andrew, *op. cit.,* Table 3.

   Item 12: 1839–59, same as item 1; 1869–89, same as item 1.

Index

Index